Melville, Thomas
    Guatemala: the politics of land owner-
ship, by Thomas and Marjorie Melville.
New York, Free Press [1971]
    xv, 320 p. illus., maps. 22cm.

    Includes bibliographical references.

    1. Land tenure--Guatemala. 2. Land
reform--Guatemala. 3. Guatemala--Pol.
& govt.--1945-   I. Melville, Marjorie.
II. Title.

GUATEMALA

GUATEMALA:
THE
POLITICS
OF
LAND
OWNERSHIP

 by Thomas and Marjorie Melville

THE FREE PRESS, NEW YORK

Printed in the United States of America

The Free Press
A DIVISION OF THE MACMILLAN COMPANY
866 Third Avenue, New York
New York 10022

Collier-Macmillan Canada Ltd.
Toronto, Ontario

Library of Congress Catalog
Card Number: 70–143523
printing number
1 2 3 4 5 6 7 8 9 10

Dedicated to: The Maya of Guatemala, especially Francisco, Santos, and Julián, and other landless peasants throughout the Third World.

the authors

Tom and Marjorie Melville were Catholic Missionaries who lived in Guatemala from 1957 and 1954, respectively, until December, 1967. While in Guatemala Tom worked as a parish priest, as well as in the organization of peasant cooperatives and in a colonization project in the area of Petén. Marjorie was a nun and sociology teacher in Guatemala City and worked with high school and university students in social improvement organizations.

Since their return to the United States, they have been studying the relations between the United States and Latin America as graduate students in the School of International Service of The American University, Washington, D.C. This book is the product of their personal experiences as well as their research into the land problems of Guatemala and the history of the solutions that have been attempted.

contents

foreword

MR. CHESTER BOWLES, former United States Ambassador to
India, stated in 1967:

Many years of observation in the developing nations of Asia, Africa
and Latin America have convinced me that in these vital areas
the most important economic and political question is: who owns
the land? Where the land is owned by a few, millions of landless
laborers are inevitably left with a deep sense of insecurity which
makes them an easy target for determined Communist agitators.[1]

It should not be surprising that Mr. Bowles considers the most
important economic and political question in the so-called developing nations to be: who owns the land? Nonindustrialized
nations are by definition agricultural, and in an economy that
is basically agricultural, there are two prime assets: the
people and the land.

Land tenure or land ownership is the basic social problem
of Guatemala, and portends to be such until some sort of
revolution can completely reverse the present patterns of ownership. This is the thesis of our book. We intend to demonstrate
it by showing: who and what is Guatemala; who among the
Guatemalans own the land; how they obtained and retain it;
and finally, why land ownership means economic and political
power.

The subject is not as esoteric as it may at first appear and
it ought to be of vital importance to anyone interested in "un-
derdevelopment" as a problem of twentieth century man.
Guatemala's land problem has had, in the recent past, grave
implications for the United States in its role as a world power,
as have the land problems of other "underdeveloped nations."
The misnamed "soccer war" between Honduras and Salvador
in 1969 concerned land ownership, or rather, the lack of

ownership. Even the war in Vietnam, according to many specialists, is essentially about land-ownership:

The importance of an effective program of land reform, one that would meet the just aspirations of the masses of farmers who work the land, has been emphasized on numerous occasions by a wide variety of authorities on Vietnamese affairs. Perhaps more than any other single program, land reform offers the opportunity to the government of Vietnam to secure the allegiance of the Vietnamese people, which is the ultimate objective of the entire range of activities known as the pacification program. One of the leading candidates in the recent Vietnamese presidential elections is quoted as saying that "Land reform is the issue of the Vietnam war, not Communism . . . Land reform is the most crucial problem . . . If a good land reform program were set up, the tide of the war would change very quickly."[2]

On March 17, 1970, the Saigon legislature finally passed a land reform bill, but it is doubtful that it can be implemented under the present Thieu regime without a massive infusion of U.S. funds.[3] It is imperative that the industrialized nations understand the meaning of land reform in the "developing nations." In recent years, peasant rebellions have become more frequent and more determined in nations such as Malaysia, the Philippines, Peru, India, Laos, and Thailand, while peasant participation in the great social revolutions of this century has been essential and decisive in Mexico, Russia, China, Bolivia, Algeria, Cuba and of course, Vietnam. The motivation for all these peoples, as diverse as their cultures are, has been basically the same: a solution to the problem of land tenure.*

If we believe that the U.S. has learned a lesson in Vietnam and is not about to repeat the same mistakes in other areas of the globe, it might be of value to offer Guatemala as a case in point, examine the nature of the problem and see how the U.S. characterizes the solution.

* See: Wolf, Eric R., *Peasant Wars of the Twentieth Century,* New York: Harper and Row, 1970, pp. 364.

We have observed that most historians and chroniclers go to great lengths to preserve and assure their objectivity. We find the task impossible for ourselves. We lived too long in Guatemala and formed too many close friendships to pretend that we are now neutral observers of what is going on there. We do not think it necessary to underscore what our personal views are—they will become obvious in the course of the book. Simply, let us admit that we have opinions and that they influence our view of the Guatemalan scene. This is not to say, however, that we have falsified, suppressed or distorted any information. It is in recognition of our lack of detachment that we have gone to great lengths to document our facts. We offer a variety of social scientists' findings, both Latin and North American, to support our interpretation of the facts. If we have done anything original, it is to offer the reader abundant material under one cover, never before found in English, and to draw some conclusions from this material which should give pause to citizens of the United States. For to know Guatemala is to better understand the "developing world" and to raise some serious questions about the United States.

We have quoted extensively from Guatemalan newspapers in order to document the happenings of recent years. Newspapers are not the best source material for a well-rounded overview of social processes and this is certainly true of Guatemala's Fourth Estate. It must be noted, however, that these accounts are largely taken from Guatemala's most conservative press, *El Imparcial* and *Prensa Libre*. If these newspapers are biased at all (and they unquestionably are), they favor the military establishment and landowners. Furthermore, these newspapers report no more than a small percentage of the social conflicts that occur daily throughout the country. Their news stories are mainly supplied by part-time reporters living in the major population centers, seldom venturing into the countryside. It may be that the limitations thus imposed on available data serves our purpose: Reality can often be more depressing and terrifying than anything conjured up by the imagination, and if we were able to paint in detail a realistic picture of Guatemala's impoverished masses, our account might be beyond the scope of the reader's imagination.

At the back of this book, the reader will find several addenda which we feel are important for the understanding of the references made throughout the book. Appendix 1, "Man–Land Relationships," will give the reader an idea of the setting wherein this history takes place. Care must be taken that the enumeration of the various laws cited does not become confusing. Guatemala has had 3 different constitutions in the last 26 years, and the enactment of each meant a new series of identification numbers for the laws promulgated under each.

Finally, we wish to acknowledge the invaluable suggestions and encouragement given us by Dr. Harold Davis and Dr. John Finan of the School of International Service of The American University and Dr. James J. Bodine of the Anthropology Department; also by Dr. Gerrit Huizer of the International Labor Organization, Dr. James Petras of Pennsylvania State College and Dr. Mario Rodriguez of George Washington University. The material, organization, and conclusions are our own and any critique of these should in no way impugn the scholarship of the aforementioned. The extensive typing assistance given by Miss Roberta Harrison is deeply appreciated.

There are many Guatemalans to whom we are also indebted, not only for much of the information and insights contained in this book, but more importantly, for helping us to realize that most difficult of all human tasks: to glimpse ourselves as others see us. We would like to name a number of them here, but know that to do so would only jeopardize them in their native land. We hope that the general dedication of this book serves the purpose of rendering them the acknowledgement they deserve. If this book in any way serves our mutual purpose, that in itself will be recognition enough.

NOTES

1 *The New York Times,* July 22, 1967.
2 Committee on Government Operations, *Land Reform in Vietnam,* Twentieth Report, Washington, D.C.: U.S. Government Printing Office, 1968, p. 14.
3 *The New York Times,* March 17, 1970.

This world divided into compartments, this world cut in two is inhabited by two different species. The originality of the colonial context is that economic reality, inequality, and the immense difference in ways of life, never come to mask the human realities.

Franz Fanon

1

a world cut in two

THE PRESENT social structure of Guatemala can be divided into three segments: the ruling class, the middle sectors and the popular class. Mario Monteforte Toledo, a Guatemalan sociologist, gives the following distribution in these three groups: ruling class, 1.14 percent; middle sectors, 17 percent; and popular class, 81.86 percent.[1]

The ruling class is determined by economic standing, inherited position, political influence and educational opportunities. To be considered of "good family" one need not be in the higher economic brackets—inherited position in the ruling class assures deference—but basically those who constitute this class have inherited or acquired wealth and position principally through large agricultural enterprises. Since the turn of the century, industrial, commercial and financial enterprises have supplemented agricultural endeavors in the acquisition of wealth. Textiles and food processing are principal industries.

High military officialdom and Church hierarchy are considered part of the ruling class because of their position of

1

power and influence. Successful professionals, mostly through their family name, but also through acquired wealth, qualify. The University of San Carlos for some opens the door to the ruling class when they obtain degrees, principally in law and medicine, that permit them to occupy positions of economic aggrandizement and political influence. Often they purchase land or acquire it through political favor in order to establish a foothold in the ruling class. The founding of three new universities in the 1960's: Landivar by the Jesuit Order, Del Valle de Guatemala by the American Community, and Mariano Gálvez by the American Presbyterian Mission, was seen by some as elitist efforts to limit access to the ranks of the ruling class and to relegate San Carlos University to the category of public education vis-à-vis private education.

The middle sectors, sometimes referred to as the emerging middle class, are urbanites who live primarily in Guatemala City and in the capital cities of the twenty-two Departments (equivalent to states). Small independent farmers, relatively few in number, belong in this group, but most are government bureaucrats, teachers, journalists, storekeepers, managers of transportation and other services, struggling professionals. Monteforte Toledo placed their income range between Q. 500 and Q. 1,022 annually in 1955.[2] In 1969 an acceptable salary for an urban teacher was Q. 1,200.

Humberto Flores Alvarado, a Guatemalan anthropologist, typifies the middle sectors as almost totally lacking class consciousness[3] and he quotes Eric Wolf's term of "power-seekers" to express the transitional class attitude of many who aspire to ruling class status. Membership in the clergy, graduation from the military academy (Escuela Politécnica), as well as a university degree are all potential passports.

After the revolution of 1944, the opportunity for political power was opened to members of the middle sectors and the hegemony of the traditional landed oligarchy was disrupted. Some members of the middle sectors identified themselves with the popular class, proposed social reforms and became mentors or even leaders of the popular class. Cases in point are Víctor Manuel Gutiérrez and Leonardo Castillo Flores who actively organized labor and attained positions of political power without forfeiting loyalty to the popular class. Since the counterrevolution of 1954, however, the traditional oligarchy has regained its control, albeit with a loss of prestige and a slight diminution of power due to expanded membership.

Many in the middle sectors look to the United States as a vehicle for their rise in position from the middle sectors to the ruling class. The prestige of a Stateside education leads them to seek scholarships there. The propaganda of the United States Information Agency, as well as North American motion pictures, are effective agents for enticing people to seek work in the United States and accrue savings that make investments in land possible upon returning to Guatemala. Training programs sponsored by United States money, such as INAD (Instituto Nacional de Administración), prepare members of the middle sectors to take managerial positions with the Guatemalan government or United States business enterprises in Guatemala and thereby provide them with stepping stones to higher class status.

The popular class is made up of laborers: agricultural, industrial, domestic, construction, and so forth; 79.86 percent[4] of them live in the rural area and are mostly subsistence farmers who own such small plots of land that they must supplement their income by seasonal labor on the large plantations. The *colonos* (tenant farmers) use small plots on the plantations in exchange for their labor.

The rural population is termed *campesino* (peasant), not only because agriculture is its chief occupation but because it is subject to the legal control of outsiders. Largely illiterate, the peasants' freedom of suffrage is limited by pressure from plantation owners or administrators and government employees. The United States has not experienced peasants in its social structure, therefore this social category is not often understood. Foster defines a peasant society as:

. . . a peripheral but essential part of civilizations, producing the food that makes urban life possible, supporting (and subject to) the specialized classes of political and religious rulers and the other members of the educated elite. This elite carries what Redfield called the "Great Tradition," which gives continuity and substance to the sequences of advanced culture, and which lies in contra-distinction to the "Little Tradition"—which characterizes villagers themselves.[5]

Mobility from the popular class is difficult because of the lack of educational facilities and the minimal work oppor-tunities. Minimum salaries for work on the plantations is eighty cents a day, while industrial and service occupations average Q. 1.50. Yet, the ILO (International Labor Organization) determined in 1962 that the mimimum daily expenditure in Guatemala for a standard of life in keeping with human dignity was at least Q. 2.75.

Guatemala, much as other third-world countries, has been said to suffer from "megalocephalia"—an uncommonly large head on a small body because of the overdevelopment of the capital city, where government, industrial, commercial and educational activities are centered, to the neglect of the rest of the nation. Guatemala City, graced with beautiful avenues and modern architecture, has a population of more than one-half million, or 10 per cent of the nation's total. Yet many of its inhabitants—90,000 according to an IDESAC (Instituto de Estudios Sociales de América Central) survey—are immi-grants from the rural area and are increasing daily. They live in makeshift, unsanitary hovels that have been thrown together along and within the ravines that surround the city. The nation has one other city, Quezaltenango, with any degree of industrialization, but even this is only one-tenth the size of the capital.

Industrial electrical power is scarcely available even in the principal cities and towns, and its lack, together with the lack of transportation facilities, is one of the reasons why industry is concentrated in the capital and Quezaltenango.

There is marked contrast between the life styles of the ruling and the popular classes. Members of the ruling class often have large homes in the city as well as summer homes and plantation residences. They employ the advantages of modern technology in their households, education and entertainment. They travel abroad and often educate their children in Europe or the United States.

The popular class generally lives in dirt-floor, one-room huts that lack all sanitary facilities. Medical attention of the most elemental kind is beyond their means. According to the 1964 census, only 25.3 percent of the total school-age population was actually receiving any instruction, which in terms of the popular class, means that education was available to no more than 8 percent of their children.[6] The city dwellers who belong to this class are often as badly off as the rural population.

The variation of the life styles and social opportunities of the middle sectors is so great that it is impossible to characterize it with any accuracy.

Of the three segments of society, the ruling class is the most effectively organized. There are regional groupings of coffee growers centralized in the ANACAFE (Asociación Nacional del Café); other agricultural associations include: the cotton growers, meat exporters, sugarcane growers, sugar producers and others. All are united in the AGA (Asociación General de Agricultores) which is the most powerful pressure group in the country, and the base from which the landed oligarchy operates.

The Cámara de Comercio (Chamber of Commerce), which includes the North American Chamber of Commerce of Guatemala, and the Asociación Nacional de Comerciantes (National Association of Merchants) are in turn formed by specific groups such as the pharmaceutical producers, the automobile agencies, the Guatemalan Association of Transportation, and others.

The Cámara de Industria (Chamber of Industry) represents industrial enterprises. Hotel owners form the National

Hotel Association. Insurance and banking is grouped under the National Association of Credit Institutions. Many of the members of these associations are also members of AGA, and often close ranks on specific issues, such as taxes.

The CCIP (Coordinating Committee of Private Enterprise) covers entities such as the Center for Development of Industrial Productivity, the American-Guatemalan Institute (for an interchange of U.S. and Guatemalan culture), and many others.

This intricate pattern of local, regional and national associations is coordinated by the CACIF (Coordinator of Agricultural, Commercial, Industrial and Financial Associations). Its role includes the arbitration of internal disputes such as that between the sugarcane growers and the sugar producers in May, 1968 over the price and amount of cane to be processed. But it serves primarily as a unified pressure group to direct the economic patterns of the country.

The principal field of interest of the ruling class is economics. Government positions have been largely relegated to the middle sectors who respond to the bidding of the ruling class. Since 1944, there have been only two candidates for president who could be categorized as belonging to the ruling class: Ortiz Passarelli who ran against Ydígoras Fuentes in 1957 and Roberto Alejos in 1963. Other candidates become members of the ruling class by running for high office and, more assuredly, by becoming president. In recent years, cabinet members have belonged to the middle sectors, except for the Ministries of Agriculture and Economy, which are usually reserved for ruling class members.

An example of effective economic pressure was the refusal of the economic organizations to accept a sales tax in January, 1968, a decision which almost toppled the government. A long delayed and still ineffective income tax legislation also reflects ruling class ability to control the government. It is important to note that these economic organizations are the bases of all political power in the country and that political parties themselves are often only temporary groupings that spring up around the candidacy of a given individual. If a party survives from one election to another, its ideology will swing to the left or right depending on the presidential candidate himself. Such an eventuality produces the "Marroquín Rojas syndrome"[7] which is nothing more than a facile switching of party allegiances. During the 1970 election campaign, the newspapers noted almost daily that entire groups of party members, often supported by political leaders, renounced membership in one party to join another. After elections it is customary to assign ambassadorial positions to high ranking opposition party members, to remove them from the local scene and thus diminish organized opposition to the new administration.

The middle sectors have sometimes organized themselves effectively. The AEU (Association of University Students) has been a champion of social justice, but since 1968 it has lost much of its unity and prestige. The Teachers' Union was powerful, effective and recently destroyed.

There are two groups that seem to straddle the middle sectors and the upper class: young clergy of the Catholic Church and junior officers of the army and air force. There are only six hundred priests in Guatemala and more than half are foreigners. This small number, led by their bishops, exerts uncommon influence through indirect political pressure. Approval or condemnation of persons and actions by them carries much weight in a society that considers itself Catholic.

In 1945 the rank of General was abolished from the army because the rank had become too common. In 1969 the rank of General was reinstated because of a prestige factor in international meetings. The upper echelon of the officer corps is composed of a small elite, who have trained together, who know each other well but who divide themselves according to personal loyalties. Such men enter the ruling class by using their power to support or oppose successfully a military coup that eventually results in personal aggrandizement. In the 1970 elections, two candidates were Army officers, Carlos Arana and Lucas Caballeros, and each boasted of fellow-officer support in case his opponent attempted a coup. This is not to say that the Army elite act only to gain wealth themselves, but usually as agents of the ruling class[8], or to defend the pride and honor of their military institutions and to develop the image and reputation of folk-heroes.

Popular class organizations such as unions and peasant leagues were begun after the 1944 revolution and were only effective during the decade that terminated with the counter-revolution of 1954.

Who rules Guatemala? Guatemala is a country that is eminently agricultural. The thesis of this book is that he who owns the land in an agricultural country, rules. Therefore, it would be best to look for the answer to the question: who owns the land in Guatemala?

NOTES

1 Monteforte Toledo, Mario, *Guatemala, Mongorafía Sociológica.* México: Instituto de Investigaciones Sociales de la Universidad Autónoma de México, 1959, pp. 587–592.
2 *Ibid.* (Q. or Quetzal is the unit of Guatemalan currency and is equal and pegged to the dollar.)
3 Flores Alvarado, Humberto, *La Estructura Social Guatemalteca.* Guatemala: Editorial Rumbos Nuevos, 1968, p. 129.
4 Monteforte Toledo, Mario. *op. cit.*
5 Potter, Jack M., May N. Diaz and George M. Foster, *Peasant Society, A Reader.* Boston: Little, Brown and Company, 1967, p. 6.
6 Guatemala: Dirección General de Estadística, *Censos de Población, 1964.* Junio, 1966, p. 27.
7 Marroquín Rojas was elected Vice President under Méndez Montenegro in 1966. He went from the Partido Redención to the Partido Revolucionario to the Movimiento de Liberación Nacional. He finished his term in 1970 denouncing Méndez Montenegro and campaigning for his party's opponent, Arana Osorio.
8 Needler, Martin C., *Political Development in Latin America.* New York: Random House, 1968, p. 107.

In song the free indian traveled his paths; after the Spaniards came, paths were opened only by cows looking for pasture or indians who wailed a dirge of agony that wolves had become men. What the landowner eats, the indian grows; like flowers that lose their scent, indians fall dead.

José Martí

2

a dirge of agony

GUATEMALA is classified as one of the six "Indian" countries of Latin America because a high percentage of its people are characterized as *Indian*. The remainder of the population is called *Ladino* which essentially means "nonIndian."[1] The distinction is largely cultural, but does have racial overtones. An *Indian* is a person who recognizes his Maya heritage by wearing one of the two hundred eighty-eight distinct indigenous costumes, by being married to a woman who so dresses, by speaking a dialect of one of the twenty-two indigenous languages, by having a value system that is more communal than individual, and/or by being considered *Indian* by his neighbors. An *Indian* can become a *Ladino* by dropping his indigenous dress and language, learning Spanish, dressing in the Western tradition, and developing more competitive and individualistic values. The process is known as "Ladinoization" and, according to the Guatemalan government, it took place in almost 13 percent of the population between the years 1950 and 1964. The census for 1950 lists 56 percent of the population as indigenous while the 1964 census classified only 43 percent of the population as such.

The difficulty with the distinction between *Indian* and *Ladino* is that the former classification is meant to connote ignorance and backwardness, while the latter often signifies intelligence and progress. Sometimes a *Ladino* is classified by his neighbors as an *Indian* if he goes barefooted or if he is illiterate, and *Indio* is used as a term of disparagement. The authors prefer not to use the term "Indian" because the people who are themselves so classified reject this label. Instead, the term "Maya" will be used, which, although it is employed often by social scientists to designate a civilization long since passed, it is an appropriate designation that embraces a value system still largely intact.

The Maya themselves most often use the terms *natural* and *indígena*. Since the latter name lends itself to an English translation, it has also been employed extensively in this book.

The term *Ladino* is more difficult to define. It is often used where there is close contact between the indigenous and Western value systems, especially among people of the lowest economic strata. The distinction is rarely used in areas that have a minimal indigenous population, although the people there would recognize themselves as *Ladinos.* The term generally refers to those who, whatever their economic standing may be, have rejected, either personally or because of cutural heritage, the Maya value system and have accepted Western culture. By definition then, the middle sectors and ruling class are *Ladino,* since entrance into their ranks presupposes the competitive and individualistic traits which are foreign to indigenous culture. The ruling class never refer to themselves as *Ladino,* since this involves a distinction between themselves and *Indian,* an implicit comparison that they find odious.[2] Nevertheless, we use the term *Ladino* and include the ruling class and all those who do not accept the Maya cultural system.

The Maya of Guatemala lack a sense of their own cultural (and largely racial) unity because of the diversity of their dress and language. As a result, they have seldom achieved concerted action on any issue, even though they constitute more than half the population of the country.[3] They participate in national life on a secondary plane and at the same time, they are the work force that makes possible the economic existence of that country. After 445 years of Spanish and *Ladino* domination, they continue to hold on to their own culture and largely refuse to be assimilated into the pattern of the Western World.

Many cultural elements, different from their own, have been thrust at them: language, dress, religion, land tenure. Some have been adopted, others rejected, some of these new cultural elements have replaced the old ways. But Maya culture persists. The concept of private property has been imposed by physical and/or legal force with persistence—often ignorant, sometimes malicious—by the full succession of governments. A Western concept of private property in relation to land is presupposed to be within the cultural experience of the indigenous population, a people with their own highly developed concept of ownership. It is presumed that the Maya understand land property in the same terms as do the governing elite who possess a Western cultural heritage.

The concept of property is a cultural universal. For a group to utilize the natural resources at its disposal with some degree of security and continuity, it must have adequate definitions as to right of ownership and use.[4] Land can be held privately or collectively, and both terms can be modified by any number of variations in the rules that limit the use of that land. The ownership of land, or natural resources such as water or forest areas, is a fundamental aspect of economic organization. Where property is held collectively, the title may be vested in the group, which in turn determines the mode of use.

In the Western mind, "private property" has come to be such a basic concept of civilization that it is seldom understood that other cultures can have different but equally valid patterns for the organization of land tenure.

Yet, this individualistic and complex system of Western countries is a comparatively recent development. It took form in the sixteenth and seventeenth centuries, when the "enclosure movement" and peasant rebellions, together with the growth of an increasingly large landless class, indicated the transformation of feudalism and collectivism into private ownership in the modern sense.

Land holding is an important element of culture since its significance involves many factors besides the economic. It affects political, religious and sentimental elements, particularly when it has been a prime concern of a people for a long period of time.

Land tenure involves the conditions under which people own or occupy land. Its subject matter is the behavior of people with respect to land as property, as a source of income, as a place of residence and family life. Tenure conditions must be judged according to how well they meet the needs of the people. Clearly, all people visualize certain goals toward which they strive and want the tenure system to help them and their society obtain these goals.

The question of how the present day Maya of Guatemala understand land tenure is a problem of history and of actuality. We know relatively little of ancient indigenous customs and way of life. However, an understanding of the complex problem of somewhat evasive indigenous attitudes toward land tenure, of their psychological dependence on the "milpa" (field of standing corn), are basic to any projected land reform or agricultural reorganization. Guatemala's social and economic progress depends on this. As the indigenous population is awakened to national and international realities through the use of transistor radios and through increased mobility, the traditional fatalism that characterizes them is being transformed into new determination. For some, this is "Ladinoization." However, their cultural heritage is still rich enough to provide them with ethnic identity, and they may soon attain that unity that will make them demand justice in no uncertain terms.

The Maya inhabited the area of Middle America which to-day constitutes the Yucatán Peninsula in Mexico and some of the southern states of that country, as well as Belice, Guatemala, Northern Honduras and Western Salvador. Beginning approximately one millennium before the birth of Christ, they embarked on a road of societal development and civilization that carried them to heights of greatness that far outstripped contemporary Europe within a few hundred years of Christ's death. Their organization enabled them to build monuments that are still the marvel of the Western hemisphere. Their mathematics and astronomy facilitated the plotting of the movements of the planets and the stars to a degree of accuracy that was not attained by so-called Western Man until more than one thousand years later. The Mayan calendar made the Gregorian calendar seem juvenile in its calculations. Their writing, art forms and architecture still intrigue our social scientists today. They accomplished all this as a theocracy, their social organization being strictly religious, under the leadership and rule of priests and with a minimum of internal conflict. This development reached its peak in the ninth century AD and then took a sudden downward turn. There is no exact explanation for this decline but it is variously attributed to the influx of warlike ideas from the Toltec nation of Mexico that converted the priest class to warriors in order to maintain control over the people, as well as to invasions of the Toltec themselves. The modern Quiché of Guatemala are the descendants of these Toltec (as were the famous Aztec of Mexico) and by 1054 AD they had established a composite civilization and had a flourishing dynasty.

In the *Popol Vuh,* sacred book of the Quiché, it is related how the conquered tribes were made vassals and were forced to pay tribute to the conquerors. Quicab was the king of the Quiché, who succeeded in dominating the surrounding tribes:

He made war on them and certainly conquered and destroyed the fields and the towns of the people of Rabinal, the Cakchiquel, and the people of Zaculeu; he came and conquered all the towns, and the soldiers of Quicab carried his arms to distant parts. One or two tribes did not bring tribute, and then he fell upon all the towns and they were forced to bring tribute to Quicab and Cavizimah. They were made slaves, they were wounded and they were killed, and for them there was no longer any glory, and they no longer had any power.[5]

The population must have grown considerably because when the Spanish came they are reported to have annihilated large hosts of other Maya such as the Mam, Pocomam, and the Zutuhil. And in the battle against the Cakchiquel they claimed that thousands had been killed. It is calculated that the Spaniards reduced the indigenous population of Middle America from 14 to 2 million within 130 years of their arrival due largely to newly imported diseases and to Spanish brutality.[6]

One source of Mayan history is the land titles that were written between 1554 and 1580 in which the Indians related the basis for their land holdings. Title to land was acquired not only through conquest but through the rights of the legend of the origins of lineage. In fact, the principal source of their rights to an area was the lineal descent from their anceint kings.

The individual farmers held their lands communally and used them according to their needs and their possibilities. They considered the land to belong to the tribal community much as does air or water. They used plots assigned to them or picked out by them. The right to work the land and to enjoy the fruits thereof might be inherited by immediate descendants in an unbroken line of succession, but the concept of private ownership of land *per se* was apparently alien to indigenous thought.[7] Private property was personal property, the fruit of one's own labors. Only society as a whole could "own" what nature and the gods had produced.

Another feature of Maya culture which helped them to develop a sense of duty to neighbor and community, besides the use of communal land, was group labor for clearing forest land, for building homes, for clearing and planting fields. A man helps a team of other men in exchange for labor on his own project. This extended the concept of communal land even to the idea of communal labor,[8] which is so prevalent throughout Guatemala today.

The Maya share a highly mystical explanation of nature with other ancient civilizations. Although some merging has occurred from a mixture of Catholicism with the indigenous religion, they still maintain many of their basic concepts regarding the nature of the world. Most of their agricultural techniques center about the cultivation of corn and these techniques are all indigenous and preColumbian. In varying degrees they still maintain the custom of elaborate prayers, fasting and continence before beginning any new stage in the cultivation of their crops, as well as consulting a *chimán* (a priest or medicine man), in order to determine the best day to initiate the work.

The Maya apologizes to the gods or saints of the earth when he cuts the trees to clear the land, when he burns the underbrush and disfigures the landscape. His prayer indicates that he feels that he owns his work and the fruit his work will produce, but that the land is there for his use, lent to him by God, whom he also identifies with the Earth.

O God, my Mother, my Father, Lord of the hills, and valleys, Spirit of the forests, be patient with me for I am about to do as I have always done. Now I make my offering to you that you may know that I am troubling your good will, but suffer it, I pray. I am going to destroy your beauty, I am going to work you that I may live.[9]

A great upheaval for the Mayan people came with the conquest by the Spanish in the early 1500's. Battle, conquest, slavery and tribute were hardships that they had known before but never to the genocidal proportions effected by the Spaniards.

In spite of brave and exceptional efforts by men such as Fray Bartolomé de las Casas, the treatment meted to the indigenous population by the *Conquistadores* was degrading domination, brutality and oppression quite in keeping with the prevalent European mentality of those times. In addition to this, the Spanish brought their own conflicting elements of culture which they both consciously and unconsciously imposed on the Maya.

Land to the early Spanish *Conquistadores* meant power and prestige, in much the same way a large landed estate or a famous name is regarded by North Americans today. As a result, land was coveted for itself, as well as for economic considerations. This meant owning, not a sufficient plot where the owner could do his own work, but rather large tracts of land where he could have slaves, peons, tenants or sharecroppers to do the work for him. The social prestige that came from land ownership was also obtained from the "ownership" of peons who worked these lands, and this too was independent of economic factors. That is to say that it was not uneconomic if one had an excessive number of laborers on a huge plantation since it only cost the owner the use of a small piece of his otherwise idle land in payment for the unsalaried and inefficient labor supplied by these tenants. The reliance of the early Spanish settlers on the exploitation of cheap labor prevented them from introducing new and more productive methods of agriculture. This practice is one of the chief causes for the present day backwardness of Guatemalan agriculture.

To the *Conquistadores,* God, as Creator, was the supreme owner of lands, and the Pope, as His representative, could dispose of them. It was thus that the Pope ceded these new lands to the King of Spain, whose subjects had "discovered" them. And so the *Conquistadores* took possession of the Maya lands. King Ferdinand V dictated in 1513 a law that stated: "It is our will that houses, lots, lands, *caballerías* and *peonías* be or may be distributed to all those who go to colonize new lands according to the will of the Governor."[10]

The land ownership pattern, begun as early as 1524, only

five years after the arrival of the Spanish in Guatemala, is
enforced even to the present. It has been the subject of dispute,
causing the overthrow of governments and it is still in need of
reform. Lands were distributed among the infantry in lots
called *peonías,* and among the calvary, *caballerías,* so that
they could support themselves. Those in higher positions in the
governing force of colonial society received *encomiendas* as
well. The latter constituted a certain number of indigenous
villages whose inhabitants could be taxed and used as a work
force in the town and in the fields. Their village lands were
not taken from them as such, but they were required to pay
such exhorbitant taxes and to render so much labor, that they
slowly lost possession of their lands, and whole villages were
enslaved.[11] On the other hand, the Spanish came to see the
tribute, not as exchange for protection and for teaching them
Catholic doctrine, but as due rent for land they began to
consider their property.

A common custom that exists in modern day Guatemala
and is the direct result of this practice is to include the *colonos*
in the enumeration of the goods of a given plantation when it
is offered for sale, enhancing the selling price. They are thus
"sold" along with the rest of the farm.

Not all the land was taken from the Maya. The *ejido*
(communal land) was established by which villages were assigned lands to be used very much the same as the indigenous
population was accustomed to. These communal lands were
inalienable and administered by the local indigenous function-
aries. They also had forest and pasture lands and the
surrounding uncultivated areas. The Maya in the *altiplano* (the
highlands) were able to conserve their lands because the Spanish
found communications so difficult in that mountainous area and
because much of that land was not worth taking.[12]

As more land was given out to the Spanish conquerors,
the need for a work force was provided by *Mandamientos,*
which were squads forcibly recruited to work for miserable
salaries. Many Maya were moved from their highland villages

to large land holdings on the coastal plain to cultivate *añil* and *cochinilla,* dyes which constituted the first agricultural export crops.

There is no question that a strong economic factor also existed in the exploitation of these lands and their workers. It was not only a power-prestige factor. The wealth produced by ownership was and is a very important consideration. Coffee and cotton are the principal exports of Guatemala and they constitute 70 percent of its foreign exchange.[13] They come largely from the great landed *fincas* (plantations). To produce these crops, the individual land holdings themselves need not be large necessarily, but the care of the plants and the harvesting of the coffee bean must be done by hand labor. If a *finquero* (plantation owner) is going to dedicate his land to coffee production, he must have a large number of hired laborers to do the work for him. Although the harvesting of cotton could be mechanized, the quality is greatly enhanced by hand labor. It is in the best interest of the Government, whose economy depends on these crops, to see that hired labor is available.

Coffee is a crop whose production apparently cannot be mechanized and which therefore requires great quantities of labor and strong initial capital . . . In the past, the Governments that were dependent on the coffee fincas for their national income, did nothing to urge diversification and thus the low standard of living in Guatemala was perpetuated as the finqueros continued to exploit their colonos and jornaleros.[14]

How better can the Government guarantee the *finca* owner a cheap source of plentiful labor and thus insure that sufficient workers will be obliged to toil for him than to see that they do not have enough land of their own? Without these seasonal laborers, known as *cuadrilleros,* the present commercial agricultural economy of the country would collapse.

Although there are laws against child labor, the migrant worker is usually accompanied to the fields by his wife and children and the whole family shares the work. In Guatemala in 1965–1966 the number of migrant laborers was estimated between 200,000 and 250,000 families, which means about 1 million persons.[15] These figures do not represent the tenant farmers living on the plantations, and even the National Cotton Council estimates that from 300,000 to 400,000 workers are needed to pick the cotton crop alone.

This work force has been obtained since colonial days chiefly by the *habilitación* system. Money was lent or goods were given on credit in exchange for work. In this way many were virtually enslaved. This method persists to the present day although Governor Alvaro de Quinónez y Osorio (1634–1642) "officially" outlawed it. Most of the money-lending today is done immediately before a local fiesta for the purchase of new clothes and enough alcohol for a celebration that lasts several days. The contract is then called up at the time of harvest when the workers are needed. Since this does not always supply sufficient workers, it is not unknown for *finca* owners to go to the Government and request aid from the army or some other security force to find the necessary but unwilling hands to do the job. This last happened in 1965. Most often it is not necessary since the amount of drinking that occurs during the days of *fiesta* will usually guarantee a sufficient supply of money borrowers and therefore contracted migrant workers. It is a system aimed at providing cheap seasonal labor at those times when the plantation owners need it. It is doubtful that the Government could go very far to eradicate the system, even if it wished to, without causing a profound social upheaval.

In 1821 with Independence, the dominion of the lands passed directly from the authority of the King to that of the newly established independent government with little change for the individual owners or for the Maya population.

The Catholic Church had accumulated large estates during the colonial period and some religious orders had exploited indigenous holdings to provide for monastery maintenance. In

1829 the government expropriated church lands and reduced
the number of indigenous *ejidos*. This caused such an uproar
that it finally brought the conservative Rafael Carrera (1847–
1865) to the presidency. He restored the lands to the Church
and ruled with a strong hand for eighteen years.

President Justo Rufino Barrios (1871–1885) was a liberal
in the great tradition of the nineteenth century. He came to
power in 1871 as a result of a revolutionary movement, and
his reforms were sweeping and profound. However, he destroyed one *latifundio* (extensive landholding) to construct
another. His confiscation of church lands was definite and
complete. He distributed these lands among some peasants, but
mostly among his supporters. His attempts to integrate the indigenous population into Western culture brought about the
strong resurgence of the forced labor practices of colonial
times. Though he made some attempts to protect the Maya,
his desire to develop the economy led him to support the landowners in the institution of a brutal system of debt-peonage
that spelled enslavement.

President Manuel Lisandro Barillas (1885–1892) was in
office long enough to demand once again that all lands be
recognized officially by a title of private property, a good way
to dispossess the Maya of their communal holdings. During
his term in office the government took great tracts of land from
the indigenous peoples declaring them to be uncultivated,
not taking into consideration that *milpa* agriculture demands
that lands be left to lie fallow for some time so that they can
regain their strength. These lands were given to *Ladinos*. From
Nahualá hundreds of Maya came to see the President:

"You have ordered us to leave our lands so that coffee can be
grown", the leader said when he was finally permitted to see the
President. "In exchange you have offered us 600 caballerías on
the coast. We know how to grow coffee—we do this for the landowners on their fincas—but we want our fathers' lands for corn.

They have always been ours. We have paid for them three times. We came to President Carrera and said, here are the titles. Then we came to President Cerna and paid for them again and we got new titles. Here they are. Then President Barrios again demanded the same thing. Here are the titles we got from him. We have the money now. How much do you want for our own lands this time?"[16]

This concept of private property seems to have become the prime concern of the *Ladinos* and their government. For them, prestige and wealth lay in the possession of land. No other form of wealth provided the sense of stability and assurance that land does. For the Maya, land also meant stability and well-being; but not to be possessed as private property, rather to be used as the communal wealth of a village. The *Ladinos* continued to accumulate lands at the expense of the Maya whose labor as well as their lands were needed so that these expanding *fincas* could be made to produce. The Maya were taken from their lands on two counts: to make their lands available to *Ladinos* and to make the Maya available as a source of cheap labor.

During his long tenure in office, Manuel Estrada Cabrera (1898–1920) welcomed foreign investors. Principal among these was the United Fruit Company, which in 1906, in the name of Mr. Minor Keith, was granted the right to finish the construction of the cross-Guatemalan railroad which was still lacking one-third of its tracks. Upon completing the railroad, the United Fruit Company received from Estrada Cabrera the ownership of the complete line and with this, one hundred and seventy thousand acres of the best agricultural land which was to be chosen by Mr. Keith himself.

Jorge Ubico (1931–1944) was Guatemala's last strong-man President on the order of Estrada Cabrera, Batista, Trujillo and Somoza. In 1934, he promulgated his "Vagrancy Laws", a new method to obtain laborers for the *fincas,* since he had already abolished "debt peonage" or inherited debts and plantation owners were feeling its effects. Those owning from 10 to 64 *cuerdas* of land (1 to 6.5 acres) had to give 100 days of work a year for wages. Those who owned less than 10 *cuerdas* were obliged to give 150 days a year. The work need not be done consecutively or for the same employer. A record of each man's labor was kept in an official *libreto* that he was obliged to carry with him. If at the end of the year a man had not completed the allotted work days, he would either be imprisoned as a vagrant or else work out the incomplete time on the construction and repair of the roads.[17] The vast majority of the peasants owned less than 64 *cuerdas* so that needed labor for the plantations was easily assured.

An agrarian law was passed in 1935 reiterating the suppression of inherited debts that agricultural workers owed the *finqueros*. However, the *finqueros* were given the right to kill any peasant who would enter a plantation or demand his rights by force. The *boletos de vialidad* were official records issued to each man in addition to the *libretos*. These were designed to provide labor for the construction of roads. On them, each man had to have recorded the thirty days of free work he had to give on the roads. *Ladinos,* or at least those who had money, could pay a fee instead, but this left the great majority of peasants with the obligation to work thirty days more without wages. In addition the *fincas de mozos* (peon farms) were reestablished: the *finqueros* on the coast had indigenous families living in the highlands on broken and poor lands who had to work on their plantations in exchange for the use of these small plots. These were obtained "mainly by invasion of community holdings . . . In consequence, the Indian [sic] although he has secured a considerable degree of emancipation, is still frequently drafted for forced labor on the *fincas*. The problem of the Indian community's relation to the white man's [sic] labor needs has not yet been solved satisfactorily."[18]

The direct relationship between small landholdings and large landholdings, poverty and riches, weakness and power, humility and prestige, is obvious. The one depends upon the other, the first feeds the second and vice versa. The two cultural patterns lend themselves to such a society, such an economy, one that spells backwardness and injustice:

Two-thirds of the total Guatemalan population or nine out of every ten rural families are engaged in subsistence agriculture, chiefly corn for tortillas grown on small plots . . . The primitive farming methods in use consist mainly of the machete, the hoe and the pointed stick. The life of the subsistence farm family is one of poverty, malnutrition, sickness, superstition and illiteracy."[19]

The mass of the population is forced up the hillsides onto slopes and soils that can only be destroyed by the methods of subsistence agriculture that are used. It not only does not matter that "the finest lands are generally held in large coffee *fincas* and ranches, or by foreign corporations"[20]; rather it is necessary that there be no alternative to working on the plantations as migrant laborers because the peasants are either entirely landless or lack enough land for even a subsistence agriculture.

The complexity of the situation has been further aggravated by the lack of understanding on both sides for the cultural values of the other. The Maya generally goes his way, suffering, patient, hardworking, living from day to day, believing that God or the gods have made him inferior and doomed him to his lot for some past sin; all the while hating those who perpetrate this system against him. The Ladino goes his way, believing the native's capacity for suffering to be infinite, that he is not conscious of his misery, that he would not have things any different even if he could change them.

There have been sufficient signs however, for those who would read them, that such a judgment is superficial. Since the death in 1524 of the great Quiché king, Tecún Umán, at the hands of the Spanish conquistador, Pedro de Alvarado, there have been other uncoordinated and spasmodic shudders of indigenous ethnic life directed against the intruders.

In 1817, Anastasio Tzul declared himself king of the Quiché (he actually was of royal lineage) and led an unsuccessful uprising in Totonicapán against the *Ladinos.* In 1898, an uprising of the K'anjobal in San Juan Ixcoy resulted in the death of all *Ladinos* in the area with the exception of a deaf mute. His powers of visual perception enabled him to anticipate the danger and he escaped to warn federal troops. When the rebellion was put down, even the few lands the Maya possessed prior to their uprising were confiscated and many of them have not been returned to this day.

In 1943, a revolt of the indigenous population aimed at recovering lands stolen from them by large landowners began in Patzicia, but Ubico was able to suppress it before it spread.[21]

The struggle continues even today in the form of guerrilla movements. Few indigenous groups have acknowledged this as a solution to the problem, however. The outside observer (U.S. social scientists and Embassy personnel) who might question the extent and depth of indigenous hostility to the *Ladino,* need only assist at any religious fiesta anywhere in the country. The Maya peasant's tongue, almost always restrained by a natural stoicism and a prudent fear, loosened by alcohol, breaks forth into anguished cries of despair: *"Soy Indio; soy hijo del Pueblo; soy de esta tierra,"* (I am an Indian—[the *Ladino* term of opprobrium]; I am a son of my people; I am of this land).

There are *Ladinos* who do recognize the problem, but it is seldom that they have the power to do anything about it. Individuals who would buck the system tend to disappear. The *finquero* who would provide better facilities or more wages to his laborers than do his neighbors, is socially ostracized and is economically obliged to recant or sell out. The Maya who would publicly dare to protest, will die from lack of work or an untimely "accident."

It should not be thought, though, that all the nonindigenous population is partisan to the exploitation and suppression of the Maya. There are many *Ladino* peasants who share, not his cultural heritage, but certainly his lot. These are the poverty-stricken *Ladinos,* those whose ancestors were both European and Mayan, who were excluded from sharing the fruits of the enslavement of the latter. These people have not been left unaffected by their close contact with the Maya. They share his poverty, but not the indigenous sense of community that springs from a common past. They are more individualistic, more ambitious and competitive. These poor *Ladinos* constitute about 28 percent of the total population and many of them live in urban centers while others make up a large part of the *colono* population. It has been this difference in cultural values among the popular class (and the corresponding distrust that it generates) that has kept the poor from a greater organization which would pose more of a threat to the ruling class. It has been principally among these poor *Ladinos* that the guerrilla movement has taken hold, but there is now some evidence that its tactics may be used by the indigenous population as well.[22]

NOTES

1 Adams, Richard N., *et. al., Social Change in Latin America Today.* New York: Vintage Books, 1960, p. 240.
2 For a detailed critique of the distinction between *Indian* and *Ladino* see: Flores Alvarado, Humberto, *La Estructura Social Guatemalteca,* Guatemala: Editorial Rumbos Nuevos, 1968.
3 The 13 percent "Ladinoization" that supposedly took place between 1950–64 was principally due to the Guatemalan government's desire to present statistics of "progress" rather than to any large scale rejection of indigenous culture.
4 Keesing, Felix, *Cultural Anthropology.* New York: Holt, Rinehart and Winston, 1958, p. 233.

5 Recinos, Adrian, *Popol Vuh, The Sacred Book of the Ancient Quiché Maya*. Norman: University of Oaklahoma Press, 1950, p. 221.

6 The "Black Legend", according to some historians, is an exaggerated report by colonial chroniclers of the loss of Indian lives during the conquest and colonization periods. Recent studies, however, confirm the original estimates of "the most careful of all bureaucratic observers." See Wolf, Eric, *Sons of the Shaking Earth* Chicago: University of Chicago Press, 1959, pp. 31 and 195; Dobyns, Henry F., "Estimating Aboriginal American Populations," *Current Anthropology*, Vol. 7, October 1966, pp. 395–416.

7 Naylor, Robert A., "Guatemala: Indian Attitudes Toward Land Tenure", *Journal of Inter-American Studies*. October, 1967, p. 622.

8 Thompson, J. Eric, *The Rise and Fall of Maya Civilization*. Norman: The University of Oklahoma Press, 1954, p. 136.

9 *Ibid.*, p. 132.

10 Comité Interamericano de Desarrollo Agrícola, *Tenencia de la Tierra y Desarrollo Socio-Económico del Sector Agrícola: Guatemala*. Washington, D.C.: Pan American Union, 1965, p. 31.

11 *Ibid.*, p. 32.

12 Higbee, Edward, "Agricultural Regions of Guatemala," *Geographical Revue*, Vol. 37, 1947, p. 180.

13 Guatemala: Dirección General de Estadística, *Anuario de Comercio Exterior*, 1962, p. iii.

14 Suslow, Leo A., *Aspects of Social Reforms in Guatemala*. Hamilton, New York: Colgate University, 1949, p. 70.

15 Schmid, Lester, "El Papel de la mano de obra migratoria en el desarrollo económico de Guatemala," *Economía*, No. 15, 1968, p. 56.

16 Osborne, Lilly de Jongh, *Four Keys to Guatemala*. New York: Funk and Wagnalls. 1952, p. 58.

17 Suslow, *Op. Cit.*, p. 85.

18 McBride, George, "Highland Guatemala and Its Maya Communities," *Geographical Revue*, Vol. 32, 1942, p. 264.

19 Hildebrand, John R., "Latin American Economic Development, Land Reform and U.S. Aid with Special Reference to Guatemala," *Journal of Inter-American Studies*, Vol. 4, 1962, p. 356.

20 Vogt, Evon Z. and Alberto Ruz, ed., *Dessarrollo Cultural de los Mayas*. Mexico: Editorial de la Universidad Autónoma de México, 1964, p. 486.

21 Naciones Unidas, *Informe sobre crédito supervisado para Guatemala*, 1952, ST/TAA/D/Guatemala/1, p. 18.

22 *Prensa Libre*, October 18, 1969.

Idealist and dreamer that he was, he did not realize that the Northamerican monopolies have today, alas, more importance for our America, than the principles of the French Revolution and the Declaration of the Rights of Man.

Manuel Ugarte

3

idealist and dreamer

A NEW DAY BEGAN for Guatemala with the fall of Jorge Ubico, the dictator who had reigned with an iron fist for almost fourteen years. The growing middle sectors with awakening aspirations of freedom, democracy and social development overthrew him, and with the revolution of October, 1944, launched the country in an entirely new direction.

Juan José Arévalo, teacher by vocation, philospher by avocation, won the presidency by an overwhelming majority, after a hard-fought electoral campaign during which his life was constantly in danger, in what was termed the freest election Guatemala has even seen.[1] He was the idol of the intellectuals, especially teachers and university students, who insisted that he return from his voluntary exile in Argentina to participate in the elections. His thought as well as his social awareness were well known to literate Guatemalans because of the diverse books he had written, principally on education. This thought and awareness made him feared and hated by the powerful few to the degree that he was loved and revered by many others.

Juan José Arévalo was an anomaly in the political life of

Guatemala. He burst upon the political scene much the way Justo Rufino Barrios had done seventy-five years earlier, breaking with all political precedent that went before him. He was an idealist who believed in the federation of the Central American countries, combining this with a nationalism that put Guatemala first in all his interests.

If any of his compatriots had any doubts about the orientation of his government, these were dispelled by his first speech as president-elect;

There has been in the past a fundamental lack of sympathy for the working man, and the faintest cry for justice was avoided and punished as if one were trying to eradicate the beginnings of a frightful epidemic. Now we are going to begin a period of sympathy for the man who works in the fields, in the shops, on the military bases, in small businesses. We are going to make men equal to men. We are going to divest ourselves of the guilty fear of generous ideas. We are going to add justice and happiness to order, because order based on injustice and humiliation is good for nothing. We are going to give civic and legal value to all men who live in this Republic.[2]

Such ideas may seem to be vague generalities, but to the quasi-feudalistic mentality that was the birthright of Guatemala's ruling class, such ideas were positively terrifying. It was not long before the epithet "Communist" was being linked to his government and to his person. He responded on May 1, 1946, in no uncertain terms:

You have all heard the cry of our common enemy. You have heard and have seen the untiring campaign of your enemies who are also my enemies. You already know that for those politicians of the traditional line, that is to say, the dictatorial line, the President of Guatemala is Communist because he loves his people, because he is on the side of the humble people, because he aids the workers, because he refuses to be an accomplice in the bastard interests of the powerful, because he refuses to make pacts with the perpetual corruptors of people in public life.[3]

His message did not seem to be getting through, so he repeated it in September, 1947, in even clearer terms:

So far in Guatemala, there are only individual Communists that believe in the Communist doctrine. Fortunately, up to this moment there are no more than a dozen Communists living in Guatemala, and this includes Guatemalans, Salvadorans, and Hondurans . . . But at no time have they been permitted to organize into a political party, openly or covertly, nor have they been authorized to exercise within the country a political creed at the service of Communist ideology.[4]

Still, it was a mystery to many influential and land-owning people in Guatemala how their President could speak of the obligation to "explore the geographical reality of our country, grade the human factor, examine new possibilities of exportation, liberate Guatemalan soil, dignify the working man, give impulse to capital"[5] without at least being manipulated by the Communists.

Arévalo himself knew the implications of the social upheaval his ideas would cause if he could ever implement them. He called himself a "spiritual socialist" and told his people: "Spiritual socialism is on the move. In this historic moment, all of us are turning toward every man, turning around egoistic liberalism toward the great social entity in which every man is immersed."[6] And in case some of his more wealthy countrymen felt that such talk was a menace to their privileged position, he attempted to placate them by comparing himself to the very admired but deceased President of the United States, Franklin Delano Roosevelt, and implied that he too had been a spiritual socialist: "He (FDR) taught us that there is no need to cancel the concept of freedom in the democratic system in order to breathe into it a socialist spirit."[7]

Thus it was that President Arévalo embarked on the most daring experiment in Guatemalan socio-political history. He called it "scientific politics" as well as "spiritual socialism." He had two fundamental aims, two fields where he intended to en-

act and implement legislation, the lack of which he felt was
at the base of the social backwardness of Guatemala: "Agriculture and popular education are the two fields that have been
orphans of official interest in Guatemala."[8] A program that
would heal the ills in these two fields (education being his
first love) was enough to strike fear into the hearts of Guatemala's oligarchy. They listened and they fretted and they
plotted against this man who talked about changing "the very
social fabric" of Guatemalan life. And the peasant, living in
his humble hut in the mountains, had yet to realize that at
last a man sat in the President's chair who spoke as a friend.

The new Constitution that had been drawn up and ratified
by the national Congress a few days before Arévalo took over
the Presidency in March, 1945, gave the new President the
basis he needed to begin the social reforms that were close to
his heart. Two articles contained the seed of the long awaited
and sorely needed land reform:

Article #91: The State recognizes the existence of private property
and guarantees it in its social function without more limitations
than those determined by law, by reason of necessity, public utility
or national interest.
Article #92: Private property can be expropriated with prior
indemnity to satisfy a public necessity, utility or social interest
which has been legally verified.[9]

The concept that the right of private property is not absolute but rather that it has a social function, was designed to
break down the quasi-feudalistic structures that had so long
strangled any type of capitalist development in Guatemala. Its
implications were unsettling for the wealthy landowners, but
no real outcry came from that quarter. The country was in no
mood for such a protest, and furthermore laws had been
written before in her history that had significance only in their
enactment, since they had never been enforced. An attitude of
"wait and see" was the order of the day.

The process was begun by minor but still important legislation. The "Law of Supplementary Title" (Decree #70) was published before Arévalo was in office one month. It ordered the registration of all lands according to ownership, category and use, and was intended to make legal all quasi-ownership titles of the poor, especially those of the Maya. A few months later, in July, 1945, another decree recuperated the lots of from 5 to 10 *caballerías* (546 to 1,098 acres) which Ubico had given in 1942, 1943, and 1944 to some of his more faithful generals, returning them to the patrimony of the nation. This was the first act of expropriation, but rather a safe one in view of the class of people that were affected, as well as the shortness of their tenure. But, for some, it was a disquieting precedent.

In October, 1945, a colonization program was started at Poptún in the Petén. This was an attempt by Arévalo to begin opening up the vast northern jungle regions as well as to quiet the voices of those who maintained that colonization of the Petén region was the answer to all Guatemala's land problems. Poptún was a favorite project of President Arévalo but it proved to be a very expensive one. The lack of communications made the effort most difficult. All labor and equipment were dedicated almost exclusively to the building of roads, at the expense of other social needs of the colonists. Malaria proved to be a big problem. By 1948, the Government had spent several million quetzales on the Poptún project, and its advisability was being questioned in some quarters. But no one could accuse the President of ignoring colonization as a solution to the land problem.

Two months before this project had been started, Arévalo had met in Escuintla with representatives of the different social and economic interests of the country to see what were their most pressing problems and the approach that should be made to correct them. Government, capital and labor were all free to speak their mind, and the meetings took on the name of "El Triángulo de Escuintla"[10] (The Triangle of Escuintla), referring to the three groups represented.

In simple language a peasant explained that he had only 4 *cuerdas* (.4 acre) on which to grow the food needed for his wife and family, and that he was paid thirty cents a day for working on the plantation when there was work. He pleaded that he had not enough to live on and that changes must be made.

A plantation owner urged the establishment of a "law of workers" to avoid the class war that could arise as the discontent of the workers grows. He felt that the greatest need of governmental aid to agriculture was in granting credits and in the organization of the world market. He ended by bemoaning the extensive use of alcohol that incapacitated so many workers.

Mr. Bradshaw, Manager of IRCA (International Railways of Central America, subsidiary of the United Fruit Company) presented his views. He maintained that a projected highway from the capital to the Atlantic seacoast, paralleling his rail lines, was not needed and was wasteful; that the money should be used on roads in the interior where there were no rail facilities, and where buses and trucks owned by his company were utilizing poor roads, with the consequent delay and deterioration of equipment.

It is not difficult to imagine what the President thought of some of these attitudes. He was never considered a great admirer of the United Fruit Company, and Mr. Bradshaw's discourse was not of the type to change his opinion. But here, too, one can consider the move to hold such meetings as the attempt of a clever politician to bring competing interests face to face, that each would know where the others would take their public stand. The presence and voice of the peasant was unprecedented in Guatemalan history. Everyone who had ears to hear knew where the government stood, even as it responded that after taking all these aspects into consideration, overdue legislation would follow. And it did.

The colonization at Poptún was one response. It was followed soon after with the publication of detailed instructions for the *Dirección General de Colonizaciones y Tierras* (Department of Colonizations and Lands). The Ministry of Economy became the Ministry of Economy and Labor and it began to work in earnest on a study of changes to be made in these fields, especially the drawing up of a labor code. The first Institute of Social Security was founded, and INFOP (Institute for the Development of Production) was established. All of these measures affected the state of agriculture and the agricultural workers.

But before any broad and basic reforms could be instituted in this field, a comprehensive study of national resources and conditions had to be undertaken. Statistical information was incomplete and unreliable. In 1947, Congress established a Commission of Agrarian Studies presided over by Mario Monteforte Toledo, President of Congress. They undertook to investigate and provide the answers by a general *cadastre* of rural property according to municipalities, based on the Real Estate Registry in Quezaltenango, the internal migration of agricultural workers, data on rural population, land holdings, agricultural production and exports. They compiled a bibliography of works on agrarian reform and a critical summary of the agrarian reforms in Rumania, Italy, Mexico and Russia. They studied rural credits in Mexico and after establishing the basis that the Constitution of Guatemala provided for agrarian reform, they presented a projected law to be studied by Congress.[11]

A preparatory law was passed in February, 1949, the Organic Law for National Fincas. This decree created a new entity for handling the almost 150 *fincas*[12] that belonged to the government. Of these, 108 had been taken from people of German descent during World War II by Ubico. Some of the owners were interned in concentration camps in Texas. Ubico was influenced to do so by Nelson Rockefeller, Assistant Secretary of State for Latin American Affairs, during a visit to Guatemala in early 1944. Rockefeller's task was to strengthen Latin American opposition to the Axis powers. These German *fincas* were nationalized and operated for the State, and the "former owners were to be paid after the war a sum determined by the declarations of the value of the property made for the payment of taxes."[13] These plantations, along with the others that Arévalo had taken back from Ubico and his generals, represented about one-third of the total coffee production in the country and provided the government with fifteen percent of its gross annual income. As the years passed their production fell off, due to the litigation in the courts and the lack of an organized entity responsible for these *fincas*. The new decree was supposed to remedy this difficulty, and at the same time give the government another opportunity to prepare the way for the real agrarian reform to come.

There were 21,378 workers in these state farms and the law provided for experimentation in order to increase the farm's productive capacity. The experimentation was to consist of the mechanization of crops other than coffee, giving preference to products for the benefit of the people, rather than for export, and improving the breeds of cattle on the experimental lands; and to found new agricultural colonies (cooperatives).[14]

The AGA was very bitter about the way the farms were being handled. It maintained that the managers and administrators were political appointees and knew nothing of their work. The AGA, the political organization of large landowners, wanted to see these farms sold at public auction to private individuals. This organization was a lobby that had been formed to protect the vested interests of the large landowners and was the strongest political force in the country defending the *status quo*.

Collective farms had been established in May, 1948, at La Blanca in San Marcos and Montúfar in Jutiapa. Both experiments were largely unsuccessful, due to the lack of coordination between different branches of the Government responsible for the experiment.[15] When it became apparent that the experiment was not going well, the two plantations were transferred from the Ministry of Economy and Labor to the new Department of Government-administered Fincas with the explanation that they were "neither collectives nor cooperatives."[16]

Such a setback was temporary but real. The idea of turning the State farms into collectives or cooperatives was of paramount importance to the Government and one that had been foreseen in the new Constitution, which declared that "the establishment of production cooperatives is of urgent social utility and similarly the need of legislation which will organize and develop them" (Article #100).[71] On August 1, 1945, the new Congress had promulgated a law which had created the Department of Cooperative Development. By December 31, 1947, there were forty-one cooperatives in the country, many of them credit unions (savings and loan cooperatives). The cooperatives continued to develop and in 1948 more emphasis was then put on agricultural cooperatives. It was a long, slow process, and when Arévalo gave his "State of the Union" message in March, 1949, on the preceding year's accomplishments, all he could say was:

With the prudence demanded by the smallness of fiscal possibilities, the Government has counted on its political policy of protection for the Indian farmers. Congress approved a sum of Q. 25,000 for the acquisition of lands in the aldeas of Ilón, Chel and Zotzil, in the Department of Quiché; the arrangements for acquiring a part of the plantation Yerbabuena in Cuilco are proceeding; also, the papers are being passed for the acquisition of lands in the aldea Zunzapote, Municipality of Cabañas.[18]

It was frustrating for Arévalo as he saw how slow the process for change actually was. This attempt to protect the Maya from losing their lands, by purchasing *fincas* for the development of agricultural cooperatives near their own highland villages, was another aspect of the Government's interest. In the light of this orientation, the failure of the two collective farms was more bitter than it might have been. And the AGA continued its outcry: "Heads of agricultural labor unions on the national farms want to form collectives in order to be directors and increase their personal gain."[19]

The labor unions that AGA referred to were another outgrowth of legislation based on the new Constitution as well as the direct result of the "Triangle of Escuintla." Emphasis was placed on labor unions of agricultural workers, an unheard of step in the history of Guatemala. To present the peasants with the legal weapon they needed to protect themselves against the exploitation of centuries' duration, was another indication of the road down which Guatemala was heading. It was the duty of these labor unions to see that the new labor code was implemented on all the plantations. They were to enforce the minimum wage requirements (another Arévalo first) as well as demand education for their children and medical protection for their families. The custom of lending land to *colonos* in payment for work was forbidden, and a requirement was made that all work had to be paid for in cash. In 1948, fifteen of these rural unions were approved by Congress and in 1949, a total of ninety-two were recognized.[20]

It was the organization of these unions, more than any other measure of the Arévalo government, that was feared by the landowners and merited the president the epithet of "Communist." Some of these unions came to Arévalo's aid in his moment of greatest crisis in July, 1949, when his conservative opponents, using the assassination of Colonel Francisco J. Arana as a banner, managed to unite enough support in the Army to almost topple the government. Suslow observed:

It is admitted by most Guatemalans that the labor organizations in the capital actually saved the day. Members of the national labor organizations located in the capital, the area where the revolutionary attack took place, obtained arms from the government arsenal and fought in the streets against the attacking antigovernment forces. They, aided by some loyal Army members and the Airforce, proved to be the turning point.[21]

More than a score of these attempts had been made against Arévalo's government, and support, such as that given by the labor organizations, only stimulated the President's desire to see the labor movement grow.

The Confederation of Workers of Guatemala (CTG) was founded on October 1, 1944, predating the revolution by three weeks, as an association of workers, since "labor union" was still a suspect term.[22] It was not until August, 1948, that this Confederation was legally registered, its statutes were approved and Víctor Manuel Gutiérrez, a Marxist school teacher turned labor organizer, was elected as the general secretary.[23] In 1950, the National Peasant Federation of Guatemala (CNCG) was founded under the leadership of Leonardo Castillo Flores, also an ex-school teacher and Marxist, and Amor Velasco de León, an agricultural worker. Two hundred delegates from four regional federations and twenty-five peasant unions assisted at the founding meeting. Certain Catholic priests tried to stop the peasants from joining by labeling the movement as "Communist"[24] but were not always successful. A State Department bulletin later noted that the CNCG had 215,000 peasants organized[25] while a Guatemalan government publication of 1956 stated that the totals had not gone above 100,000 members.[26]

On December 12, 1949, the "Law of Forced Rental" (Decree #712) was promulgated, which enforced rental of uncultivated lands. This was the first law to directly effect the personal property of the mighty landowners and was viewed as explosive. It was aimed primarily at those owners who had stopped renting land to their *colonos* within the previous four years for fear of expropriation. It stated that:

Tillers of the land that do not have lands of their own or have less than one hectare of cultivatable land can solicit lots for rental. Those interested in renting lands should solicit them in writing or verbally from the proprietor who has available lands. If he denies them or demands an excessive rent (*i.e.*, above 10 per cent of the crop), the solicitor should appeal to the municipal authorities, who will thereupon give the proprietor an audience within three days.[29]

Mention was made of the "notorious resistance of some proprietors to rent plots of land, which conforms to a concept of excessive right of private property that is so injurious to collective interests."[28] This was real ammunition for the cannons of the professional anti-Communists who hoped to shoot the President down.

But the law never accomplished what Arévalo hoped it would do. It was applied mostly to those lands that were already rented, fixing for them a rent ceiling. This hit harder at smaller land owners who were in the habit of renting out their lands to supplement their incomes, than it did the *latifundistas* whose rental activities usually consisted only in that land used by their *colonos*. One of the reasons for the failure of this law was that the request for lands had to be made to the owner himself, a man who is seldom on his own plantation. The landless peasant who dared approach the forbidden sanctuary of the *patrono*'s house, usually found that the owner was in the Capital and that the maid did not know when he would be back or what his address in the Capital was. But even if Arévalo was not getting any closer physically to a more equitable distribution of his nation's lands, psychologically he was preparing everyone for what the country knew had to come.

Clearly, this effort was too small in itself even if successful, in view of the overall needs. Something more drastic had to be undertaken. The President ordered a general census with this in view, having stated that "it is imperative that we create an agrarian reform"[29] as well as to provide the needed statistical information for the programs of health, education and social security that were to accompany it. The results of the census demonstrated a situation that was even worse than officials had anticipated. It analyzed the problem of the migratory workers, salaries, cost of living and the *cadastre* of all rural properties.

The results of the census were made available too close to the end of Arévalo's presidency for any effective land reform to be initiated, so he concentrated on creating the most favorable agro-political climate possible. He felt the publication of the new data would accomplish much in this realm.

Arévalo was not only far ahead of most of his countrymen in his theories of socio-economic development, but had also outdistanced the international institutions whose specialty was this very field. The World Bank shortly thereafter made a study of the Guatemalan economy, and although they mentioned the need for land reform, it came close to the bottom on their list of priorities, and its extent was meant to be very limited. Whether for financial, socio-political or philosophical reasons, land reform was neither a primary nor secondary target of the World Bank.

Although Arévalo had fulfilled his word of looking out for "the two orphans, education and agriculture," he closed out his term of office in 1951 without effecting all the meaningful legislation that he had hoped for in the latter field. He was the first Guatemalan president of the twentieth century to complete his legal term, but this was not the consolation it might have been. He left to his successor the rectification of the terrible imbalance of land tenure that had been Guatemala's inheritance of centuries.

NOTES

1 Suslow, *Op. Cit.*, p. 12.
2 Dion, Marie-Berthe, *Las Ideas Sociales y Políticas de Arévalo,* Chile: Prensa Latinoamericana, S.A., 1958, p. 116.
3 Alvarez Elizandro, Pedro, *Retorno a Bolivar.* Mexico: Ediciones Rex, 1947, p. 219.
4 *Ibid.,* p. 171.
5 *Ibid.,* p. 151.
6 Dion, *Op. Cit.,* p. 113.
7 *Ibid.,* p. 107.
8 Alvarez, *Op. Cit.,* p. 151.
9 Suslow, *Op. Cit.,* p. 65.
10 Díaz Rozzotto, Jaime, *El Ocaso de la Revolución Democrático-Burguesa en Guatemala.* Mexico: Universidad Nacional Autonoma de México, 1957, p. 105.

11 Monteforte Toledo, Mario, "La Reforma Agraria en Guatemala", *El Trimestre Económico*, Mexico, July–September, 1952, p. 433.
12 CIDA, *Op. Cit.*, p. 52.
13 Suslow, *Op. Cit.*, p. 65.
14 *Ibid.*, p. 68.
15 *Ibid.*
16 *Ibid.*
17 *Ibid.*, p. 49.
18 Azurdia Alfaro, Roberto y Mateo Morales Urrutia, *Recopilación de las Leyes de la República de Guatemala*. Guatemala: Tipografía Nacional, Vol. 68, p. ix.
19 Suslow, *Op. Cit.*, p. 69.
20 Azurdia, Vols. 68 and 69.
21 Suslow, *Op. Cit.*, p. 9.
22 Gutiérrez, Víctor Manuel, *Breve Historia del Movimiento Sindical de Guatemala*. Mexico, 1964, p. 32.
23 *Ibid.*, p. 46.
24 Huizer, Gerrit, *On Peasant Unrest in Latin America*. CIDA, Pan American Union, 1967, p. 204.
25 U.S. Department of State, *Intervention of International Communism in the Americas,* Department of State Publication No. 5556, Washington, D.C.: 1954, p. 75.
26 Guatemala, Secretaría de Divulgación, Cultura y Turismo, *Así Se Gestó la Liberación*. Guatemala: Tipografía Nacional, 1956, p. 353.
27 Azurdia, *Op. Cit.*, Vol. 68, p. 173.
28 *Ibid.*
29 Guinea, Gerardo, *Evolución Agraria en Guatemala*. Guatemala: La Nueva Editorial, 1958, p. 23.

The condition of the indigenous peoples can be improved in one of two ways: either the heart of the oppressor is moved to recognize the rights of the oppressed, or the spirit of the oppressed acquires the virility necessary to punish the oppressor.

Manuel Gonzáles Prada

4

one of
two ways

T HE TRANSITION of power from Arévalo to Jacobo Arbenz Guzmán was not without its difficulties. The latter had been a member of the triumvirate that had come to power in the 1944 October Revolution, and had shared the control of the government until Arévalo took over in March, 1945. He had since served Arévalo as his Minister of Defense and was one of the President's strongest backers for reform. Another member of the triumvirate, Colonel Francisco J. Arana, had been given effective control over the army, and although he identified with the conservative elements both in the army and in Guatemalan society, he refused to participate in any plans for overthrowing the Arévalo government, and at least on two occasions had foiled his fellow officers' attempts.[1] As the Arévalo term drew to a close, it was evident that Arana would be Arbenz's principal opponent in the upcoming election, and both men were actively promoting themselves.

Then tragedy struck in the form of assassin's bullets and Arana lay dead by the side of the road in Amatitlán. The driver of the dead man's car identified one of the assassins as

Mrs. Arbenz's chauffeur, and it was rumored about that the killing was the work of Arbenz to guarantee himself the presidency. The mystery has never been solved, but it has also been conjectured that many of Arana's "friends" felt that they would profit from his death since he had obstructed several coups against Arévalo, casting a shadow on his "loyalty." His murder would at one stroke remove him and cast blame and subsequent public revulsion on Arbenz.[2]

This assessment, of course, is impossible to prove, but there is a ring to it that cannot be ignored. First, there is reason to believe, judging from the eventual outcome of the elections, that Arbenz could have defeated Arana; secondly, the coordination with which a number of military leaders attacked the Arévalo government in response to the assassination casts a doubt on the spontaneity of their indignation; and thirdly, the survival of Colonel Arana's driver and his subsequent identification of Mrs. Arbenz's chauffeur as one of the assassins was more than an oversight for a man of Arbenz's abilities.

Whatever the truth may be, blame was cast on Arbenz by the right-wing forces, but not enough of the public fell into line to deny the young Colonel an impressive victory over conservative General Miguel Ydígoras Fuentes, ex-Minister of Communications of dictator Ubico, and seven other "also-rans." Arbenz polled more than 266,000 votes, 65 percent of the total cast.[3]

One last attempt to eclipse Arévalo, and with him Arbenz, was made by another young army Colonel, Carlos Castillo Armas, in the form of a military coup, but he failed and was sentenced to be executed. Before the sentence could be carried out, he made a daring and improbable escape with obvious collusion by digging a huge hole in the floor of his cell and burrowing under the prison walls. He managed to reach Honduras where he immediately began to plot his return with other Guatemalan exiles. Arbenz would live to regret this escape.

Jacobo Arbenz's succession to Arévalo was a logical one, and the only possible one if the work of the 1944 revolution was to continue. Arévalo was an intellectual and an idealist while Arbenz was a practical and energetic implementor of ideas. In his inauguration address to the nation, he outlined his plans for economic development, stating that his three fundamental objectives were to make the country economically independent, to bring about the change from economic feudalism to a modern and capitalistic system, and to do both in a way that would effect a rise in the standard of living.

He said that he intended to encourage private enterprise. Foreign capital would be welcome if it were willing to adjust to national conditions, to agree to be subject to national laws, to cooperate with the economic development of the country, and to abstain from interfering in the political and social life of the nation. This was a direct reference to United States capital investment in Guatemala, particularly The United Fruit Company, since it enjoyed an extraordinarily privileged tax position due to long standing arrangements made with dictators Estrada Cabrera and Ubico. Arévalo had already challenged the United Fruit Company by beginning a highway to the Atlantic Coast paralleling the company's rail lines, to break its transportation monopoly and the resulting stranglehold on the national economy. The company had refused to bargain with the newly formed labor union and had even ignored a presidential order to arbitrate disputes with the workers.[4] In fact, the United Fruit Company had responded to Arévalo's order by resorting to tactics that had previously succeeded in maintaining its concessions during other difficult times. It had shut down its port facilities at Puerto Barrios, crippling local industries that depended on imported raw materials. Meanwhile, in the U.S. Congress, Senator Henry Cabot Lodge from Massachusetts had denounced Arévalo on the floor of the Senate as "Communistically inclined"[5] because of the latter's attempts to control the Boston-based company. Now it was Arbenz's turn to deal with the company and the new President realized that the task was not going to be easy.

Arbenz also detailed some of his plans to carry out the agrarian reform that Arévalo had tried to begin. He proposed to liquidate all *latifundios* in order to bring about a fundamental change from the primitive agricultural methods then employed. He planned to distribute all land that was not cultivated or where feudalistic customs were practiced to the landless peasants and he hoped to introduce scientific and technical agricultural methods. He recommended that all *fincas* should be considered and handled by their owners as capitalistic enterprises in their methods of exploitation of natural resources as well as in their labor relations.

Arbenz announced the plans for his presidency, declaring his intentions in unequivocal terms. He said that it was not his purpose to divide all large rural properties in order to distribute them to those who worked that land. This would be done only with *latifundios* or uncultivated areas, but not with large economic agricultural units of a capitalist pattern.

He considered that there were four principal hindrances to progress: first, the Maya communities that produced only for their own subsistence; second, the feudalistic practice of usurious loans; third, the lack of labor for national economic development due to an excessive labor investment in harvesting; and fourth, the large *fincas* where much of the land was not cultivated. This last point he elaborated adding that many owners did not try to obtain the most production possible by the use of select seeds, fertilizers, and modern machinery. They rented their land to subsistence farmers in exchange for labor or a part of their harvest; they lent money to those renting in addition to buying most of their crop at miserable prices. They paid their laborers in species or with hunger salaries. He suggested that the best of national lands were not being exploited and that the use of the land should be given to the landless so that they could enlarge small holdings in order to make them productive.

He concluded with five proposals: first, landowners should convert their properties into remunerative enterprises; second, help should be given to peasants so that the land distributed to them would be productive; third, small farmers should be protected from the exploitation of usurers; fourth, enough credit should be made available at cheap interest rates and at opportune times; and fifth, technical assistance should be made available in the fields of education, equipment, seed, fertilizers, and the utilization of credit.[6]

The Arévalo government had named a commission to study proposals for the agrarian reform. Arbenz now invited proposals from other groups. Clemente Marroquín Rojas, a well-known maverick politician and sharp-tongued newspaperman, a defeated candidate in the 1950 presidential elections, presented a law in which he proposed that uncultivated government lands be made available and that *latifundios, fincas* with a land extension above 5,000 hectares (12,350 acres), be subject to partial confiscation with due indemnization.[7] The Arévalo census of 1950 had yielded the following: the largest *fincas* in the country were 32 whose land extension was from 4,480 hectares to 8,960 hectares (11,066 acres to 22,131 acres) and another twenty-two *fincas* whose lands exceeded 8,960 hectares (22,131 acres). The total land held by these *fincas* was 696,251 hectares (1,719,740 acres) of which 637,725 hectares (1,575,181 acres) was not cultivated.[8] According to Marroquín's proposal the lands to be given out to the peasants were uncleared and uncultivated government lands and a small part of these 637,725 hectares (1,575,181 acres) from the privately held *fincas* that were not being cultivated.

The agricultural commission of the Congress presented their projected law in April, 1951. The principal authors were Víctor Manuel Gutiérrez and I. Humberto Ortiz. The general consideration that introduced the projected law formulated the social development of Guatemala. The law itself called for the establishment and internal organization of the National Institute for Agrarian Reform (INRA),[9] and was quite distinct in its social orientation from that of Marroquín Rojas.

Neither of these two projected laws was to become the final draft, however, but that presented by the Congressional Commission did provide a number of elements that were taken into account. Víctor Manuel Gutiérrez had positive ideas on how agricultural development was to take place. He explained that in the United States "agricultural enterprises evolved which favored the formation of capitalist small farmers with productive farms."[10] He emphasized that the agrarian reform was not intended to create many new small landholders who were to continue with a subsistence economy, but rather it was meant to establish a "capitalist system in agriculture that would bring economic development to the whole country"[11] as it did in the United States. He continued on to say that the best way to bring economic development to agriculture was to confiscate private unused lands. His ideas on indemnization of confiscated lands were even stronger: "No indemnization at all is more just, since these landowners have already profited from the lands."[12] "In any case," he added, "the Government will have to pay with long terms because it does not have sufficient funds and because it must not favor in this way, those who have tenaciously opposed the work of the Revolution."[13]

On August 28, 1951, a special commission was named by Arbenz to study the national *fincas* and how they should be developed and utilized. Three members of the commission were representatives of private enterprise: Roberto Berger, member of the AGA and a large cattle rancher; Minor Keilhauer, who owned a vegetable oil enterprise; and Ralph Bellamy, manager of El Salto, a huge sugar refinery in Escuintla.[14]

Arévalo's "Law of Forced Rental," (#712) promulgated in 1949, had proven itself largely ineffective. As the problem of the landless peasants grew without any immediate prospect of a strong agrarian reform law being passed, Arbenz saw need to modify this law in order to cover the situation until he could be sure that his agrarian law would be received satisfactorily. On November 28, 1951, he passed his own "Law of Forced Rental" (#853).

It changed Arévalo's law (Decree #712) by saying that: "The owner of lands who is not using them for agricultural production or cattle is obliged to make them available so that those who lack lands can rent them."[15] The previous law had limited this obligation of rental to those who had discontinued renting those lands during the previous four years. Also, the old law had put the rental fee at no more than 10 percent of the production obtained, while the Arbenz law lowered this fee to 5 percent. This had to be paid in cash and it was prohibited that anyone should be required to provide labor in exchange for rental.

The former decree had limited the obligation of rental to those who owned less than 1 hectare (2.47 acres) or none at all. The new law provided for anyone who wanted land and who could work it. If the rented land was left unattended for two months, the right to use it was forfeited. The Arévalo law had stated that a person wanting to rent land must present himself to the owner. The Arbenz decree modified this, giving an indication of the problems that had been encountered. It stated that a man should present himself with two witnesses, either to the owner or to his representative, since absentee owners were just not available to those requesting lands.

This new law guaranteed more equitable prices for rental and meant to provide more lands for anyone who could work them. Its weakness, in the judgment of Mario Monteforte Toledo, lay in its implementation in that "the revolutionary bourgeoisie was impotent in giving it a character of genuine progress from feudalism toward capitalism, while the political and labor sectors failed to make it an instrument for social change toward socialism."[16] It was not in accord with national reality, however, and focused almost exclusively on the elimination of idle lands, excluding fundamental social concepts. Nevertheless, its failure opened the way to the agrarian reform law in an even more patent manner.

The idea of a Guatemalan land reform had begun to draw the attention of governments and international agencies. The Mexican Ambassador to Guatemala praised Arbenz' efforts to plan for a good agrarian reform law. His message appeared in the *Diario de la Mañana* (the *Morning Daily*) on August 6, 1951:

In Mexico, the agrarian reform, the expropriation of the oil, and the conquest of workers' rights which constitute the best of our revolution, caused, nevertheless, great problems nationally and internationally. Misunderstanding was very great at the beginning, almost incredible and desperate, especially for a country that has lived in darkness for generations. Without these three capital steps, all in the best democratic traditions, my country would never have reached its present stage of development. For this reason, I am captivated by the determined and brave stand of President Arbenz.[17]

In the United Nations, the United States made recommendations for FAO's program for raising the economic level of countries in order to obtain world stability:

Land reforms are difficult to achieve and may involve substantial investments that are hard to finance. However, in underprivileged nations where peasants now have a deep-rooted feeling that whatever they do they cannot prosper by their own efforts, land reform may prove to be the most productive of all improvement programs.[18]

Four tenets for land reform were stated by FAO as follows: First, land reform must come largely from national governments, not from the outside. It requires conviction of the people who live on the land as well as that of the government. Secondly, every country must determine its own solution to its land-tenure problems. Thirdly, technical assistance can be requested from other governments. Fourthly, land reform must come NOW. There is little time to ponder over the perfect or ideal schemes.[19] Perhaps it was this last recommendation that most impressed Arbenz. Nevertheless, he took all of them to heart.

The President came before Congress in March, 1952 for his annual report. He stated: "In the field of economy, the agricultural question occupies first place."[20] He brought up several of the more outstanding features of the disparity in land tenure that the 1950 census had verified. He promised that the

law for agrarian reform would soon be ready for the consideration of Congress and that it would follow the 1945 Constitution. He indicated that he was determined to act NOW, as
FAO had recommended.

Meanwhile, a difficulty between the United Fruit Company
and its labor union developed. A wage dispute was reported
in the American Press as a purely political question. Wage
increases had been asked for on the basis of the new labor
code. The company again refused to grant the demands of the
workers or to submit the dispute to arbitration. In fact, it began
to use the same economic tactics that for decades had guaranteed its position and had recently proved effective against
Arévalo. It again sharply curtailed ship traffic to Guatemala,
reducing both imports and exports.[21] Guatemala's need for
foreign exchange also was used as a lever by the company to
exert pressure in its favor.

Arbenz had already detailed some of the aspects of the
difficulties with United Fruit in his address to Congress.[22] He
stated that in answer to the wage demands of the United
Fruit Company's workers, Mr. Walter Turnbull had come from
Boston representing the presidency of the company on October
22, 1951, and had demanded that the previous work contract
be renewed for three more years. He also asked that the
Government promise not to increase the company's taxes and
should there be a decrease in the rate of exchange of the
Guatemalan currency, a guarantee be given that United Fruit
would not be affected by it. None of these requests were aimed
at endearing the company to the Guatemalan Government.

On November 10, the government answered that if the
contract were extended, the company would first have to agree
that the government would be the arbitrator of all disputes
between workers and management and that the Constitution
and laws of Guatemala would have to be respected. It further
stated that the nation's sovereignty would not permit the government to give legislative preference to a foreign company
any more than to national companies or individuals. The
guarantee against a decrease in currency exchange rates was

viewed as an intentional insult, since the country's currency had been stable for twenty-five years. The Guatemalan government presented seven counter-propositions of its own. They were the following:

(a) Any contract between labor and the company should be in accord with the Constitution.

(b) The docks owned by the company in Puerto Barrios should be improved.

(c) The company should begin paying export duties, and all exonerations previously granted should be reviewed since they were outdated.

(d) There should be government revision and control of contracts made by the company with individual fruit growers.

(e) Compensation should be paid to the government for the "exhaustion" of lands used by the company.

(f) Periodic revision of contracts must be made.

(g) Railroad transportation costs should be reduced.[23]

The company regarded these propositions as a frontal attack on its privileged position as well as a lack of gratitude on the part of the government for the contribution made by the United Fruit Company to the development of the country. They were all of this, but nobody could dispute the fact that the United Fruit Company had taken out of Guatemala far more in excessive profits than it ever put into that poverty-stricken nation. The International Development Bank had reported in 1951 that IRCA, the United Fruit Company railroad monopoly, was charging the highest rates in the world.[24]

The company answer to the seven government proposals was to lay off 4,000 workers. It was then that the court ruled that a 26,100 acre farm belonging to the United Fruit Company in Tiquisate be confiscated as guarantee for the back-wage demands of the workers. Finally, in March, the company was able to defeat Arbenz just as it had done with Arévalo and got what it wanted when Arcadio Chávez, representing the labor union, agreed to end the dispute by signing a renewal of the old three-year contract in exchange for the $650,000 in back wages. *Time* magazine referred to Mr. Chávez as the

Union's "nonCommunist" leader,[25] since any anti-American Guatemalan of the day was commonly regarded as a Communist. That Mr. Chávez would agree to the company's demands made him proAmerican and "nonCommunist."

On June 17, 1952, the Arbenz Agrarian Reform Law (Decree #900) was finally approved and promulgated. Various peasant rallies had been held during the previous months in Guatemala City to pressure Congress into action and to give thousands of peasants a sense of participation in the making of legislation that was to govern them.[26] It was ultimately the work of Arbenz himself, who had proven to know much more about the national land situation than the many members of Congress or AGA who had been consulted on possible solutions to the land problem. The greatest outside influence on Arbenz and his law was thought to be a Mexican agrarian lawyer and sociologist, Licenciado Lucio Mendieta y Nuñez.[27] Congress passed the law with a smaller majority than Arbenz had expected. It was criticized in the conservative Guatemalan press and by the landowners as antiscientific, premature, vague and unconstitutional.[28] But the real basis for opposition was political:

The fervent nationalism which forms the main drive of this revolutionary movement has been harnessed to a principal purpose, which appears to be the liquidation of all foreign land holdings of any size and the reduction of all native land holdings to manageable proportions.[29]

The United Fruit Company was the largest single landowner in Guatemala, possessing more land than that owned by 50 percent of the total population.[30] The company had demonstrated in its recent difficulties with Guatemalan labor that it not only did not respect the rights of the Guatemalan government over its own internal affairs, but also had the ability to put a stranglehold on the economy in pursuit of its own interests. Its monopoly on rail lines, international communications, and port facilities made it a very dangerous enemy and one whose power had to be broken. No one could deny that it provided jobs for thousands of workers, but at what price to the country? Besides the affront that the very existence of such a company rendered to the concept of national sovereignty, the taxes it paid were negligible. International Railroads of Central America, as a United Fruit Company subsidiary, had not paid any taxes to the government since its incorporation more than fifty years earlier.[31] The very visible benefits provided to its workers in the form of living quarters, hospitalization and higher-than-average wages, were indirectly paid for by the government many times over by virtue of uncollected taxes. Added to this was the fact that the United Fruit Company kept more than 90 percent of its lands in reserve, giving Arbenz plenty of economic as well as political reasons for going after it. Its lands seemed to be a much more likely subject for expropriation that the German *fincas,* since the owners of the latter at least had lived and worked in Guatemala, not as foreigners, but as immigrants and citizens.

The United Fruit Company was not meant to be the only object of the new law, despite its claims to be such. Arbenz was also interested in applying the weight of the law against native landowners for two basic reasons: most of the laborers were working under medieval conditions, receiving little cash wages which left them economically marginal; the 1950 census showed that *latifundistas* with land holdings over 900 hectares (2,223 acres) were keeping 60.7 percent of their cultivatable lands idle, while hundreds of thousands of landless peasants did not have any place to grow the food needed to feed their families. David Stern, an American lawyer, in a commentary on the new law, stated:

The law was the blending of various traditions. One was the American land-grant tradition to open new frontiers. Another was the revalidation of the civil law tradition that all arable lands and national wealth are essentially endowed with the public interest. The third tradition in the new decree was its affirmation of the

validity of private property notwithstanding its socialistic overtones.[32]

He also went to the very core of the matter and indicated one
of the basic motives for its enactment: "A fair, impartial and
democratic administration of this law would go very far toward
destroying the political power of the minority . . . who are
vested property-holding interests, both native and foreign."[33]

The first article of the new law gave its purpose: the
liquidation of all feudal property. The second stated how:
abolishment of all types of servitude since all labor must be
adequately remunerated. The succeeding articles determined
that some expropriated lands would be first nationalized and
subsequently given out to the landless in usufruct or rental.
Other lands would be expropriated in favor of the beneficiaries
and given as private property in lots not exceeding 25 *manzanas* (42.5 acres). All lands belonging to a single owner
would be considered as a single piece of property regardless
of the location, and indemnization would be made with government bonds of twenty-five years duration at 3 percent
interest. Value of the land would be determined by the declarations made for tax purposes as of May 9, 1952.

The vagueness of the wording of many articles determining what lands would be expropriated and what lands exoner-
ated caused unnecessary doubt and subsequent opposition. No
one knew what "two-thirds cultivated" or even "uncultivated
lands" were supposed to be, nor was it certain how it was to
be decided if lands were cultivated "for" the owner. And what
product was not necessary for the national economy? The
generality of these elements provided for much uncertainty as
to what the law meant.

The biggest stumbling block of all, if we can pin the blame
on any one aspect of a law that was meant to revolutionize
Guatemalan society to its foundations, was the naming of persons or agencies responsible for expropriations, the manner
in which these were to be made, the time given for effecting the
same, and the process of appeal from their decisions. The fact

that appeals could only be made to the President himself, eliminating effectively the judiciary from participating in the machinery of expropriation, frightened many. That the declarations or denunciations were made by peasants to peasant organizations without landowner representation, scared many others. What affected the *latifundistas* the most was the summary nature of the expropriation procedure which enabled the whole operation to be accomplished in six weeks. In a country accustomed to red tape and bureaucracy, where "wait and see" is a way of life, where social legislation in the past had always been circumvented, this was going too far.

When United Fruit Company officials first read the law, they were concerned, but they considered the company exempt because its lands were "cultivated."[34] They should have known better. In other sectors, due to the preparation made by both Arévalo and Arbenz, the law had been expected for years so it came as no surprise. Yet there was immediate reaction throughout the country—both of hope and of fear. Near the eastern frontier, peasant members of CNCG had even anticipated the law by publishing lists of landholders whose lands they considered would be eligible for expropriation. When the law was promulgated, they began to measure off these same lands. Small farmers with machetes seized police headquarters in San José Arcada, and in Camotán a Union leader was killed by a group opposing land reform. An amendment was proposed to the three-day-old law: "Landowners who oppose the agrarian reform law by violent or subversive means will be totally expropriated without regard to the limitations and indemnization provided by the law."[35]

It was not the law itself that was now causing the greatest difficulty, but the manner of its implementation. Analysis and commentaries on the law were favorable, despite its glaring generalities and lack of preciseness on many points. Local agrarian committees were being formed in order to determine what lands were to be expropriated and to carry out the procedure. On August 6, 1952 the regulations for these committees were approved by Congress.[36] They consisted of five members: one government representative, one municipal representative and three peasant representatives. The latter were to be members of any local union, cooperative or other peasant organization. There was no representative from the landowners. Usually, the government representatives would be considered on the side of the landowners, but not in this government. For the first time in the history of Guatemala instructions such as these had been issued to government employees: "In any dispute between a peasant and a landowner, the peasant is to be given preference; in any dispute between labor and management, labor is to be given preference."[37]

Although AGA had been invited to send representatives and spokesmen to the planning sessions for the agrarian reform law, they refused so as to indicate that they were opposed to the very concept of land reform and the "social function of property." Now that expropriations were to begin, many felt it was fitting that they not be invited to participate or have representatives on the committees.

It was not until six months after the law's promulgation that the expropriations began. The first order was approved on January 5, 1953, expropriating a total of 24.2 *caballerías* (2,658 acres) which were assessed at $10,622. From this date on, the expropriations continued quickly, amid disputes and violence on both sides. Marroquín Rojas gleefully published accounts of these in his newspaper, *La Hora,* seeing in this a vindication of himself and his own rejected project for a land reform law: January 3: three peasants killed by landowners in San Cristóbal Verapaz and Santa Ana Huista. January 9: twenty-three houses burned and people ousted, light and water cut off because the landowners feared expropriation. January 22: peasants invade lands that had been refused to them in customary rental. January 23: two-hundred peasants on rented lands invaded and ousted by other peasants. January 30: fences of small farms removed so that the cattle invaded and destroyed the crops. February 4: small farms invaded. February 14: agrarian committees request permit to carry arms. The agrarian committees were having as much trouble controlling the peasants who saw the immediate hope of acquiring lands as they had controlling the landowners who tried to impede the law's application through terrorism and deceit.

On January 22, Ernesto Leal Pérez, a large landowner affected by an expropriation decree, put in an appeal to the Supreme Court. The law specifically stated that ultimate recourse was to the President and that appeals on land reform questions were not subject to the Supreme Court. However, the judges decided to consider the appeal and deliberations began. The country waited. On February 2, 1953, the justices declared that "the right of appeal could not be invalidated by the agrarian law"[38] and on February 5, a final vote of 5 to 4 gave approval to admit appeals on the land reform law, suspending further expropriations until the law itself could be studied further. Congress convened that very night to discuss the constitutionality of this declaration.[39] Víctor Manuel Gutiérrez spoke to Congress and said: "One can live without tribunals, but not without lands."[40] The President, with approval from Congress, dismissed the dissenting members of the court and replaced them with judges more favorable to the new outlook. In civil law countries, says Stern, this lack of judicial review is not unusual.[41] Nevertheless, this new action indicated to all that Arbenz would brook no opposition in the realization of the fundamental aim of his government. The landowners were stunned. There were discussions and declarations by law students and lawyers throughout the country. Most supported the President's action.

The ultimate interest of the agrarian reforms was the good of the peasants, but this was not obvious to many of the peasants themselves. Some were able to interpret it, but others were convinced by local authorities, landowners and even the clergy that land reform was not in their interest. Still, others, in their haste for land, were upsetting the operation by invading the property of people as poor as themselves.

Monseñor Mariano Rossell y Arellano, Archbishop of Guatemala, was deeply concerned over the inroads being made into the established social order by the government of Arbenz. He launched a far-reaching procession that carried the venerated image of the "Black Christ of Esquipulas" along dusty roads, into towns and remote villages. He sometimes accompanied the procession himself and everywhere large gatherings materialized while he led prayers to end the "Communist regime."[42] He said that the Christ of Esquipulas would not return to His altar until the government was changed. Then on April 4, 1954, the Archbishop used a Pastoral Letter to denounce Communism, which brought a storm of governmental protest and the applause of the opposition. These acts, perhaps more than anything else, awoke and solidified opposition to the Arbenz programs.

From January, 1953, to June, 1954, when Arbenz was finally overthrown, a total of 1,002 plantations were affected by expropriation decree. Only eleven of these were expropriated in their totality for being either "peon colonies" or for having been completely leased. The total area of all the affected plantations was 1,091,073 hectares (2,694,950 acres), but only 55 percent of their land was taken, or 603,615 hectares (1,490,929 acres).[43] This was considered to be 16.3 percent of the country's total idle lands in private hands available for cultivation.[44] The value of the indemnization bonds for the expropriated properties amounted to Q. 8,345,544.[45]

The three Departments most affected were Escuintla, Alta Verapaz and Izabal. The twenty-two largest farms in the whole country were all located in Escuintla, where a total of 176 *fincas* were affected, yielding 24.9 percent of the total lands expropriated. In Alta Verapaz, 117 *fincas* yielded 15.6 percent of the lands expropriated, while Izabal provided 13.7 percent from fifty-three *fincas*. It is interesting to note that 40 percent of the total lands expropriated were owned by twenty-three persons in lots of more than 100 *caballerías* (10,980 acres) each.[46] These rather boring figures are mentioned in detail because in recent years, some authors have maintained that the Arbenz reform was more propaganda than fact.

Along with the expropriation of private *fincas,* the national *fincas* were also being distributed. Although their production provided the largest segment of government income, it had been decided that they would be given out to the peasants who were working on them, either in usufruct or on a cooperative basis.

By December, 1952, the national *fincas* had been declared to be in their liquidation phase.[47] Three men were named to the liquidation commission. They were instructed to take the necessary measures to safeguard the interests of the nation. They were also encouraged to make the liquidation as quickly as feasible and to encourage the peasants to organize in cooperatives wherever possible. Many of the *fincas* had been run as large industrial enterprises and the yield of money crops was more readily assured if they were not divided into small holdings but worked as cooperatives.

A total of 107 national *fincas* were distributed, 61 to 7,822 farmers in lots of from 5 to 10 hectares (12.4 to 25 acres) of cultivated lands and 15 to 25 hectares (37 to 62 acres) of uncultivated but cultivatable lands. Another forty-six farms were given to the peasants to operate as cooperatives.[48]

In January, 1953, one of the big problems that arose was the fact that in forty-six national fincas that were in the process of being distributed, the peasants had not been paid their usual salaries amounting to Q. 255,000, and many of them were afraid that they might be left out of the land distribution and deprived of their back salaries as well.[49] It was organizational failures such as this that caused much of the unrest in regard to the application of the law.

NOTES

1 Baker, Ross K., *A Study of Military Status and Status Derivation in Three Latin American Armies.* Washington DC: American University, Center for Research of Social Systems, 1967, p. 51.
2 *Ibid.*
3 Johnson, Kenneth. *The Guatemalan Presidential Election of March 6, 1966.* Washington DC: Institute for the Comparative Study of Political Systems, 1967, p. 3.
4 Rodríguez, Mario, *Central America.* Englewood Cliffs, New Jersey: Prentice-Hall, 1965, p. 143.
5 *Ibid.*
6 Estrella de Centroamérica. *Transformación Económica de Guatemala: Hacia Una Reforma Agraria.* Guatemala: Tipografía, Nacional, 1951, pp. 7–15.
7 *Ibid.*, p. 114.
8 Monteforte Toledo, Mario, *Guatemala: Monografía Sociológica.* México: Universidad Nacional Autónoma, 1959, p. 412.
9 Estrella, *Op. Cit.,* p. 151.
10 *Ibid.*, p. 171.
11 *Ibid.*
12 *Ibid.*
13 *Ibid.*
14 Azurdia, Vol. 70, p. 347.
15 *Ibid.*, p. 102.
16 Monteforte Toledo, *Op. Cit.,* p. 436.
17 Estrella, *Op. Cit.,* p. 27.
18 *United States Department of State Bulletin,* September 17, 1951, p. 467.
19 *Ibid.*, p. 474.
20 Azurdia, Vol. 71, p. v.
21 *The New Republic,* January 28, 1952, p. 7.
22 Azurdia, Vol. 71, p. xi–xiv.
23 *Ibid.*, p. xiii.
24 In March, 1960, the case of 27 minority stockholders of IRCA vs United Fruit Co. finally was decided in the Court of Appeals in New York after 11 years of litigation. They had claimed that their company undercharged UFCo. for banana transportation and overcharged its other patrons. The Court decided that the United Fruit Company should pay $4,531,055 for losses to IRCA up to December, 1955. Prices were stabilized after that date adding up to millions more. No reimbursement was made to overcharged Guatemalans. (*El Imparcial,* March 24, 1960).

25 *Time,* March 17, 1952, p. 36.
26 Huizer, *Op. Cit.,* p, 205.
27 Monteforte Toledo, "La Reforma Agraria en Guatemala," *Op. Cit.,* p. 393.
28 Stern, David, "Guatemalan Agrarian Law," *The American Journal of Comparative Law,* Spring 1953, p. 235.
29 *Ibid.,* p. 235.
30 Beals, Carlton, "Guatemala Takes Land from Peasants," *Christian Century,* September 8, 1954, p. 873.
31 *El Imparcial,* June 23, 1958.
32 Stern, *Op. Cit.,* p. 236.
33 *Ibid.*
34 *Time,* January 23, 1952, p. 37.
35 *Ibid.*
36 *Revista de la Facultad de Ciencias Jurídicas y Sociales de Guatemala,* "Cuatrocientos Cuarenta y Cuatro Años de Legislación Agraria," Epoca IV, Nos. 9–12, Enero-Diciembre de 1960, p. 772.
37 Author's personal interview with labor court official, June 1965. See also Whetten, Nathan, *Guatemala: The Land and the People.* New Haven: Yale, 1961, p. 166.
38 *La Hora,* February 2, 1953.
39 Rosenthal, Mario, *Guatemala, The Story of an Emerging Latin American Democracy.* New York: Twayen Publishers, 1962, p. 247.
40 *La Hora,* February 6, 1953.
41 Stern, *Op. Cit.,* p. 237.
42 Guatemala: Secretaría de Divulgación, *Así Se Gestó La Liberación,* 1956, p. 93.
43 CIDA, *Op. Cit.,* p. 41.
44 Paredes Moreira, José Luis, *Aplicación del Decreto 900.* Guatemala: Facultad de Ciencias Económicas, 1964, p. 16.
45 CIDA, *Op. Cit.,* p. 41.
46 Paredes, *Op. Cit.,* p. 16.
47 Azurdia, Vol. 71, p. 617.
48 Fuentes Mohr, A., "Land Settlement and Agrarian Reform in Guatemala," *International Journal of Agrarian Affairs,* January 1955, p. 34.
49 *La Hora,* January 2, 1953.

One day, the apolitical intellectuals of my country will be interrogated by the simplest of our people. They will be asked what they did when their nation died out, slowly, like a sweet fire, small and alone.

Otto René Castillo[1]

5

sweet fire, small and alone

WHEN ARBENZ addressed Congress in March, 1953, he spoke strongly about the land reform:

The most important point in the Government's program as well as that of the October Revolutionary Movement, is a profound change in the backward agricultural production of Guatemala, which will be realized by means of an agricultural reform that will end *latifundios* and semi-feudalistic practices.[2]

There was no doubt that the principal object of this agricultural reform would be the United Fruit Company, largest *latifundista* in Guatemala. The United Fruit Company, with more than 500,000 acres in its possession, was affected by the law in four different decrees of expropriation. On March 3 and 5, 1953, some 209,842 acres were taken from their properties in Escuintla and given to the peasants as private property; on February 25, 1954, it was 171,159 acres in Izabal. This made a total of 386,901 acres.[3]

Although the expropriation had been feared, it was still a shock to the United Fruit Company once it became a reality. The U.S. State Department addressed the Guatemalan Ambas-

sador on the subject. Their principal objection was in regard
to the indemnization offered. The State Department claimed:
"The fixing of the amount of bonds on the basis of tax value
of the properties, especially in light of tax evaluation procedures followed in the present case by the Guatemalan
authorities, bears not the slightest resemblance to just evaluation."[4] The State Department went on to cite the obligations
imposed by international law whereby a government is called
to pay a just or fair compensation at the time of taking the
property of foreigners. International law, they said, cannot be
abrogated by local legislation, even though they had suggested
identical compensation in the case of Ubico's takeover of the
German *fincas*.

The property that was expropriated was registered in the
name of Compañía Agrícola de Guatemala, a Delaware Corporation duly registered to do business in Guatemala and a
completely-owned subsidiary of the United Fruit Company.
The result of the action of expropriation, according to the
State Department, was the undermining of the confidence of
foreign investors.

It is interesting to note that of the 209,842 acres expropriated by the first two decrees, the company claimed that a
total of 111,577 acres were leased to two individuals for cattle,
and to another for agricultural purposes. They also stated that
another 11,500 acres were for the growing of vegetables for
consumption in the company mess halls and hospital.[5] The
government claimed that these extensions were grossly exaggerated, as well as falling within the category of "leased lands."
The United Fruit Company felt otherwise, as did the U.S.
State Department.

The company was offered $612,572 for the 209,842 acres
that were taken. This amounted to $2.86 per acre while the
company had paid $1.48 an acre when they bought the same
land.

The President of the company was quoted in the *Times
Picayune* of New Orleans as saying that he would ask the
State Department to make some kind of claim in regard to the

expropriation of company land should this occur.[6] When it did happen, the State Department acceded to the request. On April 20, 1954, there was a formal claim filed against the Government of Guatemala for $15,854,849 in indemnities. The value of lands and improvements in Tiquisate were said to be $6,984,223 and the damages to other lands, including severance damages were figured at $8,737,600.[7]

The same claim went on to say that in 1928, 302,000 acres had been purchased for $3,130,634 and that subsequently from 1936 to 1952 they had invested a total of $25,942,026 for facilities and the improvement of the lands. The one million dollars that they were being offered for land expropriation under all four decrees did not compare to the $15 million dollars that they were demanding.

The United Fruit Company claimed that they needed great amounts of reserve lands because the "Panama disease," which attacks bananas, necessitates flood-fallowing of lands before they can be used again. However, on the Atlantic coast they had only 4,000 acres planted and had a reserve of 88,000 acres. Even if they doubled their production and did not effect flood-fallow, they had enough reserve land for 110 years more.[8] Some Guatemalan agriculturists pointed out that bananas wear out the soil more quickly and more radically than any other of Guatemala's crops.

When Arbenz addressed Congress in March, 1954, his main concern again was the application of the agrarian reform law. He expressed the fear that the law and its implementation would be the excuse of foreign intervention in Guatemala's internal problems: "The cause of political controversy and social struggle in 1953 was principally the agrarian question."[9] He rejoiced in the positive fruits reached even in so short a time. He stated that some new landholders had received a profit of more than Q. 1,000 in their first year of ownership in comparison to the Q. 200 to Q. 300 which were the average incomes previously. The law had not produced the ruin or the misery of the peasants, as some had claimed, but rather devel-

opment for many who had been favored by it so far. Then
he asked, almost seeming to plead with his fellow citizens,
"Aren't there better possibilities for the future of thousands
of Guatemalans with the expropriation of these United Fruit
lands?"[10] He gave the totals of what had been expropriated and
distributed up to January, 1954: Total hectares distributed,
247,833 (612,148 acres) to 55,734 peasants; 13 national
fincas to 16,200 peasants (a total of 175,418 acres); and
forty-four national *fincas* given as cooperatives to 6,634
peasants.[11]

He did recognize the weaknesses of the application of the
law and he hoped that the government would put forth
greater effort to correct these weaknesses:

There have been some radical deviations in the application of
the law such as the illegal occupation of lands or the invasion of the
lands by some peasants in detriment to others. These questions
are being corrected by the agrarian authorities, but it is necessary
that the directors of the peasant organizations themselves take
care that the application of the agrarian reform law be according
to its fundamental tenets, orientating the agricultural workers
adequately for their own good. There have also been deviations
to the right but these are less grave because the law itself provides
for their correction.[12]

He also mentioned to Congress that the U.S. Department
of State had sent two representatives asking that greater consideration be given to the United Fruit Company in regard to
the expropriation and indemnizations. The President had
answered that the law was legitimate and constitutional and
that foreigners were just as subject to it as were nationals, and
that no type of preferential treatment would be given to
anyone.[13]

A very important aspect of the law was the need for a bank
to handle the credits for the new class of small farmers that
was being created. The Agrarian Bank (Banco Agrario

Nacional) was approved by Congress on July 8, 1953, but the National Mortgage Bank (Banco de Crédito Hipotecario Nacional) handled all the transactions from March, 1953, until the new bank was ready to function in October, 1953. In the eighteen months that these two banks operated, they made loans to 53,829 small farmers amounting to Q. 11,881,431.[14] Of the beneficiaries, 87.4 percent were men who had received lands under the agrarian reform program, and the rest were small farmers who had never before received the benefit of credit. The National Mortgage Bank alone had loaned more than 3 million dollars from March, 1953, until June, 1954, and it had recovered 90 percent of these loans by July,1954. This was an unprecedented and unequaled movement of Guatemalan capital in small loans.

The law was in effect for only two years and was actually implemented for only eighteen months. Its immediate benefits can be enumerated, but its long-range benefits, those that the law primarily meant to effect, were annulled before they could even be observed. Its errors were present for so short a time that it was not possible to correct them before the law itself, judged by many as one of the best agrarian reform laws ever actually implemented, was cancelled.

By June, 1954, about 100,000 families, or approximately half a million people, had received lands. The amount of private land distributed was 603,615 hectares (1,490,929 acres), besides the 101 national *fincas* that were given out.[15] This signifies that the plots of land received by these peasants were sizable and together with available credit, destined to eradicate the *minifundio* (landholdings capable of providing subsistence or less) and the *latifundio,* and to establish a large class of farmers; farmers that would either produce on their own small farms or in cooperatives on the large coffee and sugar plantations.

The 1945 Constitution and the First and Second Governments of the October Revolution did not establish different regulations for the Maya and *Ladinos,* but very definitely the

Government did not agree that the former should continue to live as a foreigner in his own land. The *Instituto Indigenista* had been founded by Arévalo to study specific indigenous problems and to look for solutions within indigenous culture. "Principally, the Government of the Revolution accuses these people of not consuming enough and it disputes their right to continue dying of typhus. It also denies them their traditionally accepted right not to possess land, a really serious matter."[16]

The land reform program was accused of taking the Maya from the protective *patrón-peón* relationship and putting them at the "mercy" of the state. It was asked if the *indio* would be capable of being his own boss. One of the differences was that under the new program, they would pay 3 to 5 percent of their annual harvest as interest to the state instead of one-third to one-half to the *patrón*. It perhaps occurred to many that the state's "mercy" was more beneficial than the *patrón*'s "protection."

An effect of the agrarian reform was that it created an "agrarian climate" in other Departments of the Government. Public health began to broaden its services to previously neglected rural areas. The national education system inaugurated two regional schools for the training of rural teachers—many of whom spoke the indigenous dialects; a program for the study of indigenous languages was begun. A hospital in San Juan Sacatepéquez began to train auxiliary rural nurses. Roads to many villages were constructed, giving the small coffee growers freedom to choose their buyers. Joaquín Noval, a Guatemalan anthropologist, concludes this list of "indigenous projects" by saying: "Who knows whether the poor rural *Ladinos* or the poor urban people should envy the Indians or vice versa? With the new factors now at work in Guatemala, they may merge together as a better nation."[17] One thing was certain: if the Maya was now to be envied, it was indeed a social revolution of fantastic proportions.

As more peasants began to get better income from their new lands, they came to form part of the money economy. As a result, many merchants began to appear in Escuintla, Retalhuleu, Mazatenango and Coatepeque.

The minimum wage in the national *fincas* had been set at eighty cents a day. When the agrarian reform made labor more scarce for the large landowners, they were forced to increase the wages to their workers. Previously, the government attempted to enforce the minimum wage law artificially. Now, the law of supply and demand began to take effect.

It is no great criticism of the Arbenz Government to admit that the principal defect of the law was mainly in its implementation. The agrarian committees had a difficult time controlling the peasants. In San Miguel Petapa on June 11, 1953, a local agrarian committee took lands belonging to the village composed of 2,500 people and gave them to sixty peasants from other towns. The people, small farmers themselves, appealed to the Government for redress of the injustice and the Government sent a representative to hear the facts and try to correct the abuse.[18] On February 12, 1953, it was announced in *La Hora* that any agrarian committees that committed errors would be fined. The newspapers later reported that the threat had been carried out, with the firing of some officials and the fining of others.[19] The explosiveness of the need for land was the real cause of the turmoil and it is difficult to look back even now and to say how it could have been avoided.

The second most noteworthy deficiency was the tendency of the law to punish the more generous landowners. Some of the landowners who had given better treatment to their *colonos* and provided them with larger and better plots for their personal crops, suffered more than those who were more selfish, since the law stipulated that plots being used by *colonos* were to become their property. Another point of contention was the stipulation that where fifteen or more families were living together on a plantation, the site of the houses was to become their property and the area was to be designated a municipality, making the settlement into a rural village. Land had to be set aside for this. These two points of the law tended to divide property since most of the landowners had their *colonos* living on one side of the plantation and the lands assigned to them might be on any other part of the *finca*. When these lands were expropriated in favor of the *colonos,* the owner found himself with split property which made it difficult to maintain a unified farm.

The vested interests of the landowners constituted the major reason for their condemnation of the law. It was declared unconstitutional because the right of appeal was limited and an owner who believed himself cheated had no recourse which would favor him. This accusation of unconstitutionality was found to be erroneous after Arbenz was overthrown and the issue brought before the Supreme Court (*El Imparcial,* August 10, 1954).

The price being paid for the expropriated lands, determined by the tax declarations made before May, 1952, suited none of the landowners. Hernán Santa Cruz, regional director of FAO for Latin America, said:

An agrarian reform always carries with it an element of confiscation in the general interest of society, and for this reason long delayed payments must be accepted at no less than twenty years payment, with low interest rates and at prices much lower than the market values, which in Latin America are usually much inflated.[20]

Raúl Branco, of the Center for Development Planning of the United Nations, states:

Given the assumption that land reform will be carried out by due legal process, who would pay for the land confiscated and how would payments be made? Since the landless peasants are by definition poor, the government will have to pick up the tab, even if only to finance the sale to the peasant. If the 'rights' of the landowning class were fully taken into consideration, payments would tend to be made in cash and at rates far above the capitalized value of the land. Obviously, no country could afford to carry out an extensive land reform program with such a procedure. Thus, payments must be necessarily made mostly in bonds, which will be strongly resisted by the present landowning class. Even if a compromise is reached involving limited land reform with a part of the compensation paid in cash, I fail to see the economic rationale of using scarce government funds to finance the transfer of ownership titles of existing immovable assets, when the same funds could be used for financing the creation of new productive capacity.[21]

The formation of cooperatives was compared by some,[22] not unintentionally, to the Russian kolkhozes, and they were generally feared as were the rural unions that had been encouraged since the time of Arévalo. The agricultural labor unions had been one of the first tools used by the government to provide the rural workers with an effective lever with which to demand their rights from the landowners.[23] The landowners historically had had the protection of the government for securing plenty of cheap labor. This was the second government (and the last, unfortunately) that had given preferential treatment to the workers and peasants.

The unrest felt by the landowners was made evident by the political pressure they tried to use in order to change the state of affairs. One of their most effective weapons was the use of the label "Communist" to discredit the government and put fear in the hearts of the peasants. In the use of this weapon they found the Church and its ministers to be particularly good allies.

There is no doubt that there were Marxists in the Guatemalan government. Two of them were particularly active in the formulation and administration of the agrarian reform law: Víctor Manuel Gutierrez and José Manuel Fortuny. Carlos Manuel Pellecer, another Marxist, was the head of the agrarian committee in Escuintla. The Guatemalan Labor Party (Partido Guatemalteco del Trabajo) established at the end of Arévalo's government, was the Communist party in Guate-

mala. The U.S. Department of State published a study about
Communist "intervention" in Guatemala in August, 1954, in
which they describe the PGT as follows:

The PGT is a party of young *ladino* intellectuals of the lower middle
class. Its founders and present leaders are young school teachers, ex-
university students, journalists, white collar workers and former
employees of U.S. and foreign enterprises in Guatemala. This was
the sector of society most frustrated under the archaic social structure of Guatemala . . . which, until after World War II, remained
a backward dictator-ridden agricultural country where two percent
of the landholdings covered seventy percent of the arable land and
over half of the population consisted of illiterate Indians living apart
from the currents of twentieth century life.[24]

The party members, during Arévalo's Government, had
become involved in reform and had invited experienced men
from other countries to help them in their organization programs, especially in the fields of labor and education. The
General Confederation of Workers of Guatemala became a
member of the World Federation of Trade Unions (WFTU).[25]
They worked very hard under the guidance of Víctor Manuel
Gutiérrez and the special tutelage of Lombardo Toledano, a
highly respected Marxist from Mexico, to establish unions and
educate the workers in organization. Lombardo Toledano, as
head of the WFTU's Mexico-based affiliate, the Confederation
of Workers of Latin America, was instrumental in bringing
the Guatemalan Confederation into the WFTU.

One would have to consider membership in the CGTG or
the CNCG to being identical with membership in the Communist party, in order for the list of peasants from San Ray-
mundo, qualified as Communists in the House Hearings Report
of the 83rd Congress, to be considered a valid accusation.[26]
The names of the peasants listed there are all indigenous
names. It hardly seems possible that illiterate men, just four
years after the founding of the labor confederation, could have

been converted to and instructed in political Communism in so short a time. (See p. 92.)

In 1952 the labor and peasant confederations joined forces and began to work more closely together. In May, 1952, there were 568 unions and in February, 1954, they had grown to 1,758.[27] Even the Department of State Report admits that "the PGT exerts its influence to a somewhat lesser degree over the CNCG than it does over the CGTG."[28] This same Report goes on to explain the plans of the Communist party:

In International affairs, the party (PGT) has emphasized as its first task the 'Peace Campaign' which is defined as preventing the harnessing of Guatemala to the 'war chariot of imperialism'—i.e. preventing Guatemala from taking its role in the defense of the Western Democratic community grouped around the United States. As the corollary in domestic Guatemalan politics, the PGT has announced as its first task the implementation of Guatemala's 1952 agrarian reform law which is designed to transfer much of the country's potential arable land to new small farmers, and as its second, the heightening of the struggle against United States 'monopolistic' companies operating in Guatemala. These domestic programs tend toward the breakdown of the established order and are simultaneously adapted to the immediate objective of weakening Guatemala's position in the Western community and the ultimate objective of preparing the ground for the Communists coming to power.[29]

In even clearer terms the party outlined its *Camino Guatemalteco* (Guatemalan Way) in seven points to be followed after their May, 1953 plenary session:

(a) The application of the agrarian reform must be carried on.

(b) Intensify the fight against the foreign monopolies and increase the antiimperialistic sentiment of our people, especially against the United Fruit Company, IRCA, and the *Empresa Electrica* (American and Foreign Power Company subsidiary).

(c) Denounce the counterrevolutionary activities of feudal and imperialistic reaction.

(d) Give increased support to progressive measures undertaken by the democratic government of President Arbenz, such as the highway to the Atlantic which will allow Guatemala, by competing with U.S.-owned IRCA to free itself from monopolistic exploitation.

(e) Improve the living conditions of the people, especially by struggling for a minimum daily rural wage of eighty cents and an urban wage of Q. 1.25.

(f) Cultivate and strengthen organic unity and united action in the working class, by fighting against diversionism in labor organization.

(g) Tighten the alliance between the workers and the peasants.[30]

The party membership was difficult to ascertain. The director of the Departmento Nacional Agrario (DNA) was Major Alfonso Martínez Estévez, considered to be an opportunist nonCommunist. But seven inspectors of the DNA were publicly registered as Marxists and seven others had been identified as such. Another twelve out of the 350 employees of the DNA were "known" to be Communists, for a possible total of twenty-six Marxists in all.[31]

U.S. Ambassador John E. Peurifoy had come to Guatemala from Greece in the early 1950's, where he had been very active and successful in fighting Communism. When he appeared at the Congressional hearings in August, 1954, after the Arbenz overthrow, he claimed that the "Communist party used the agrarian reform as a weapon to gain political control over the farm workers and the landless peasants."[32] This was the cry of the expropriated landlords, and the United States Government obviously agreed. Nathan Whetten, traveling through Guatemala during the time of the agrarian reform, observed the following:

The Communists were under strict discipline. They worked day and night to put their program across. They traveled throughout the country under difficult conditions in order to learn the problems of local and national concern. When there was land to be distributed to peasants by the government, they were the first to arrive on the scene and the last to leave. They seemed to accumulate more information about local problems than anyone else; and the peasants gradually began looking to them for advice.[33]

He also describes a visit to the headquarters of the CNCG where the men were available at all hours of the day and night to counsel peasants with great patience and solicitude.

The government of Guatemala was not a Communist government. Communists held only four out of fifty-six seats in Congress. There was much political activity and freedom and the newspapers of that time demonstrate that there was also freedom of the press and free elections for Congress. There was much made of the fact that José Manuel Fortuny, a very well-known and active Communist, lost the election to Congress in 1952. And President Arbenz had continually reiterated his intentions of converting Guatemalan economy from "feudalism" to capitalism, hardly a Communist goal.

The U.S. Government had followed the expropriation of United Fruit Company lands with great concern. When the first expropriations had taken place in March, 1953, the State Department had sent a message to the Guatemalan Embassy in Washington, saying:

The Government of the United States sees with great concern the way the agrarian reform law of Guatemala has been applied to the property of the United Fruit Company in Guatemala . . . The Guatemalan Government seems to be applying the law in such a way as to make impossible the continuation of United Fruit activities in Guatemala.[34]

Viewing what the United Fruit Company activities had been, there is no reason to doubt the truth of this allegation.

Guatemala answered the message as follows:

The agrarian reform law is a general law, applicable equally to any person, natural or juridical—national or foreign—who owns rural lands in the national territory. Its application constitutes an act of inalienable sovereignty, therefore the government of Guatemala cannot consider at present, nor in the future, the possibility of converting this business into a matter for international discussions.[35]

The expropriations of the United Fruit Company land continued. But several attempts against the government were made. Arms were found on company property. The struggle between the Guatemalan government and the company became more and more evident.

In March, 1954, the tenth Inter-American Conference was held in Caracas, Venezuela. The U.S. Secretary of State, Mr. John Foster Dulles, assisted at the Conference until a seventeen-to-one vote had been passed whereby the countries of Latin America agreed to their unity and mutual defense against "Communist aggression." Guatemala voted against the agreement which gave the United States freedom to intervene anywhere in the Americas in the defense against Communism. Mexico and Argentina abstained, and Uruguay voted in favor of it but its representative told reporters afterwards that they were very unhappy about it but felt forced to vote affirmatively because of U.S. pressure.[36] After Mr. Dulles left, the Conference ran for two more weeks. They had just begun to work.

The Latins are not unaware of the threat to their security implied by International Communism, but they have long felt that they cannot solve effectively their social and economic problems, which are indeed the breeders of Communism, without substantial help from one or more of the great industrial and capital exporting nations. This was the problem they had come to Caracas to discuss and Mr. Dulles' proposal received their support because the present U.S. administration has made it reasonably clear that only nations which take approved views of International Communism can expect to be recipients of economic aid or technical assistance without much American grumbling . . . Mr. Dulles' departure was, in their eyes, tantamount to saying that he was concerned only with their support, and could not take time to discuss Latin American internal problems since they were not of sufficient importance.[37]

A month later, in April, 1954, the Department of State made a formal claim to the Guatemalan Government for $15,845,849 for the expropriated lands of the United Fruit Company. The Guatemalan Embassy in Washington answered in May and said, among other things:

If the government of the United States continues to act in favor of the illegitimate pretensions of this company, the Government of Guatemala cannot but consider such an attitude as the insistence of intervening in the internal affairs of the Republic of Guatemala, contravening in this way the most solid principles of the Inter-American community.[38]

Mr. Dulles held a news conference on May 25, 1954, after receiving Guatemala's answer to his claim in favor of the United Fruit Company. He accused the Guatemalan government of being infiltrated with Communists. He based his judgment on three significant factors: first, Guatemala was the only Latin American State that did not ratify the Mutual Defense Treaty of Rio de Janeiro, drawn up at the Inter-American Conference of 1947, during the Caracas Conference; second, Guatemala was the only country that voted in Caracas against the statement that the domination of the political institutions of any American State by the International Communist movement would constitute a threat to the sovereignty and the political independence of the American States; and third, Guatemala was the only American State that had been the recipient of a shipment of arms from behind the Iron Curtain.[39] It was obvious that Guatemala could not vote for a treaty that was tantamount to giving foreign governments permission to intervene in its internal affairs.

The Secretary of State failed to mention that the shipment of arms from Czechoslovakia was precipitated because the United States had maintained an effective arms embargo against Guatemala ever since 1948 by all nations in the U.S. sphere of influence.[40] Later it became public knowledge that the United States was supplying arms in 1953 and 1954 to the governments of Honduras and Nicaragua, as well as to Guatemalan exiles in both these countries and El Salvador for the express purpose of overthrowing the Arbenz Government.

Dulles then went on to quote a statement by Guillermo Toriello, the Guatemalan representative to the Caracas Conference, and to refute it:

The Guatemalan Government boasts that it is not a colony of the United States. We are proud that Guatemala can honestly say that. The United States is not in the business of collecting colonies. The important question is whether Guatemala is subject to Communist colonialism.[41]

As the United States continued to arm and train the Castillo Armas forces in Honduras, Guatemalan protests in the United Nations were met by the U.S. delegate and acting president of the Security Council, an old defender of United Fruit Company in Guatemala, Henry Cabot Lodge:

While the reports that we receive on the situation in Guatemala are incomplete and fragmentary, the information available to the United States thus far strongly suggests that the situation does not involve aggression but is a revolt of Guatemalans against Guatemalans.[42]

On June 30, 1954, when the military invasion against Arbenz had succeeded, Dulles addressed the United States in a radio and television newscast:

Communist agitators . . . dominated the social security organization and ran the agrarian reform program. The judiciary made one valiant attempt to protect its integrity and independence. But the Communists, using their control of the legislative body, caused the Supreme Court to be dissolved when it refused to give approval to a Communist-contrived law.[43]

It must be remembered that the Communists were only four out of fifty-six in Congress, hardly "control of the legislative body." The Secretary of State continued:

Throughout the period I have outlined, the Guatemalan Government and Communist agents throughout the world have persistently attempted to obscure the real issue—that of Communist imperialism —by claiming that the U.S. is only interested in protecting American business. We regret that there have been disputes between the Guatemalan Government and the United Fruit Company. We have urged repeatedly that these disputes be submitted for settlement to an international tribunal or to international arbitration. That is the way to dispose of problems of this sort. But this issue is relatively unimportant.[44]

If this issue was "relatively unimportant," Dulles had not made the basic issue any clearer by making such insistent demands in the United Fruit Company's favor. Nor did he think it very important that the issue of the $15 million dollars payment be submitted to an international tribunal. The United Fruit Company's word was sufficient for the United States to back their claims. The fact of the matter is that Dulles, as a senior partner of the Cromwell-Sullivan law firm, the United Fruit Company's lawyers, had been personally instrumental in drawing up the contract between the United Fruit Company and Dictator Jorge Ubico in 1936, and his continued support of the company's claims left his motivation open to criticism.

Castillo Armas was the man chosen by the United States State Department to be the beneficiary of arms, money, planes, pilots and advisors. He was to be the hero of the day, the man who would push back the tides of the "international conspiracy" that had prompted this "Communist-contrived" law.

He was to be the savior of the landowning class and the protector of the United Fruit Company's interests. And so, with complete disregard for the freedom and self-determination of the Guatemalan people, the United States added one more page to its long history of intervention in Latin American affairs under the banner of the highest idealism, while seeking principally the furtherance of U.S. economic interests at the expense of Guatemala's poorest people.

NOTES

1 Guatemalan poet killed by government forces in April, 1967, in the ambush of a guerrilla band.
2 Nájera Farfán, Mario, *Los Estafadores de la Democracia,* Buenos Aires: Editorial Glem, 1956, p. 156.
3 Paredes, *Op. Cit.,* p. 30.
4 *U.S. Department of State Bulletin,* September 14, 1953, p. 357.
5 *Ibid.,* p. 358.
6 Selser, Gregorio, *El Guatemalazo.* Argentina: Editorial Iguazu, 1961, p. 32.
7 *U.S. Department of State Bulletin,* May 3, 1954, p. 678.
8 Fuentes Mohr, *Op. Cit.,* p. 34.
9 Azurdia, Vol. 73, p. v.
10 *Ibid.,* p. vii.
11 *Ibid.*
12 *Ibid.,* p. ix.
13 *Ibid.,* p. xxiii.
14 CIDA, *Op. Cit.,* p. 43.
15 CIDA, *Op. Cit.,* pp. 40 and 42.
16 Noval, Joaquín, "Guatemala, The Indian and the Land," *The Americas,* March, 1954, p. 6.
17 *Ibid.,* p. 43.
18 Guatemala: Dirección General de Asuntos Agrarios, *La Evidencia de los Hechos.* Guatemala: 1957, p. 99.

19 *La Hora,* May 29, 1954.

20 Paredes, *Op. Cit.,* p. 16.

21 Branco, Raúl, "Center for Development Planning," *Journal of Inter-American Studies,* Vol. 9, 1967, p. 234.

22 Nájera, *Op. Cit.,* p. 157.

23 Adams, Richard, *Cultural Surveys of Panama, Nicaragua, Guatemala, El Salvador.* Washington; Pan American Sanitary Bureau, 1957, p. 297.

24 U.S. Department of State, *Op. Cit.,* p. 36.

25 The WFTU was founded shortly after World War II by the British Trade Union Congress, the North American Congress of Industrial Organizations (CIO), the French General Confederation of Workers and the Soviet Trade Unions. The American Federation of Labor (AFL) refused to join the WFTU because of Communist participation in the new organization and set about gathering support to oppose the WFTU. This organizational campaign, with United States State Department backing, eventually resulted in the formation of the Interamerican Organization of Workers (ORIT), which as a Subcommittee Report (published July 15, 1968, p. 8) of the Senate Foreign Relations Committee says: "ORIT has never quite solved the problem of emphasis as between fighting Communism and strengthening democratic trade unions." ORIT later endorsed the CIA sponsored overthrow of President Arbenz, as well as the Bay of Pigs and the Dominican Republic invasions. George Meany, president of the AFL-CIO, denounced the Subcommittee report and refused labor's official support for the Subcommittee chairman, Wayne Morse, in his reelection bid less than four months later. Senator Morse lost the election by a very close margin.

26 House Hearings, *Ninth Interim Report on Hearings Before the Sub-committee on Latin America on Communist Aggression in Latin America.* Washington, D.C.: U.S. Printing Office, 1954, p. 271.

27 Schneider, *Op. Cit.,* p. 169.

28 U.S. Department of State, *Op. Cit.,* p. 39.

29 *Ibid.*

30 *Ibid.,* p. 66.

31 *Ibid.,* p. 70.

32 House Hearings, *Op. Cit.,* p. 115.

33 Whetten, Nathan, "Land Reform in a Modern World," *Rural Sociology,* Vol. 19, 1954, p. 334.

34 Toriello, *Op. Cit.,* p. 58.

35 *Ibid.*

36 *New York Times,* March 7, 1954.

37 Taylor, Philip B., "The Guatemalan Affair," *American Political Science Review,* September 1956, p. 791.

38 Toriello, *Op. Cit.*, p. 258.
39 *U.S. Department of State Bulletin,* June 7, 1954, p. 873.
40 Toriello, *Op. Cit.*, p. 143 and Taylor, *Op. Cit.*, p. 794.
41 *U.S. Department of State Bulletin,* June 7, 1954, p. 873.
42 U.S. Department of State, *Op. Cit.*, p. 14.
43 *Ibid.*, p. 31.
44 *Ibid.*, p. 32.

The United States appear to be destined by Providence to plague America with misery in the name of liberty.

attributed to Simón Bolívar

6

misery in the name of liberty

COLONEL CARLOS CASTILLO ARMAS, despite the fact that he was obviously a strongwilled person, was in many ways a helpless figure. Caught up in the turmoil of strong cross-currents of political ideologies, Guatemalan economic and social backwardness of abysmal proportions, with ties to powerful national and international blocks not always of his own choosing, he took the reins of Guatemalan government in the early days of July, 1954, and held them until his assassination in August, 1957. That he managed to survive at the head of his government for three years is a tribute in itself.

Castillo Armas became official head of the new government through an election held within the reigning military Junta on July 7, 1954. He had already been included as a member of the five-man military Junta due to the "Pact of El Salvador"[1] which had taken place on July 2, 1954, under the auspices of the President of El Salvador, Colonel Oscar Osorio. Present also at the meeting were José María Peralta, President of the National Congress of El Salvador; Archbishop Genaro Verolino, Apostolic Nuncio of the Vatican in Guatemala and El Salvador; Colonel J. Alberto Funes, Ambassador of Salvador in Guatemala; Colonel Elfego Monzón, reigning member of the military Junta which had taken over after Arbenz had stepped down; and Colonel Carlos Castillo Armas, head of the National Liberation Movement.

After Castillo Armas had won his "military victory" at Chiquimula, he had returned to El Salvador to await arrangements for his inclusion in the new government. This was effected by the "Pact of El Salvador" at which time it was agreed that an election would take place within fifteen days from among the Junta's five members (besides Monzón and Castillo Armas, they were Colonels Cruz Salazar, Dubois and Oliva) and a new head of the government would be declared. It was a foregone conclusion that the winner would be Castillo Armas, which is exactly what occurred in Guatemala on July 7, 1954. At the same time, Colonels Cruz Salazar and J. Mauricio Dubois resigned.

We refer to the "military victory" of Castillo Armas at Chiquimula for want of a better expression. It is doubtful that much of a battle took place. The Guatemalan newspapers of those days are filled with photographs of soldiers of the "Liberation Army" lolling around in the sun, conversing lazily in the shade of tropical trees or simply practicing marksmanship. Nowhere is there a picture that resembles a military encounter. The foreign press was excluded from the "battle area" for unexplained reasons, one of which may be that there was no real battle. It is true that skirmishes occurred, but their limitation seems to be reflected in Castillo Armas' own words:

In the wars of all times and countries, that which counts and makes history is not the number of effective soldiers or the quality of its armaments, but the socio-political results which are obtained as a consequence of victory; and in this case, the Battle of Chiquimula has national importance, because it was there that the liberty of Guatemala was won.[2]

Even the radio address of Arbenz on June 27, 1954, as he handed over the Government to a military junta headed by Colonel Enrique Díaz, did not reflect a preoccupation with the military capacity of the "Liberation Army":

The military situation of the country is not difficult; quite the contrary. The enemy, the foreign mercenary bands recruited by Castillo Armas, are not only weak but incapable and cowardly. We have proven this in the few battles we have sustained. The enemy managed to advance and capture the Department of Chiquimula only because of the attacks of the mercenary aviation. I do not think that our armed forces will encounter great difficulty in defeating them and expelling them from the country.[3]

There is much contained herein that is still shrouded in mystery. If Arbenz did not fear a military defeat, why did he resign? Some claim it was sheer cowardice. Those who know him best claim he is incapable of cowardly conduct. Another explanation was that he feared imminent and massive United States participation (the bombings had already had a demoralizing effect on the population) and felt that he could best avoid this by stepping down himself and turning his government over to Colonel Enrique Díaz, his Minister of Defense, and two other Colonels. Most observers feel the reason was that Arbenz could not convince his supporters in the army to fight nor would they agree to arm the thousands of peasants who were ready to duplicate the feat of repelling counter-revolutionary forces as they had done for Arévalo in July, 1949. Such a switch of Army loyalty was not without precedent. The President apparently thought that Colonel Enrique Díaz might have more influence at this time with some of his fellow officers.[4] Díaz immediately stated his firm intention of expelling Castillo Armas from the national territory and almost as immediately was replaced by Colonel Elfego Monzón, the second member of the new Junta. The maneuverings of U.S. Ambassador, John E. Peurifoy, played a big role in this substitution. He was present when the change of power occurred,[5] and there is little doubt that he promised and threatened that the United States would see Castillo Armas in the president's chair and that the Junta had better accept it.

Arbenz and his followers today admit that he made a grave mistake in not remaining to fight.[6] There was at least one

peasant force already assembled in Cobán in central Guatemala, preparing to leave for the battlefront that wept openly
upon learning of the President's resignation.[7] There is little
question that Arbenz could have gotten much support if he
had gambled for time. When he did resign, he did not believe
that Castillo Armas would be successful.[*]

One of the elements that Arbenz mentions in his speech is
the "foreign mercenary bands" and "the mercenary aviation."
He was referring to the fact that the forces of Castillo Armas
had been trained, equipped and financed by the United States
Government and his air force (six P-47's) was donated and
flown by personnel of the Central Intelligence Agency, then
under the direction of Allen Dulles, brother of the Secretary of
State. Despite Cabot Lodge's disclaimer in the United Nations,
the U.S. interference in Guatemala was public knowledge and
its brazenness shocked many U.S. allies. Prime Minister
Clement Attlee of England wanted to know "how U.S. support
of an antiCommunist faction in Guatemala, differed from, say,
Chinese support of a Communist faction in Vietnam."[8]

Many authors have since minimized United States military
participation, yet the CIA air force was better equipped than
Guatemala's own, the head of which, Colonel Rodolfo Men-
doza Azurdia, had already been convinced to desert to Salvador by the former Deputy Air Attache at the United States
Embassy . Nor should the psychological impact of the threat of
intervention by the world's strongest military power in a nation
of just over three million people be minimized. United States
participation was significant enough that President Dwight
Eisenhower, after his retirement, listed the defeat of "Communism" in Guatemala as one of the highlights of his administration.

But to say that Castillo Armas was only the tool of United
States foreign policy in Guatemala would be an exaggeration.
He had proven his capabilities and sentiments in late 1950
when he attempted a military coup against the Arévalo government and was condemned to death. His dramatic escape

* Personal interview with exiled Arbenz aids in Mexico, March, 1968.

from prison put him high on the list of *macho* (virile) heroes for many Guatemalans. But it cannot be ignored that he had received much help and support from the United States and thus became a participant in the international cold-war battle between the United States and Russia, between the "international Communist conspiracy" on one side and the "democratic free world" on the other. He could not now ignore a moral debt of gratitude, nor, for that matter, his monetary obligations to the government of the United States.

It would be incorrect to suppose that his antiCommunism was generated by United States sponsorship of his movement, as well as to think that he was indifferent to the United States' applause for his antiCommunism. He was obviously a firm advocate, if not necessarily a believer, of the international conspiracy concept and a cold war gladiator in his own right. His *Plan de Tegucigalpa,* which had been formulated the preceding year in the capital of Honduras and named for that city, was a general statement of his aims, indicating that the primary principle of his movement was the *desovietización*[9] of Guatemala. In one of his first statements as head of the new government, he declared he would "satisfy the needs of the people, destroying the arguments that Communism uses to rob the world."[10] Most of his legislation contains preambles denouncing the "Communism" of the Arbenz government. All of his public statements attempt to show that the failures of the preceding governments were such because they were Communist-inspired and Communist-directed, and that he would be successful by not only avoiding that route but by vigorously closing it to others.

The danger of viewing all social reforms through the cold war prism lay in believing that all measures passed by the Arbenz government were bad because they were inspired by Russians for the purpose of turning the country over to Russia. Who actually believed this, and who merely stated it because it fitted his own purposes, is hard to tell. But the AGA proclaimed it as their official doctrine. That it fitted their purposes, there is no doubt. To prove to themselves, to all

Guatemalans and to the world that the land reform program of Arbenz was an integral part of the international conspiracy, was the order of the day, every day.

There is no question that the members of AGA, along with The United Fruit Company, were the staunchest opponents of the Arbenz agrarian reform, as the ones most affected by it. They gave money, food and men to the Castillo Armas crusade, for they were the ones to benefit most by his success. After the Castillo Armas triumphal entry into Guatemala City (on a flight from Salvador in the United States Ambassador's plane) the AGA made a big fuss over sending food and supplies to the victims of the battles in Chiquimula.

It was a formidable array of opponents for Arbenz and backers for Castillo Armas: the United States government, the United Fruit Company, the AGA, the Catholic Church and every self-proclaimed antiCommunist on the two continents. Emotions had been heated to the boiling point and when Castillo Armas finally managed to take over, many people were not just looking to him for action, but were demanding it of him.

Despite the fact that Castillo Armas had said that "In this crusade, there joined together men and women of all groups and social sectors; old fighters and young enthusiasts; professional people, workers, peasants, soldiers, farmers, businessmen and industrialists,"[11] it is certain that his support was not that broad. His army was estimated at 1,000 men, most of them political exiles living in Honduras, Salvador and Nicaragua, plus the few peasants that he had picked up on his journey from the Honduran border.

Castillo Armas recognized the lack of support among the peasants and this is evidenced by the fact that one of the new Junta's first decrees was the cancellation of the voting franchise of illiterates. This effectively closed the door to 72 percent of the Guatemalan population to participation in the Liberation government and it served as a warning to the peasants as to how Castillo Armas regarded them—certainly not as supporters.

Castillo Armas was in power only a few days when his regime had to face the fact that some of the landowners had already begun to take "justice" into their own hands and reclaim their expropriated lands, as is evident from newspaper accounts. On July 12, 1954, "AntiCommunism Day", in his first public discourse, Castillo Armas found it necessary to say that:

For national recuperation and for the establishment of social justice, the immediate collaboration of the *finqueros* and *patronos* is indispensable. It ought to be understood that the MLN cannot be a pretext for committing injustices and taking vengeance. Those who do it, far from cooperating to heal the country, are sabotaging our Movement. Neither the firing of workers nor the recuperation of lands can serve as a base for a just restructuring of the Nation. To eradicate Communism does not signify to persecute the worker and the honest peasant who in every case merits the protection of the government.[12]

That such a stand was necessary is corroborated in the newspaper accounts of those difficult days. *El Imparcial* for July 2, 1954, stated that "seventeen workers were killed in Tiquisate by antiCommunists." July 6 reported a fight between "four hundred Communist *Indians* and antiCommunist *Ladinos* of San Juan Sacatepéquez in which seventeen *Indians* were killed and many wounded." On July 8, the Minister of Interior, Jorge A. Serrano, said that the jails are full of "aroused peasant farmers," and on July 13, he announced that 4,000 "Communists" were in jail throughout the country. *El Imparcial* of July 9 told of the "arrest warrants against the humble peasants of Progreso as Communists." Who was a Communist and who was not, who had received a piece of land legally and who had not, who was being excessively vengeful for personal reasons and who was not, were the problems of those days and the Head of State was not finding it easy to encounter a solution.

An interesting study was made at this time of a sampling

of 250 prisoners in three Guatemala City jails from a total of
1,600 who were there accused of Communism. The study was
conducted immediately after the fall of the Arbenz government by Stokes Newbold, who has since been identified as the
American anthropologist, Richard Newbold Adams, an
authority on Guatemalan affairs. The study is called "Receptivity to Communist Fomented Agitation in Rural Guatemala"[13] and accepts the basic premises of the cold war conflict:

This awareness of a new sociological potential had its distinct ideological aspects; the sociological changes themselves involved vast
alterations in the traditional ways of thinking. It was probably of
little importance to the rural people involved in this process
whether it was done under one name or another; what was important was that there was, for the first time, a series of channels of
communication and permissive activity between themselves and
authority. That Communism abused these channels to the point
that a change in government was brought about through revolution
is a tragedy of history.[14]

Actually the study proves just the opposite of "Communist
abuse" of the channels of communication, but since the survey
was obviously made with the cooperation of the Castillo Armas
government, perhaps these conclusions were meant to be
proven by the investigation. One wonders why such an eminent
scholar would use an "alias" for the study which is actually
very objective. In describing the political orientation of the
interviewees, the author states:

I gradually started to believe that many, if not all, the persons who
claimed ignorance of the issues actually knew little or nothing about
them. Support for this is to be found in the fact that a person who
claimed not to recognize the name of the Communist labor leader,
Víctor Manuel Gutiérrez, would also not recognize Mariano
Rossell, the Archbishop of Guatemala. By the way in which some
of the questions were answered, it was quite apparent they had
actually not heard of the "struggle between the classes," the
"dictatorship of the proletariat," the "Communist Manifesto," and

various other ideas and organizations mentioned. . . . All the inter-
viewers agreed that voluntary responses on the part of the interviewees consisted principally in comments to the effect that (1)
they knew nothing; (2) they were poor, illiterate people; (3) they
were in favor of the government in power; (4) they wanted only to
return to their families and work, and (5) they were Catholics. The
"know nothingness" was apparent throughout the interviews. In
response to a question as to whether they thought (an opinion,
not a statement of fact) the new government would continue with
the agrarian reform, the labor code and the labor unions, 67 percent, 66 percent and 84 percent of the persons said they did not
know; when pressed, most said they would not presume to say
what the government would do.[15]

The author then goes on to show some of the ideas that the
prisoners had picked up since 1944:

There is little doubt that some of those interviewed were not so
concerned by the change in government as they were that they
had landed in jail as a result. On the other hand, there were also
70 (and may well have been more who felt it may not have been
politic to give such an answer) who said that "a government
selected by the people" was an important part of a democratic
country. This was the second most popular response to the question concerning the characteristics of such a country; "protection
of the poor" was first. In view of the common opinion that illiterate
people are apolitical, it is of interest to note that 62 percent of
those who chose "a government selected by the people" as a char-
acteristic of a democracy, were illiterate. It would appear that the
efforts of the post-1944 governments did have some effect in
putting this idea into circulation.[16]

All in all the study proves to be a strong indication that
there was little political manipulation or indoctrination of the
peasants with Communist ideology by the Arbenz government.

Castillo Armas knew he had to undo the Arbenz Agrarian
Reform Law (#900) because this promise was the basis of

his movement, but he didn't know exactly how to go about it. He had to move slow enough to prevent organized resistance on the part of the peasants and fast enough to avoid the precipitous actions of the landowners. On July 20, 1954, he made another appeal to the landlords not to take justice into their own hands.[17]

But it seems that his efforts were not very successful. The General Confederation of Workers compiled a list in February, 1955, of names and places where murders had taken place in those first few weeks of the "Liberation."[18] It lists 217 persons and states that thirty-eight peasants were killed in Las Cruces, forty-nine peasants killed in Rio Shusto, eighteen peasants killed in Los Cimientos, twenty-nine peasants killed in San Juan Sacatepéquez, two members of the agrarian committee killed in San Juan Acasaguastlán, and other laborers, truck drivers, train workers and soldiers murdered. It goes on to state that "lists of people assassinated in other areas of the country are being compiled and will be published as soon as the data can be verified."[19] The exact figures will never be known because the government made sure that no open investigations were ever made. In fact, many of the murders were later blamed on the Arbenz government, which had executed an undisclosed number of opponents thought to be assisting Castillo Armas in those last fateful days of June.*

It was in an effort to accomplish the mandate that he had been given in Tegucigalpa, Honduras, to return the expropriated lands to their original owners while still avoiding chaos, that Castillo Armas promulgated his first agrarian decree (#31) before he was a month in office. It was meant to be "translated into a gradual but firm repeal of the agrarian reform as institutionalized by Decree #900 (Arbenz Agrarian Reform) of the national Congress."[20] This new law of Castillo

---

* Arbenz opponents claim the figure is in the vicinity of 800 but for years they could never produce more than two hundred names of people who disappeared from the Castillo Armas forces. It is likely that both sides were guilty, though Castillo Armas was more vindictive.

Armas denies categorically that the agrarian reform law of Arbenz produced any benefit. Then it goes on to admit implicitly that there were such benefits by stating that the peasants and agricultural workers who had received parcels, credits and other benefits from the application of the agrarian reform would remain under the same conditions and obligations, in possession, use and usufruct of the same until a new agrarian reform law could be enacted.

Perhaps the fairest index of the new government's mentality would be to quote the preamble of the new agrarian decree. It reads as follows:

Considering that the agrarian reform law promulgated by the previous government bequeathed to the nation grave problems whose immediate solutions are demanded by all sectors of our society . . . and that it converted the Guatemalan peasant into a political instrument by tying him to the government and to the oligarchic groups within the official political party . . . and that it overtly tried to destroy the institution of private property, upon which the social structure of Guatemala is based, producing a lack of confidence in the economic sector and the flight of capital necessary for the development of our resources; and despite offering to the peasants and indigenous peoples that by means of the agrarian reform they would obtain immediate benefits in the economic order and an improvement in their standard of living, the reality showed that instead of improving, their situation tended to become more and more precarious and anguishing . . . and that the sectarian application of Decree #900 gave results radically opposed to an increase in our agricultural production, producing discontent in our labor relations and a sharp struggle between classes in the rural sector.[21]

Here is the rationale that was used by the new government to begin hacking away at the Arbenz agrarian reform. It is doubtful that Castillo Armas believed all that is stated here, but it is certain that he wanted everyone else to believe it and hammered constantly at these points. They are worth examining.

There is no question that the attitude of the Arbenz government had produced a lack of confidence in the economic sector that resulted in the flight of capital of the wealthy, especially foreign capital. It is also obvious that the decree was never meant to stimulate harmony between the peasants and landowners, since their interests were diametrically opposed. It was blatantly untrue that "it converted the Guatemalan peasant into a political instrument" to a degree that did not exist before nor exists now as a result of the Liberation government's measures.

The peasants' economic situation is just too precarious for them to maintain any marked degree of political independence. Their vote continues to be bought and sold with impunity, often for a package of cigarettes. For this to be done by a government for a piece of land, cannot be taken as a serious indictment of the Arbenz government.[22] Could Castillo Armas's revocation of the voting franchise to the unlettered be considered any less sectarian?

To claim that the institution of private property would have been destroyed by the Arbenz agrarian reform is also untrue. The Law did allow for the continuance of private property up to 70 idle acres and even more, if such lands were producing. It also allowed for the development of a new land-owning class, awarding ownership titles to more than a quarter of the recipients who benefitted by the reform. To say that the right of private property is not absolute, or is one that can be curtailed by the government in the name of the common good, would be more exact. No one claims, for instance, that the conversion of 50 percent of Mexico's lands to the public sector in the formation of *ejidos* destroyed the institution of private property in that country. We think that the phrase "upon which the social structure of Guatemala lies" is the key to the accusation that the institution of private property would be destroyed. In the preceding chapters of this study, it has been shown that the whole socio-political and economic structure of the country depends upon a small landowning class and a large landless class. The destruction of this relationship was bound to effect basic changes, and indeed was the very reason for the law's enactment and implementation. If Castillo Armas was protesting the destruction of the *status quo* as it had existed in Guatemala since the arrival of the Spaniards, he was correct in his assertion. To equate this to the disappearance of the "institution of private property" is quite another thing.

Arbenz did not offer the peasants and indigenous peoples "immediate benefits in the economic order and an improvement in their standard of living." Such fundamental changes as those envisioned by his law, as well as the new tensions produced by its implementation, could hardly have resulted in immediate and universal benefits. The new landowners had to learn many skills and acquire management techniques that had never been demanded of them as migrant laborers or subsistence farmers. John Powelson says:

It is scarcely possible to carry out any change in land tenure without adverse effects on production . . . The upheavals of any agrarian reform are such that farmers must grit their teeth and expect early losses.[23]

This is an obvious consequence of any drastic program such as that implemented by Arbenz. It really should not surprise anyone that his reform program could have produced, as stated by Castillo Armas, "results radically opposed to an increased agricultural production." Yet its effects were not that devastating, and in many cases were quite the opposite.

The legal effect of the Castillo Armas law was not to abrogate Arbenz' reform but merely to stop any further execution of it, while giving the landowners the permission to begin turning the clock back. It declared that all expropriations made under Article #91 of Decree #900 were invalid. It was this particular article that had caused so much furor by giving the government the power to expropriate in their totality and without indemnization the lands of those owners "who oppose the application of the agrarian reform by violent or subversive means."[24] It was felt that "subversion" was a term with too indefinite a meaning and could apply to anyone who merely protested.

The law returned to the original owners "all dwellings built at their expense" and gave all those who suffered expropriation of lands the right to appeal the decision to the newly created *Dirección General de Asuntos Agrarios* (DGAA, Department of Agricultural Affairs). Nathan Whetten says that on the basis of this, "in most instances, decisions were made favorable to the landlords. The agrarian recipients were gradually removed and the land returned to the original owners."[25] He concisely notes where the government's heart is:

In some cases, agrarians who felt that they had received the lands in good faith from the previous government, resisted evacuation and were removed by force. Some observers declare that during the Arbenz regime the government was invariably on the side of the peasants and workers in any dispute involving the landlords; in the post-Arbenz period, just the reverse was true.[26]

This was bound to be true since under the Arbenz government the agrarian committees did not have landowner representation, while under the Castillo Armas government, following Guatemala's historical pattern, it was the peasants who had no representation. Castillo Armas' new decree (#31) declared that the Departmental Agrarian Committees would be composed of the Governor of the Department, who is a presidential appointee, the Mayor and the first *síndico* (trustee) of the Departmental capital. The latter two would be elected officials, and almost certainly members of the land-owning class, due to the population makeup of Departmental capitals.

The decree also stated that any recourse against a decision of the DGAA had to be made to the Minister of Interior and beyond him there was no other recourse. Since Miguel Ortíz Passarelli was Minister of the Interior and the owner of huge properties in Alta Verapaz, some of which had been affected by the Arbenz Reform, it was obvious on which side his loyalties lay. So, though Arbenz had been roundly criticized in international circles, namely the United States, for not allowing appeals on expropriations to be made to anyone other than himself, Castillo Armas effectively blocked any objective recourse to the revocations executed by his government by giving Ortíz Passarelli the same power.

This same law also abolished the "Laws of Forced Rental" of the two previous governments and the tenants were given until March 31, 1955, to get off the lands. This was to give them sufficient time to bring in the crops that had already been planted. It is also stated in the law that its implications must be explained verbally to the peasants affected by it.

It was obvious that the new law was almost exclusively negative in its propositions. Under the "Liberation government," the peasant began by losing his vote, and now he was losing his newly acquired lands. Whetten, with the ring of prophecy, said:

There are many *campesinos* who received lands under the agrarian law of 1952 only to have them taken away again after the fall of the Arbenz government. They might be receptive to any revolutionary scheme that promises to restore to them the land of which they were the proud possessors for such a short time.[27]

It was perhaps with such a glance at the future, that Castillo Armas did offer a hope of sorts to the *campesino* in what he calls the "fundamental principles" of his new law, even as he must have recognized the obvious contradiction of these principles with the nature of the law itself. He states:

Every Guatemalan has a right that land, necessary to insure his economic subsistence and that of his family, be given to him and fully guaranteed as his private property. Such property so created by virtue of this norm shall be considered as family patrimony, and shall enjoy all protection and support.[28]

He thereupon indicates how and where this would be done:

By opening up those regions of the national territory that have remained at the margins of the national economy for lack of communications, irrigation, healthful conditions and inhabitants. Consequently, it will be a fundamental policy of this government. . . . an intense colonization of the national territory.[29]

It was clear that he was talking about the Petén. The AGA had been vociferously demanding such a program ever since Arévalo started talking about agrarian reform, even though the latter's attempt in Poptún had shown the costs to be prohibitive.

Another fundamental principle of this decree does recognize that there are huge tracts of idle lands in private hands and that something should be done about it, "consequently, the government will take every opportune measure necessary to reduce it."[30]

Perhaps the most humane principle of all, but one that must be regarded as demagogic in view of the cancellation of the two "Laws of Forced Rental," is that which declares:

Every type of gratuitous labor in the fields, wounds the Guatemalan as a free man in the most profound depths of his human dignity; workers will never be obliged to fulfill any contract of work or duty in exchange for compensation of services of any kind.[31]

Despite Castillo Armas's criticisms of the Arbenz Reform and the man who preceded him in the presidency of Guatemala, Powelson was able to say:

The Reform Law of 1952 was based on the Constitution of 1945, introduced after the overthrow of the Dictator Ubico and the restoration of a popular government. The Agrarian Law provided for the liquidation of feudal properties, prohibition of all forms of servitude and distribution of land to the landless. It was no more radical than what would be acceptable today under the Alliance for Progress.[32]

Thus it was that Castillo Armas began the legal and physical process of *desovietización* of Guatemala.

On August 20, 1954, three weeks after the first agrarian decree was issued, the new government promulgated its second agrarian law. If anyone had any doubts where the new regime was going and what its intentions were, this law effectively served to enlighten the nation once and for all. It called for the rehabilitation of the national *fincas* into the patrimony of the nation. The reasons for such a move are stated clearly in the law itself, but again Castillo Armas was exaggerating in his attempts to make Arbenz look bad and himself look good.

This Decree (#57) begins more or less with the same broadsides as all the other laws of the Liberation government:

Considering that the partitioning of the national *fincas,* . . . favored only that sector that was most militant in its Communism and created a state of discrimination among the *campesinos,* who in their majority have categorically shown their willingness to return to a system of salaries . . . also produced negative results in fomenting anarchy and consequently brought about a reduction in the national production and the destruction of the enterprise as an economic unit, the majority of the plots being found in total abandonment . . . and that the goods of the Nation ought to bring general benefits to everybody and not go astray for motives of partisan politics, as occurred in the application of the agrarian reform law.[33]

But not everyone believed what was said, even if they had to obey these decrees:

In order to give credence to this infamy, the dictatorship had the audacity to deduce that the *campesinos* in their majority "wished to go back to a system of salaries" and in order to aid in this fallacy, proceeded to take away the plots of land on the national *fincas* that the Government of the Revolution had distributed, and along with them took away "their movable property, their ripening harvests, animals, houses, constructions, installations, vehicles, machinery, seeds, fertilizers, tools, equipment of whatever type, products in storage and all other goods." All this in exchange for being "liberated from international Communism," the peasant had the exciting prospect that the DGAA, on its own judgment would give them in "concrete cases" some compensation for the work and improvements that they had effected.[34]

This was written by Guillermo Toriello, who, as foreign minister under the Arbenz government, had spent months in the United Nations trying to mobilize action against the U.S.'s arming of Castillo Armas in Honduras. And even as a member of Castillo Armas's administration, the first Minister of Interior, Jorge A. Serrano, in speaking to reporters of the number of people in jail, admitted that very few of them, if any, were Communists.[35] It is difficult even to this day to imagine any group of peasants anywhere in the country that would have knowledge of what Communism is. Certainly the U.S. Ambassador to Guatemala did not know when he testified before the Senate Subcommittee:

Ambassador Peurifoy: Communism, in my opinion, is a religion, Mr. Feighan. I don't think there is any doubt about that. And anyone who thinks it is a theory . . .
Congressman Feighan (Ohio): It is a religion. It was originated in hell, with the assistance of Satan and all the evil forces.
Peurifoy: That is a better definition than mine.[36]

It seems that the new government judged as Communists those who were most in favor of the land reform program—on such a basis, it is fair to assume that three-quarters of the total population were also "Communists."

It is difficult to believe that the peasants did want to return to the "system of salaries," as Castillo Armas states in the preamble of this law. It would not have been difficult to convince them that their best interests lay in being paid a salary, in view of the new government's attitudes toward "agrarianists." It is evident that these people were very much afraid of what the government would do to them, as is shown by the fact that many had already fled, leaving their plots in "total abandonment." But to maintain that their best economic and social interests actually were procured by taking back the lands from them and returning the people to dependence on salaries from the government flies in the face of Guatemala's history.

There is no question that there were difficulties on the national *fincas*. Many of the *colonos* thought that the *fincas* should be exclusively theirs and resented the intrusion of the newcomers, some of whom received more and better lands than the *colonos* themselves. Disputes broke out, and these perhaps represented the "anarchy" that the new law referred to.

The real crux of the problem though, lay in "the reduction of national production and the destruction of the enterprise as an economic unit." During Arévalo's presidency, these plantations were producing as much as eight million quetzales for the national budget in 1947 and though it dropped to five million quetzales by 1950, this represented from ten to fifteen percent of the total government finances. This was just a little bit too much money for Castillo Armas to lose. Arbenz may have considered taxing the country's oligarchy to replace this source of income, but this was something that Castillo Armas could never consider doing.

This law declared that all *fincas* be returned to the national patrimony no matter in what form or to whom they had been given, be they individuals or cooperatives.[37] It also stated that all the belongings of the *fincas,* such as those mentioned by Toriello, also be returned, and that the peasants be paid for any work or improvements that they had made since the harvests would belong to the government. It was recognized that injustices would be committed in carrying out this law. The legal standing of all cooperatives existing on these plantations was cancelled, while giving the ex-members the choice of staying on and working for a salary like any other *colono*. It is perhaps from this time on that the official toleration and unofficial disdain of cooperatives dates. In many quarters of Guatemala, to this day, cooperative is synonymous with Communism.[38]

This decree had a somewhat ominous tone when it stated that the law was "of public order and has the character of a security measure"[39] which meant that arrests could be made and individuals held without the usual right of bond and hearing if the government so decided.

It was about this time that many observers became aware of the fact that the Liberation government was not only anti-Communist but was using this label as an umbrella to protect itself from the fallout that was developing due to its attempts to return the country to pre-1945.

It was one thing for Castillo Armas to return expropriated properties to the United Fruit Company and powerful national interests. It was quite another to take back even the government's own plantations. If the workers on these farms wanted it that way, why did this law need to be considered "of public order and a security measure?"

The dissolution of the cooperatives was a step consistent with the policies of the new government. All worker and peasant organizations were suspect. One of the earliest creations of the Liberation government was a National Committee for the Defense Against Communism, whose job it was to ferret out Communists and Communist sympathizers. This was meant to take the witch-hunting activities out of the hands of the landowners, who had been taking the administration of "justice" unto themselves, and put it into the hands of the government. The labor movement had been the principal object of attack from the landowners and industrialists. Seven leaders of the United Fruit Company's labor union had been some of the first to be murdered,[40] and they were followed by many others. Partly to forestall repetition of these incidents and partly to rid the country of its "subversive" elements, before the month of July was out, Castillo Armas had ordered the CGTG and the CNCG disbanded. He cancelled the legal registrations of 533 unions and amended the labor code so as to make effective unionization impossible.[41] Two of the first unions to be dissolved were SETUFCO and SETCAG, both of which were worker unions of the United Fruit Company. The company's assistance in the overthrow of Arbenz was being rewarded.

A few days after the national *fincas* were returned to the patrimony of the nation, another decree was promulgated under the title, "Preventive Penal Law Against Communism." It was this law, called "savage" by the editors of *Christian Century* magazine,[42] that legislated the death penalty for a series of "crimes" that could be construed as "sabotage." It was a concept broad enough to include labor organization and strike activities. Under its umbrella, even those laws left standing in the labor code could not be enforced by worker pressure. Minimum wages were effectively abolished, the work week was again extended to forty-eight hours and paid vacations were terminated. Firing for "political reasons" was encouraged and no indemnization was granted for such a loss of employment. A report made by the United Nations' sponsored International Labor Organization in 1965 mentioned that only sixteen peasant unions existed in Guatemala at that time, portraying a "deficient and almost nonexistent syndical organization."*

Castillo Armas' persecution of those who had participated in the reforms of Arbenz or who had worked in rural unions resulted in passive resistance in large areas of the rural sector.[44] This passive resistance is translated even today into peasant distrust for any reform program in many parts of Guatemala. Union organizing is often as feared by the workers themselves as it is by the landowners.

Other laws governing the agrarian situation were enacted. In September, 1954, a decree was promulgated which effectively terminated the operations of the National Agrarian Bank

* It was reports such as these that generated opposition to the ILO on the part of George Meany (President of the AFL-CIO) and ORIT (Regional Interamerican Organization of Workers) which resulted in U.S. Congressional refusal to continue funding the organization in 1970 as a "Communist front." (See footnote 25, Chapter 5.)

as a source of credit to small farmers who otherwise had in-adequate security.[45]

By December, 1954, when the landowners were again per-mitted to pay their workers by lending them small plots of lands for their seasonal crops, there was no question that Castillo Armas would fulfill all his commitments to the planta-tion owners. In order to make this law (#170) seem more palatable, the proprietors of extensive holdings were told that they had the "obligation of providing gratuitously that land to which their *colonos* were accustomed."[46] With the removal of the minimum wage enforcement, the fact that the lands were given gratuitously had no meaning whatsoever since the wage agreement reached was again governed by the mutual under-standing between owner and laborer. The lands lent to the *colonos* would again play a major role in determining such understandings, "maintaining at the same time the workers' dependence on the landowner."[47] The law also stated that in no case would such lands be the object of expropriation. The assurance was superfluous.

An interesting insight is given in the preamble of this law into Castillo Armas' claims against Arbenz and the effects of his own policies:

Considering that the agrarian reform and other dispositions dictated by the previous regime in relation to agriculture, ruined totally the national agricultural production, causing a positive and evident injury to the economy of the country . . . the alarming and progres-sive decline of the production of articles of prime necessity in the Republic is one of the most felt effects of the above mentioned dispositions, as is shown by the decrease, since 1950, of four million *quintales* of corn, which constitutes the staple of our peo-ple's diet . . .[48]

The part that is blatantly inaccurate in this statement is the figure of a four million *quintal** decline. In 1950, the Guatemalan harvest yielded 8,217,000 *quintales* of corn; in

---

* *quintal*—one hundred pounds.

1952, it increased to 10,711,000 *quintales;* in 1953, it descended to 9,400,000 *quintales* and then in 1954 to just under 9,000,000 *quintales,* but still far above the 1950 yield. However, in 1955 the total dropped almost one million *quintales* from what it had been in 1954, and continued to drop further in 1956.[49] It seems that the Liberation government saw what was happening to the corn production because of its own policies, and thought it could blame this decrease on its predecessor. The mistake that Castillo Armas made was in miscalculating the loss at 4 million *quintales,* which would have been of famine proportions, instead of the 1 million *quintal* loss that actually occurred.

The four Departments that were most affected by the agrarian reform, Escuintla, Alta Verapaz, Izabal, and Quiché, all experienced marked increases of corn production in 1953–1954 over the preceding years and big drops the following year, the first of Castillo Armas's regime.[50]

The Liberation government had been in power six months as the year 1954 came to a close. It had accomplished what it had set out to do, that is, stop the "sovietization" of the nation. It had done this mainly by reversing the land reform policies of the previous government. Now it was time to look toward some positive measures of its own, something to combat the social problems that had been building for centuries. The impetus of a negative movement that is only anti-something is not sufficient to justify the existence of any government. It was now a case of producing, or turning the government over to civilians, something Castillo Armas was not prepared to do.

In October, 1954, the Government had asked for a demonstration of popular backing by holding a plebiscite and giving Guatemala's general electorate the opportunity to say either "yes" or "no" to Castillo Armas's accession to the presidency. Journalists estimated that no more than 400 negative votes were cast.[51] Certainly, it was not safe to admit publicly that one was voting against Castillo Armas.

NOTES

1 Azurdia, Vol. 73, p. 69.
2 *Ibid.*, Vol. 74, p. 44.
3 *Ibid.*, Vol. 73, p. 68
4 Baker, *Op. Cit.*, p. 48.
5 Taylor, *Op. Cit.*, p. 797.
6 Guillen, Fedro, *Guatemala, Prólogo y Epílogo de una Revolución,* Mexico: Cuadernos Americanos, 1964, p. 72.
7 From the authors' personal interview with participants.
8 Stebbins, Richard P., *The U.S. in World Affairs, 1954,* New York: Harper Brothers, published for the Council on Foreign Relations, 1956, p. 383.
9 Azurdia, Vol. 73, p. xii.
10 DGAA, *La Evidencia. Op. Cit.*, p. 7.
11 Azurdia, Vol. 74, p. 42.
12 *Ibid.*, Vol. 73, p. 71
13 Newbold, Stokes, "Receptivity to Communist Fomented Agitation in Rural Guatemala," *Economic Development and Cultural Change,* Vol. V, No. 4, 1957, pp. 338–361.
14 *Ibid.*, p. 361.
15 *Ibid.*, p. 352.
16 *Ibid.*
17 *El Imparcial,* July 20, 1954.
18 Toriello, *Op. Cit.*, p. 331.
19 *Ibid.*
20 Monteforte Toledo, *Guatemala . . . Op. Cit.*, p. 437
21 *Revista de la Facultad de Ciencias Jurídicas y Sociales, Op. Cit.,* p. 803.
22 According to John D. Powell, the function of the Venezuelan land reform for the government in power was also to gain the votes of the peasants and *campesino* payoff came about as well in the form of goods and services provided in the government's agrarian reform program. (Preliminary Report on the Federación Campesina de Venezuela, Land Tenure Center. University of Wisconsin, 1964. Mimeo. p. 71.)
23 Powelson, John P., *Latin America: Today's Economic and Social Revolution,* New York: McGraw-Hill, 1964, p. 65.
24 Azurdia, Vol. 71, p. 30.
25 Whetten, *Guatemala, Op. Cit.*, p. 166.
26 *Ibid.*
27 *Ibid.*, p. 356.

28 *Revista de la Facultad de Ciencias Jurídicas, Op. Cit.*, p. 804.
29 *Ibid.*
30 *Ibid.*
31 *Ibid.*
32 Powelson, *Op. Cit.*, p. 55.
33 *Revista de la Facultad de Ciencias Jurídicas, Op. Cit.*, p. 812.
34 Toriello, *Op. Cit.*, p. 202.
35 *El Imparcial,* July 8 and July 13, 1954.
36 *House Hearings, Op. Cit.*, p. 131.
37 *Revista de la Facultad de Ciencias Jurídicas, Op. Cit.*, p. 813.
38 It often takes more than a year to get official recognition of a cooperative's statutes, while government bureaucrats examine the purposes of the cooperative and the backgrounds of the prospective members.
39 *Revista de la Facultad de Ciencias Jurídicas, Op. Cit.*, p. 814.
40 *El Imparcial,* July 2, 1954.
41 Huizer, *Op. Cit.*, p. 207.
42 *Christian Century*, September 8, 1954, p. 1060.
43 Oficina Internacional del Trabajo, *Informe al Gobierno de Guatemala de la Misión Interagencias sobre Colonizatión e Integración de Poblaciones Indígenas.* Geneva: OIT, 1965, pp. 46–49.
44 Huzier, *Op. Cit.*, p. 207.
45 *Revista de la Facultad de Ciencias Jurídicas, Op. Cit.*, p. 817.
46 Azurdia, Vol. 73, p. 170.
47 CIDA, *Op. Cit.*, p. 46.
48 Azurdia, Vol. 73, p. 170.
49 *Guatemala en Cifras*, Guatemala: Dirección General de Estadísticas, 1944–1957.
50 *Ibid.*
51 Johnson, Kenneth, *Op. Cit.*, p. 193.

Would anyone of you, fathers, give his son a stone, when he asks you for bread? Or would you give him a snake, when he asks you for a fish?

Matthew 7:9

7

stones for bread?

O N DECEMBER 30, 1954, the first step was taken toward a positive program of land legislation drawn up according to the principles of the Liberation Movement. A commission was established to study the situation and present suggestions for a new agrarian law.

The new commission was to be made up of five members, picked by five different entities: the Ministry of Agriculture, the DGAA, the AGA, the banking institutions, and the National University of San Carlos. The first two were appointees of the government, the next two were appointees of big money interests, and the last one can be considered a neutral party. The neutral member of the commission, the appointee of the University of San Carlos, can be regarded as the only one of the five who might represent the interests of the peasant and not be threatened by what was done by the previous regime. There is no question where AGA and the banking institutions stood on land reform. The Ministry of Agriculture and the DGAA were the government and cannot be viewed as any less antiCommunist, any less antiArbenz, or any less anti-Decree #900, than Castillo Armas himself.

The *Acuerdo* (agreement) that establishes this commission is also interesting in that it lays down the "fundamental principles" that will govern the MLN land reform:

The land will be given as private property; technical and financial assistance will be given to those who receive lands; the under-populated areas of the country will be converted into centers of agricultural labor, by means of internal migration, so that there be an effective increase and betterment of the national agricultural production; the idle lands of the government will be justly distributed; agricultural zones will be opened by means of new roads or the betterment of the means of communication already existing; the *latifundios* will be taxed in a reasonable and progressive way so as to effect their disappearance in the least possible time; with the intention of forming new agricultural and cattle units, long term credits will be given at low interest; in the political-social order, true harmony will be established for the sake of the national welfare.[1]

After more than a year of labor, the agrarian commission presented its work to the newly elected Congress. On February 25, 1956, the Agrarian Statute (Decree #559) of the Castillo Armas regime was promulgated. It confirmed the DGAA as the official governmental entity, replacing once and for all the now defunct *Departamento Agrario Nacional* and entrusting it with the realization of the new agrarian legislation of the Liberation.

The DGAA, because of the National Liberation Movement, substituted the ex-DAN. Its efforts since that time are too many to enumerate, but they can be synthesized in two fundamental aspects: first, liquidation of the policy of attack in the rural areas, which in the name of Decree #900 found ample and irresponsible support from the government; second, the creation of new lines, conveniently harmonized, of an adequate agrarian policy. In both of these aspects, it has worked with determination, counting on the collaboration of diverse entities and persons, and has come a long way on these points: it is about to liquidate the situation inherited and there is now in progress a new program that, without going to the extreme of despoliation, is realizing the rehabilitation of the peasant within a framework of legality that is his best guarantee for both the present and the future.[2]

What made the Castillo Armas government's policies more legal than the Arbenz reform is not indicated. On August 10, 1954, after Castillo Armas's accession to power, the Supreme Court had declared the Arbenz Agrarian Reform Law (Decree #900) constitutional on the basis of the Constitution of 1945. Perhaps this is the reason that Castillo Armas felt obliged to suspend the 1945 Constitution and why he asked his Congress to enact a new one. Only on this basis was his new agrarian statute (#559) legal and constitutional while the old one (#900) was not.

Since the "inherited situation was about to be liquidated" we might expect a more positive attitude on the part of the Liberation government. In this light, the new decree (#559) states:

The DGAA consequently, has all the attributes, both sufficient and final, to permit it to develop with efficiency the principles contained in the new agrarian statute which, in synthesis, has as its object, to effect a better distribution of the land and a better use of the same for the benefit of all.[3]

It represents progress to hear the Liberation government talk about a "better distribution of the land and a better use of it for the benefit of all" after hearing its negative pronouncements for almost two years. With the above statement, it can be said that Guatemala had been brought full circle in little over ten years and was now back to where it started in 1945. At last, Castillo Armas was going to attempt "land reform" himself.

The new decree, despite the propaganda that the government made to the contrary, was not a revolutionary law. It established three types of lands where the agrarian reform would be effected.

The zones of agrarian development will be established preferably in large unused extensions of land as the following: (a) unused lands that are the property of the nation; (b) the national plantations that have been exploited in a defective or deficient manner; (c) private property that the State may acquire by whatever means after the promulgation of this law.[4]

The private properties to be used for this program were certainly not going to be the objects of expropriation. The government would acquire them by what Monteforte Toledo calls *la via persuasiva*[5] and this persuasion was to be effected by taxing idle lands out of existence, forcing the owner to either sell or cultivate. *Time* magazine refers to this taxing proposition as the "most revolutionary part of the law."[6] It goes on to say that "though low, the tax strikes hard at the principle of holding land not for farming, but as an inflationproof investment."[7] It also states that if the lands remain idle, the tax will increase by 25 percent the following year and keep going up until after five years the tax will be 100 percent or twice as much as the original calculation.[8] Powelson, in describing the pitfalls of using taxation as a means of enforcing land reform, states:

One method is to tax idle land at a higher rate than productive land. A major difficulty, however, is the definition of productive land. How much of a crop does a landowner have to plant in order to avoid the high idle-land rate? Will a few stalks of corn scattered here and there be enough? If so, the introduction of this tax would soon lead to the extinction of all land registered as idle but not to increased production. This problem should not be minimized by the suggestion of certain criteria or controls. They will have to be pervasive, and rigid inspection will be necessary to see that lands are properly categorized. Often the difference between idle and productive will be a matter of opinion, and underpaid tax-assessors may be suceptible to monetary persuasion . . . Finally, the implementation of a land tax will be no better than the tax machinery with which the country is equipped. So long as the tradition of tax paying is not established, land surveys not made, books and records not adequately kept, and officials subject to bribery, taxation will not be an effective instrument of agrarian reform.[9]

The first "loophole" provided to the landowners was contained in the law where it gave them the right to classify their own lands. Gerardo Guinea, a defender of the government and its policy, in reference to this privilege granted to the landowners, says:

One might believe that such a measure, because of the special circumstance of leaving it to the responsibility of the farm owner to classify his own lands, lends itself to fraud and trickery designed to avoid the tax he is obliged to pay. But no! The DGAA will make a study of the data contained in the sworn declarations and will verify them if it deems it necessary.[10]

He does not state how the DGAA will judge a statement as false, and it is doubtful that this entity had the money, manpower or will to do anything about it anyway. It is a fact that Guatemalan landowners have known for generations how to skirt or avoid the tax laws, aided by the lack of any real tax collecting system or agency. This made the possibility of taxing the large plantations out of existence highly unlikely.

The lands that were to be given the agrarians from national holdings and *fincas* were to be paid for over a period of ten years. The price was to "be decided by DGAA and in no case was it to be greater than the price, at the time of concession, that would correspond to other lands of the same quality in the same area."[11] That is to say that the new owners would have to pay the market price for their lands, which according to economists is inflated beyond its true value because of its role as the only insurance against inflation.

The government describes the types of landholdings that the new law would create:

(a) economic type farms and (b) subsistence type farms. The farms of an economic type classification are those that, because of their extention, offer the possibility of becoming farms of great productive capacity. It is thought that the peasant who receives a farm of this type ought to have a true dedication to agricultural activity since the land will demand from him and his family a maximum effort. The results will repay him abundantly as he makes himself into an economically independent rural owner. The subsistence farms are those that will have an undetermined area that will always be smaller than the economic type farms. These will be given to peasants who have incomes from small manual industries or salaries that they receive as laborers in some enterprise. It is, in synthesis, a complement to the economy of the rural worker.[12]

It is obvious that the second type of landholdings created by the law are nothing else but *minifundios* for a continuation of subsistence farming. It is hypocritical of the government to attempt to explain them away by saying that they are only meant to supplement the peasant's income. It has been shown that it is because of a lack of a real income other than insufficient amounts from farming, that the vast majority of the population lives in poverty. To give landless peasants a less than subsistence plot does not eradicate the poverty and misery of the beneficiary.

The law also clearly states that the recipients of the new lands will be Guatemalans, between the ages of 18 and 60, mentally and physically capable, and not already possessing lands that allow them and their families a decorous subsistence livelihood. Since the government recognized that the people fulfilling these qualifications were many more than the lands to be given, preference would be given to those people who fulfill the greatest number of the following conditions:

(a) those who have farming or husbandry experience or knowledge; (b) those who live in the area or a neighboring area of the agrarian zone to be partitioned; (c) those who habitually live in the rural areas; (d) those who have families that are dependent upon them, giving preference to those with small children; (e) those who have tools or animals or other things that would facilitate the exploitation of the land.[13]

The selection of the beneficiaries according to these qualifications is justified with the possible exception of "those who live in the area or neighboring area of the agrarian zone." People living in an area where large extensions of land go untouched are not apt to be as badly off as those living up in the highlands. It is the Maya who have been forced back up into the mountains with only the most miserable plots to sustain themselves who are most in need of lands. And this provision eliminated them.

One other aspect of this same decree (#559) that we might examine is the Fifth chapter, where it states: "For this reason, the DGAA will answer directly to the President of the Republic and its jurisdiction will extend to the whole of the national territory."[14] It seems that Arbenz's idea of having the agrarian policies of the country under his own eye and control had not been lost on Castillo Armas. There was here no accusation of unconstitutionality, as there could not be. The new law was written to conform to the new constitution. Castillo Armas need not be afraid of submitting any disputes that might result from the application of this law to the judiciary, because its provisions effectively looked out for everyone's interests but those of the landless peasant. The danger of a peasant taking any landowner or the government to court to force the State to protect his rights as a citizen was minimal, if not absolutely nonexistent.

Thus it was that Guinea could, on this basis, make the comparison between the Arbenz (#900) and the Castillo Armas (#559) Decrees:

The big difference that exists between one and the other "instrument" is immediately obvious. Juridically, the Agrarian Statute (#559) is delineated by the constitutional precepts that guarantee respect for private property. The President of the Republic is no longer the supreme organ of the law, but rather the authorities who, by constitutional right, have the obligation to watch out for the application and observance of the laws of the executive branch.[15]

Nevertheless, Castillo Armas did make the agrarian policies his special domain by determining that the DGAA would answer directly to him.

A few weeks after the law was promulgated, Castillo Armas appeared before the Congress, on March 14, 1956, to render his first "State of the Union" message to his new colleagues in government. The speech he delivered at that time was a 10,000 word document, of which less than 300 words were devoted to the explanation of his agrarian policies.

Special emphasis was put on the amounts of money and technical aid to be invested in colonization, as well it might. It was obvious to everyone who had thought about the project, that this activity was to be a very costly endeavor. Castillo Armas was not afraid to face the prospect since he could count on his good friends to the north to supply him with monetary and technical help, an advantage that was never available to his two predecessors.

The main vehicle for United States technical assistance in the program was the Inter American Cooperative Service for Agriculture (SCIDA) that had been established in Guatemala during the Second World War when Roosevelt was trying to line up opposition to the Axis powers. It disappeared under Arévalo and Arbenz but was revived in order to aid Castillo Armas carry off his new program. By the end of 1956, its personnel had been expanded to include twenty specialists from the United States and 215 Guatemalans.[16] Under succeeding governments, the program ran into difficulty when the Ministry of Agriculture "made repeated assertions that the United States was dominating the program and ignoring the wishes of Guatemalans in some of the projects."[17]

Meanwhile the International Cooperation Administration (ICA) was funneling money into the colonization program as fast as it could be absorbed. By the time Castillo Armas presented his plans to Congress, the United States had already given him $2,400,000 for land resettlement[18] and during the succeeding five years a total of $12 million was expended on the program.[19]

The new law made provision for avoiding the reabsorption of lands given to the peasants by contrary agrarian pressures that tend to reconcentrate the newly acquired property in a few hands, as had repeatedly occurred in other moments of Guatemala's history. This was assured by denying the beneficiary the right "to mortgage, alienate or divide in any manner, for twenty-five years, the lands that he had received."[20] This, of course, was an excellent idea, meant to guarantee the children of the beneficiary the family patrimony that the large landowners had always been so adept at swallowing up. The government's good resolution to protect the small holdings lasted until the end of June, 1957, when a law was passed that gave the new landowners the right to sell their farms for "industrial purposes, paid for by shares in the company or in cash."[21]

So it was that the Liberation government recognized that "the greatest need . . . is a vigorous program of land colonization, reclamation and resettlement. It is argued that families needing land should be colonized on land not in use, instead of disrupting the productive enterprises that are already in operation."[22]

The actual figures on the distributions vary among different authors and can become very complicated. The CIDA report gives figures that seem to be the most faithful to what actually happened. There are three types of holdings worth noting and a fourth that is included in the statistics, but which was never meant to remedy the agricultural situation, consisting of 628 titles to urban plots averaging .11 hectares (.27 acres) each.

The CIDA work classifies the three agricultural types of holdings as: agrarian zones, microplots and communities.[23] The first category, agrarian zones, is the colonization program about which much propaganda was made by all the friends of the Liberation government as they contrasted it with the Arbenz program. This was the most promising of the three types and its objectives can be summed up as comprised of four stages: (a) redistribution of landed property; (b) credit for an adequate exploitation of the redistributed land; (c) technical assistance; and (d) social assistance to attain a higher material and moral level of life.

With such ends in view, 2,814 families received landholdings that averaged 19.2 hectares (47.4 acres) in the agrarian zones. There is little record of financial credits being given to these peasants that would enable them to obtain the designs held out for them by the government. In fact, in later years it became obvious that some of this credit was forced and onerous (see page 211). From the photographs reprinted in government publications and taken at Nueva Concepción, it can be supposed that the government did carry out its promise for some technical help. Upon visiting the area in 1963–64, the author found that many lots were being rented out to sublessees for the price of clearing the jungle growth from the lands, and very little technical aid was available. There was no evidence of "higher material and moral levels of life" among the new landowners.

In the second category, small individual plots of land were distributed in an attempt to liquidate the agrarian program of the Arbenz government. As noted previously, after the overthrow of Arbenz, most of the expropriated properties were returned to the previous owners. "This second type of holdings was a matter largely of granting titles to persons permitted to keep some of the land allotted to them by the Arbenz regime."[24] There were 3,953 recipients with an average of 2.6 hectares (6.4 acres) per family.

The third type of holdings was described thus: "small farms were distributed to the workers, each to be operated on a collective basis with ownership in common. The land in this program amounted to 45,834 hectares (113,210 acres) which were distributed to 8,590 recipients, an average of about 5 hectares (12.4 acres) per family."[25] These are what CIDA calls *comunidades* and would be similar to either cooperatives

It is not correct to call this an agrarian reform and we or the Mexican *ejidos*.

cannot properly compare these totals to what Castillo Armas said he would do. Many of these distributions were made before his Agrarian Decree (#559) was passed by Congress, recognizing *de facto* distributions made by Arbenz, and Castillo Armas lived less than eighteen months after its promulgation in which to put it into practice. Yet the government insisted on making propaganda in its own behalf, mixing all these totals together, confusing the actual amount of land distributed and then talking about 15,000 families or more as having received their own farms. We can best see what the law actually accomplished by examining the meaning of the totals.

Table 7.1
Land Distribution by the Liberation Government

Year	AGRARIAN ZONES		MICROPARCELS		COMMUNITIES		URBAN	
	No. of lots	Avg.*	No. of lots	Avg.*	No. of lots	Avg.*	No. of lots	Avg.*
1955	153	19.2	1,663	2	251	3.5	0	0
1956	1,262	19.2	1,838	1.8	1,972	10	402	.11
1957	1,399	19.2	452	8	5,876	3.3	226	.11
Total	2,814	19.2	3,953	2.6	8,099	5	628	.11

* Average size of lot in hectares.

Of the titles given out in "communities," only the 1956 distribution approximated family-sized farms and can be considered part of a legitimate agrarian program. These recipients, plus the 2,814 who received lands in the agrarian zones during the Liberation government's three years, total 4,786 beneficiaries of the Castillo Armas program. This does not mean that all recipients were landless peasants, however. When Rodolfo Castillo Armas was fired as head of the DGAA after his brother, the President, was assassinated, eighty-seven people immediately had their titles cancelled for not having fulfilled the conditions of the law (they were not poor peasants) and another 214 were investigated "among them were judicial police, military men and public employees."[26]

The land distribution worth noting during this period was

effected on July 3, 1956, on the second anniversary of the installation of the new government Junta. It was the fourth distribution to be made and involved over 50,000 hectares (123,500 acres) on twenty-two different plantations. Property titles were said to have been given to 3,346 families who received lands averaging 15.1 hectares (37.3 acres) each. This was close to the planned size set by the government. The largest area of land was at Nueva Concepción, a tract of 34,909 hectares (86,225 acres) that had been obtained by the government from the United Fruit Company under terms that were never made public. Twelve hundred families were supposed to be situated there, receiving 20 hectares (49.4 acres) each, and the rest of this land was to be utilized for communal and urban facilities and roads. Actually 1,194 farms were distributed there, but in the list of new proprietors published by the government, only 849 names appear,[27] or 351 less than the projected aim, that results in over 7,000 hectares (17,290 acres) being "misplaced" or given to people whose names could not be listed.

The distribution at Nueva Concepción was considered the beginning of the colonization program based on the concept of agricultural zones. In its publication, *Tierra en Propiedad,* the DGAA demonstrates the government's plans to provide for the complete development of the settlers by building schools, clinics, storage facilities, recreation hall, offices, roads and other installations. It is obvious that a lot of money was being invested. No one could fault the government for such a program, but it must be considered in perspective. Where would the money come from to help, on this same scale, the numbers of people that actually needed help in Guatemala? The high cost can be seen further from a governmental *Acuerdo* dated June 20, 1956, that authorized the DGAA to purchase the plantation, Trapiche Grande, in the Departments of Retalhuleu and Suchitepéquez, from the Guatemala Plantations Akiebolag Company for the price of $500,000.[28] This, too, was to be made an agrarian zone. If such an amount of money could be used to purchase lands, one might judge that the Castillo Armas program was not meant to go very far, and would not go very far without massive infusions of money.

A comparison between the Arbenz agrarian reform and the Castillo Armas agrarian program would be a valid basis for judging the two governments. CIDA makes a mathematical comparison between the two when it notes that the Revolutionary government distributed an average of 33,500 hectares (82,745 acres) a month while the Liberation regime gave out 19,000 hectares (46,930 acres) a year.

A better contrast can be seen from the goals both presidents set for themselves. In his annual message to Congress in 1954, Arbenz stated that there was no reason why every Guatemalan should not have a family-sized farm before he finished his term of office in 1957. At the rate his program was going, there is no question that he would have attained his goal. Castillo Armas said that his government would distribute lands to 25,000 families in five years, a defeatist program not intended to keep pace with the population increase, and certainly not a remedy for the existing problem. Even this minimal pace he was unable to maintain.

Castillo Armas constantly accused Arbenz of political manipulation as the motivation of his land reform. The basis for the charge was that Arbenz gave the land for life-long "usufruct" and not as "private property." It is doubtful that a piece of paper registered as a private title would make peasant manipulation any more or any less difficult. Such a view flies in the face of the peasants' historical experiences at the hands of most national governments, and certainly Castillo Armas himself proves this point with the ease that he abrogated another piece of paper—the Constitution.

Yet, in spite of all the furor over the private property versus usufruct, Arbenz gave out more private property titles (approximately 27,000) in his year and a half program than the Liberation government intended to do in five years. This fact, plus the circumstance that over ninety percent of the Guatemalans have no other legal title to their lands than "usufruct," gives a better perspective to the "Liberator's" charges.

In early August, 1957, the reins of Guatemala's government were snatched from Castillo Armas' hands just as he had taken them up—through violence. He was shot down in the presidential palace by a member of his personal guard, who in turn succumbed to an immediate hail of bullets fired by members of the president's staff. It was generally conceded that the young soldier was not the author of the assassination plot and rumors flew that individuals very close to Castillo Armas were responsible. The immediate death of the assassin sealed his lips forever, but in so doing, only managed to inflame imaginations that speculate to this day. But just as the deaths of Col. Francisco J. Arana (1949) before him and Mario Méndez Montenegro (1965) after him, remain shrouded in the shadows generated by political passions, so, too, the real source of the bullets that ended Carlos Castillo Armas's life will probably never be known. He will long be remembered in Guatemala's history as the great savior of the landed oligarchy, as an "authentic martyr" of the Catholic Church[29] and as a typical president to the poverty-stricken masses.

NOTES

1 Johnson, Kenneth, *Op. Cit.*, p. 494.
2 DGAA, *Tierra en Propiedad*, Chapter 1, p. 1.
3 *Ibid.*
4 *Ibid.*, p. 92.
5 Monteforte, *Guatemala, Op. Cit.*, p. 437.
6 *Time*, March 12, 1956, p. 40.
7 *Ibid.*

8 *Ibid.*
9 Powelson, *Op. Cit.*, p. 60.
10 Guinea, *Op. Cit.*, p. 86.
11 *Ibid.*, p. 94.
12 DGAA,*Tierra en Propiedad*, Chapter 4, p. 1.
13 Guinea, *Op. Cit.*, p. 111.
14 *Ibid.*, p. 87.
15 *Ibid.*, p. 82.
16 Whetten, *Op. Cit.*, p. 171.
17 *Ibid.*
18 *Time,* March 12, 1956, p. 40.
19 Hildebrand, *Op. Cit.*, p. 358.
20 Guinea, *Op. Cit.*, p. 95.
21 Azurdia, Vol. 76, Decree 1187, Article 89.
22 Whetten, *Op. Cit.*, p. 166.
23 CIDA, *Op. Cit.*, p. 49.
24 Whetten, *Op. Cit.*, p. 170.
25 *Ibid.*, p. 169.
26 *El Imparcial,* March 11, 1958.
27 DGAA, *Op. Cit.*, Chapter 4.
28 Azurdia, Vol. 75, p. 240.
29 Proclaimed as such by Archbishop Mariano Rossell.

> In a corrupt age, greatness can be attained only by immoral means.
>
> **Machiavelli**

8

a corrupt age

NINETEEN-FIFTY had not been the year for the ex-Ubico aid, General Miguel Ydígoras Fuentes, to throw his hat into the electoral ring against Colonel Jacobo Arbenz Guzmán. It had been obvious then that the former had inherited much of the conservative support that would have gone to assassinated Colonel Francisco J. Arana, but Guatemala was still feeling heady over the social implications of the 1944 Revolution, and that year, 1950, conservatism was not the wave of the future. January, 1958, however, was a completely different story. The presidential elections that followed in the wake of the Castillo Armas assassination were tailored to order for Ydígoras Fuentes. The reactionary forces that had been set loose across the land by the Arbenz overthrow were still impossible to contain. The murder of Castillo Armas, if it had any effect on conservative passions, had only inflamed them more.

A quickly called election gave the presidency in October, 1957 to Miguel Ortíz Passarelli, heir apparent and ex-Minister of the Interior under Castillo Armas. Ydígoras cried "fraud" and threatened the capital with reprisals at the hands of faithful followers if the Army did not annul the results. His comrades-in-arms complied, calling for new elections in January, 1958.

This second election proved indecisive since none of the three candidates got the absolute majority of votes needed for election.[1] The decision was then thrown into the unicameral Congress, and the deputies themselves were given the honor of selecting the next president of Guatemala. Ydígoras again made threatening noises about not being chosen, and Congress in what is called a "secondary election," again bowed to the threats of the "Old Fox."

It is not difficult to characterize the government of National Democratic Reconciliation or "Redemption" as Ydígoras called his regime. It was ideologically conservative, blatantly dishonest, and consistently erratic. He had enemies on the right who charged him with being soft on Communism, among them Ortíz Passarelli[2] and later his own Minister of Defense, Colonel Enrique Peralta Azurdia. He had enemies on the whole spectrum of the political left, all of whom he himself accused of Communism, including the municipal authorities of Quezaltenango, Guatemala's second city,[3] Galich, the mayor of the capital,[4] and Mario Méndez Montenegro, his opponent for the presidency, whom he graphically and falsely denounced as having inflicted some grotesque tortures on political prisoners under the two revolutionary governments.

Not many people believed his protestations of antiCommunism, least of all Monseñor Mariano Rossell, the Archbishop of Guatemala:

These are not the antiCommunists who have sealed with their blood their conviction that Guatemala had to be freed from the atheistic ideology of Marxism. These are not the antiCommunists faithful to the ideals of the *caudillo* of the Liberation, creator of the plan of Tegucigalpa and sincere protagonist for social justice and for a New Life, a better life for his people: Carlos Castillo Armas, whom for these same ideals, we count today among the martyrs of an authentic antiCommunism.[5]

And in case the new president did not quite understand that the archbishop harbored little admiration for him, he concluded this same speech:

When will the day come that Guatemala may merit another energetic and sincere defender of the interests of the poor, of the weak,
of the exploited, of the same calibre as Castillo Armas?[6]

Perhaps the Archbishop did not believe that after refusing to
aid Castillo Armas in the 1954 invasion, Ydígoras still had the
right to call himself an antiCommunist.

The General disagrees and offers us the following description of himself in his autobiography, *My War With
Communism*:

I fought Castro-Communism from the outset and from the first days
of 1959, I was a victim of Fidel Castro's aggression. I frustrated
his invasion of Panama in March of 1959; I broke off relations
with his government in April of 1960; I withstood two military up-
risings inspired by his money and his agents; I cooperated with
antiCastro groups to train 2000 Cubans and launched them against
the Soviet bastion in the Caribbean; I put down an incipient civil
war in March, April and May of 1962; I swung a submachine gun
around my shoulder in November of 1962 and put down a rebellion
of the Guatemalan Air Force.[7]

Many observers of the Guatemalan scene will question the
accuracy of the above description, including people high in the
Ydígoras government itself. Ralda Ochoa, acting as his Vice-
President, called the claims a good joke.[8] In any case, although
Ydígoras was no friend of Castillo Armas's political party, he
did not consider himself to the left of it. As such, he continued
the general outlines of the Liberation government's agrarian
program. He did this, however, without the same cooperation
the U.S. government had afforded to his predecessor.

It is not clear exactly why Ydígoras was not appreciated by
the Eisenhower administration, as he also attests in his book.
He complains of the chilly reception given him by John Foster
Dulles during his visit to Washington while still President-
elect in February, 1958, and compares himself and his trip to
the icebreaker that was working in the Potomac River at the

time. Foster Dulles is quoted as greeting Ydígoras with a very curt speech:

We welcome President-elect Ydígoras Fuentes. We want him to know that it is our desire to maintain our friendship with Guatemala, united in our efforts to fight the common enemy: international Communism.[9]

Even though Ydígoras replied that it was his intention to organize a government on "strict antiCommunist lines to stand shoulder to shoulder with the U.S. at all times in the war with Communism," it may well have been a doubt about this very point that had provoked the hostility. Ydígoras had not been as cooperative as the U.S. apparently desired when it began arming Guatemalan exiles against Arbenz in 1953 and 1954. He tells how it happened:

A former executive of the United Fruit Company, now retired, Mr. Walter Turnbull, came to see me with two gentlemen whom he introduced as agents of the CIA. They said that I was a popular figure in Guatemala and that they wanted to lend their assistance to overthrow Arbenz. When I asked their conditions for assistance, I found them unacceptable. Among other things, I was to promise to favor the United Fruit Company and IRCA; to destroy the railroad worker labor union; to suspend claims against Great Britain for the Belize territory; to establish a strong-arm government, on the style of Ubico. Further, I was to pay back every cent that was invested in the undertaking on the basis of accounts that would be presented to me afterwards. I told them that I would have to be given time to prepare my conditions, as theirs seemed to me to be unfavorable to Guatemala. They withdrew, promising to return; I never saw them again.[10]

Ydígoras goes on to say that he found out a short time later that Castillo Armas had accepted the conditions and was being prepared for the invasion in Honduras. A "gentleman's agreement" was arranged with Carlos Castillo Armas as to what role Ydígoras would play in the new government (he was to participate in elections shortly after the takeover) but Castillo Armas did not abide by the agreement and Ydígoras remained outside the country during the Liberation government's rule.

This antagonism between Ydígoras and Castillo Armas can perhaps explain some of the difficulties the new president was having with the U.S., especially financial. He speaks of his meeting with Eugene Black, head of the World Bank, during the same visit to Washington. Black told him he could expect "not one cent of help from the U.S. or other World Banks," and cited among other reasons that "previous governments of Guatemala were indebted to certain American citizens and corporations" and that he, Eugene Black, "acting on instructions from President Eisenhower, had loaned Castillo Armas the amount of $18,200,000."[11]

Ydígoras says that it was made clear to him that if he did not make good "on these oppressive claims," the doors of all banks would be closed to his government. To make matters worse, he was approached at this same time by some men whom he describes as follows:

A group of sinister individuals, all dressed in black, informed me that they were representatives—and members of—a Washington law firm. They told me that they had financed the "liberation movement" of Castillo Armas, who had committed himself to certain payments. On his death he still owed them $1,800,000, and as they considered me to be his "heir," they held me responsible for payment of this monumental debt.[12]

The President-elect sent them packing according to his account, despite the threats that retaliation would be made against his government in the Department of State and in the U.S. press.

Yet, Ydígoras writes his book as a great friend and admirer of the U.S. and his charges cannot be written off as an anti-American diatribe. Although there are many statements in the book that can be questioned, there is no doubt that his government was often in serious financial difficulties. It is possible, also, that this lack of U.S. financing played more than a small role in his decision to lend Guatemalan territory to the CIA to train the Bay of Pigs invasion force, despite strong domestic opposition, a concession that got him in very serious trouble.

When Ydígoras became president in March, 1958, he continued the same general lines of the agrarian policy of the previous government. In October, 1959, he announced that he was having a new agrarian law drawn up by a Spanish technician. When it was presented to Congress, it was intensely criticized, particularly because a foreign technician, who "did not understand the national situation" had drawn it up. It was obstructed especially by the Christian Democrats who wanted a real reform law. They presented a counterproposal emphasizing the social function of land, but Ydígoras said: "I will give land to all who need it without touching what others have inherited."[13] The law was discussed and set aside.

At a land distribution ceremony in January, 1960, Ydígoras said: "The agrarian reform being realized is a scientific one due to the help of USICA (United States Inter American Cooperation Administration)."[14] In June, 1960, Col. Enrique Peralta Azurdia, then Minister of Agriculture, appealed to Congress to approve the fourfold agrarian reform plan still pending their consideration. It consisted of four laws: (a) Law for land distributions in lots, (b) Law for agrarian development zones, (c) Law regulating idle lands, and (d) Law for INTA (Instituto Nacional de Transformación Agraria).

The law establishing INTA was discussed again in Congress, with the Christian Democrats still pushing their version. AGA, the large landowners' lobby, wrote a detailed public letter to the Christian Democrats and complained, especially about the articles dealing with the definition of idle lands and with expropriation. The Association of Economists said that the new law being discussed would not produce good results since it was improvised, empirical and was looking for the economic progress of the country apart from the consideration of the misery of the majority of the population. Congress was discussing details of the articles, they charged, without even considering their false base.

On September 27, 1962, in four hours, Congress approved the remaining 248 articles after it had been discussing the first thirteen on and off for three years. A Christian Democratic congressman, René De León Schlotter, said:

The articles approved in this manner, against the regulations (there was no opportunity given to propose amendments) are null and void. The law will be inoperable and it is only being published so that the government can ask for money from the Alliance for Progress programs.[15]

On October 17, 1962, the new law was finally published. The President described it as an "antiCommunist and Christian answer to Decree #900" (Arbenz's Agrarian Law).[16]

If the INTA (Ydígoras) and DGAA (Castillo Armas) laws are compared, not many differences can be noted. The size of the *fincas* subject to expropriation was raised to those over 100 hectares (247 acres) that had more than 50 hectares (123.5 acres) of idle lands. Regulations for agrarian zones, credits and family patrimony are similar. Expropriation procedure is a little more difficult. In fact, the CIDA report states:

Especially in the regulations relative to taxation and expropriation of idle lands, it can be said that the new law represents the most conservative expression that has ever been known on this subject in Guatemala.[17]

The two laws determine four types of holdings for the lands to be distributed:

(a) Zones of agrarian development are colonies of family-type farms established by DGAA and INTA on large extensions of idle lands from national *fincas,* government lands or lands purchased from private estates which need government resources to initiate their exploitation. These parcels are to be given to landless peasants or to those who have insufficient land.

(b) Family patrimonies are individual farm lots, large enough to support a family and to market produce, taken from cultivated farm lands that have been donated to the government, expropriated, or taken from national *fincas.*

(c) Agricultural communities are lands to be exploited communally and whose topography does not permit their partition into lots.

(d) Urban lots are for building homes and are given out in urban zones or in agrarian zones where urbanization is desired.

Perhaps the best analysis of the Ydígoras attempts at agrarian reform can be made from a study of what he did with the national *fincas.* It will be remembered that Arbenz had distributed these during his reform program, only to have Castillo Armas take them back a few weeks after he took over the government. When Ydígoras came to power in March, 1958, the State owned 132 of these plantations which could have been used to alleviate the needs of many landless peasants. On April 25th, the new president named three large landowners to take charge of selling or otherwise disposing of the national *fincas:* Julio Héctor Leal, Roberto Berger and Manuel Ralda Ochoa.[18] The latter two are the largest cattle ranchers in the country.

The Department of Agrarian Affairs suggested that some of these lands be given to those employees who had lost their jobs when the new administration had taken over.[19] The Association of University Students (AEU) demanded that the national *fincas* be given to the peasants living on them.[20] Back in 1957, in a public debate on the national *fincas,* the Association of Economists and Public Accountants had declared itself in favor of using these *fincas* to solve the peasants' need for land.[21] Ydígoras stated that the confiscation of German properties had been a "national shame" and since the "State was a bad administrator," these lands should be sold.[22] They were worth Q. 150,000,000 and therefore could greatly help resolve the government's budgetary problems.[23]

But the *fincas* continued to be returned to their original owners, to be sold to pay government debts and to be given to individuals in exchange for goods and services.[24] Approximately twelve of these *fincas* were used for agrarian distributions.[25] Others were given to government or public agencies, either to be sold or to be managed in order to supplement the agencies' budgets.

The Revolutionary Party[26] said that it was opposed to the sale of these plantations since a correct distribution of these lands could substantially help to solve the agrarian problem.[27] Some of the first "buyers" were 200 military officers who received urban lots from two *fincas* on the outskirts of Guatemala City. The price: five cents a square meter.[28] Congress complained, but to no avail.

The production of corn threatened to be low in 1959. A shortage of this basic staple affected the whole nation. Coffee growers must feed their harvesters and a daily ration of corn is necessary. Ydígoras made a public plea that idle lands on national *fincas* be rented free and that the private lands be rented for the legal fee. "It would be a national shame to have to import corn."[29] But a plea carries no executive force.

In October, 1959, five peasants came representing forty others to ask Ydígoras to sell them two small national *fincas* on credit. "We have never been able to have any economic security. We are not asking for a gift. We will pay for this land."[30] The President's declarations on land reform had reached their ears and they had mistaken political promises for sincere concern. Their petition was ignored.

The President had spoken the truth when he had said that the state is a bad administrator. Disinterested public service is not common. When Nery Rendón, the cashier for the national *fincas,* announced that there were some shady business deals going on, especially in the finca Palo Gordo, he was immediately fired and his accusations were declared false.[31] The public, however, was not fooled nor surprised when on January 12, 1960, Alfonso Alejos, personally representing Ydígoras, earned a neat Q. 5,800 in one day at the coffee auction where he sold 58,000 quintales (hundred-weight) of national *fincas'* coffee charging a ten-cent auctioneer's fee per bag. He had a lot of answering to do but his profit was not declared undue nor illegal.

The Department of National Fincas had bought two cargo ships in August, 1959. They constituted the beginnings of the "Great Central American Merchant Fleet." Guatemala could begin to use its own freighters and not depend exclusively on foreign shipping. However, Congress questioned the constitutionality of a government agency's unauthorized expenditure, especially when the national *fincas* were consistently declared to be functioning at a loss.[32]

The Minister of Agriculture, Colonel Peralta Azurdia, clarified this concept. He said the national *fincas* were producing well, better in fact than when the Germans owned them. From 1954 to 1959 they had provided more than Q. 6 million for the public treasury.[33] (This was Q. 6 million in five years. In 1950 alone it had been Q. 5 million.) Still, Congress, on February 18, 1960, declared that the purchase of the freighters had been unconstitutional despite the availability of money.

Peralta had been trying to consolidate the agricultural enterprises of the government. He felt it was the duty of the Minister of Agriculture alone to direct the nation's agrarian policy. He was finally successful on June 14, 1960, when the DGAA and the national *fincas* both came under his administration. The next day it was announced that three more *fincas* were to be sold to private enterprise. Peralta Azurdia appointed a new director for DGAA, Crisóstomo Castillo, who in turn announced a new policy for the Department:

The policy of agrarian development has produced few results. Lands must now be given to the middle class. Native peasants lack sufficient preparation, laboriousness and a spirit of initiative.[34]

Peralta supported him in his declaration and a week later added that the purpose of selling the national *fincas* was to benefit the middle class.

In spite of increased profit, an announced Q. 2,500,000 in each of the two previous years, it was decided to cut back on the number of employees in both the DGAA and the national *fincas*.[35] Both groups went on a short-term strike of protest. Nevertheless, the budget of the national *fincas* was cut in half. Their normal allotment had been Q. 10 million from the BNA (Banco Nacional Agrario). They had almost 20,000 workers and totalled sixty-one *fincas* in all at this time.[36] Of the country's 11,094 coffee plantations, 327 produced from 1,000 to 5,000 *quintales* of coffee; and of these, forty-five were national *fincas*. Another thirty produced more than 5,000 *quintales* and of these sixteen were national *fincas*. The latter, therefore, were among the most productive in the nation. The average profit was Q. 6.00 a *quintal*.

Four months later, on October 26, 1960, Crisóstomo Castillo was out and Angel Augusto Pellecer replaced him. A conflict had developed over the sale of the national *fincas*. The same policy, however, was to continue as Pellecer declared:

The granting of lands to the middle class as an established policy I will continue according to the economic possibilities of the department and according to the international agreements signed by the Guatemalan and the U.S. governments through the ICA (International Cooperation Agency).[37]

At the same time he announced that six more *fincas* were up for sale. Castillo's mistake had been that of arranging for personal friends of his to receive preferences and advantages in these sales.

The corn shortage was again a threat in 1961 and again a plea from the Minister of Agriculture went out to landowners to rent their idle lands so that landless peasants could plant corn.

On November 13, 1961, it was finally decided to transfer the incipient shipping enterprise, Great Central American Merchant Fleet, into private hands. Earlier that year, on June 27, 1961, Congress had discussed the financial problems of the national *fincas*. From 1954 to 1956 there had been a Q. 14 million profit and now they had a debt of Q. 9 million. The explanation Congress received was that payment on the debt was not due until 1962 and there were enough products in the *fincas*' storehouses to pay at any moment. Furthermore, the high 1954–56 profit had been due to the fact that it represented the harvesting of products planted by the peasants who had received those lands under Arbenz which had then been returned to the national patrimony. An added factor was the high price of coffee during these years. Previous administrations had approved a number of questionable expenditures including Q. 1,200,000 for the political campaign of Ortíz Passarelli, Q. 2,500,000 for the purchase of the two freighters as well as the acquisition of a fleet of cars and an airplane for the use of the Agricultural Department. Twenty-five plantations more had now been sold.

A month later, R. Montenegro, who had followed Peralta as Minister of Agriculture, resigned because he felt he was not given sufficient authority over the national *fincas*.[38] Once out of office, he declared that these *fincas* should be used to resolve the problems of the peasants and not be sold to private individuals. Pedro Mombiela, a well-known cattle rancher, was named to be the new Minister of Agriculture.

The public debate about the national *fincas* reached a high pitch when on January 4, 1962, it was announced that the Department would cease to exist by March 31, 1962. Sixteen *fincas* were being returned to Nottebohm, one of the dispossessed Germans, who had won one of his suits before an international court in Geneva. Eight of these alone were valued at Q. 2,791,170. INFOP was to receive plantations worth Q. 8,200,000 and the BNA Q. 7,000,000.[39] Others were to be given to the Banco de Crédito Hipotecario and the rest were to be sold. Someone finally remembered that these *fincas* had workers living on them. Twenty thousand families would be affected. Their daily wage was supposed to be eighty cents but in fact it was often reduced to sixty cents or less. Food allotments, customary on coffee *fincas,* were reduced as was the amount of land each family could use for its own crops. The administrators and agronomists would simply be fired. As an editorial on January 5, 1962 in *El Imparcial* expressed, many people were bothered with the obvious personal benefits being taken by unscrupulous persons who as buyers or intermediaries were obtaining profits that could only hurt the national patrimony.

Nevertheless, the sale and personal business deals continued. On January 11, 1962, it was made public that Juan Mini was to receive plantations valued at Q. 953,260 in exchange for the land he had ceded to the government on the outskirts of Guatemala City for the construction of the Roosevelt Hospital. The evaluator, Ramiro Samayoa, a movie theater magnate and personal friend of Ydígoras, got one finca, Xolhuitz, worth Q. 239,960 for his services.

Palo Gordo, the center of the dispute between Willy Dorión and some sugar growers, was finally to be sold to a "cooperative" of large sugar producers, 200 shareholders, with Alfredo De la Hoz as president. Ramiro Samayoa received another plantation El Perú valued at Q. 435,580 in exchange for the Rancho Nimajay, an old hotel in Antigua, Guatemala.[40] Concepción and Castañaz, the former being one of the largest *fincas* in the country, went to Herrera, Dorión and Company. All of these were valued at Q. 25,000,000.

In all, the Ydígoras government disposed of 115 plantations as follows: eleven to public entities, some of these for distribution; thirty were exchanged for lands and for constructions that were given to the government; four were for "personal services;" sixteen were returned to previous owners:

disposessed Germans or Ubico politicians; and seventeen were turned over to the BNA to pay obscure government debts. The destiny of thirty-seven other *fincas* is impossible to trace. This left seventeen plantations in the hands of the government by April, 1963, with a total of 22,548 hectares (55,694 acres), in spite of the March, 1961, goal to be rid of them all.[41]

There is no question that these dealings involving the national *fincas* were not motivated by concern for the needs and rights of the nation, nor were these transactions legal. This can best be seen by the actions of the Peralta government that followed Ydígoras and its attempts, often successful, to repossess these plantations for the State.[42]

As early as June, 1958, when the Ydígoras government was not four months old, an accusation had been made in the newspapers that forty-five sales of government properties had already been consummated for "laughable prices" including one piece of land that was sold for Q. 200 and then mortgaged the following week for Q. 48,000.[43] There were many other accusations of fraudulent deals, some of them involving the President's son, Miguel Ydígoras Laparra.[44] However, some of the money must have found its way into the government treasury to alleviate the dire need for funds, as indeed this was one of the reasons that had been suggested for the sale of the national *fincas*.

Marroquín Rojas, Ydígoras's first Minister of Agriculture, had made this proposal on several occasions[45] as a solution to aid the President in raising Q. 40 million that he had been requesting from Congress. The Legislature had rejected the request since Ydígoras refused to divulge what he wanted the money for. Then in October, 1959, the President made a public declaration to the effect that he no longer needed the Q. 40 million from Congress,[46] and although Marroquín Rojas presented his plan for the sale of some of the *fincas* to raise this money, and the plan was subsequently studied by Congress, Ydígoras maintained his stance of indifference. Marroquín shortly thereafter resigned, saying later: "I refused to be a laborer for the North American foreman who is governing us."[47]

It is not easy to understand: Ydígoras needed money, and his requests for Q. 40 million had been insistent; he also needed to effect at least a token land reform. Yet he sold the government plantations to private individuals at "laughable prices" which effectively closed the door to the use of these *fincas* to solve one or both of these problems. But apparently his need for money disappeared in October, 1959, as he himself stated. It is not clear where the money came from. Subsequent events, however, seem to indicate that a new understanding was reached with the Eisenhower administration, and this might be sufficient explanation.

In April, 1960, public outcries appeared in the papers saying that Cuban exiles were being trained in the *finca* Helvetia, property of an Ydígoras friend, wealthy Roberto Alejos. Ydígoras labelled the charges as false and invited the OAS to send an inspection team to verify his denials.[48] His protestations were not universally believed, despite the invitation to the OAS. He either thought they would not come, or if they did, that they would not make their findings public. He published his own denunciations that Cuba was preparing to invade Guatemala, until a Congressman, Villagrán Kramer, in a telegram to the OAS[49], denounced the whole thing as a farce and an attempt to divert attention from what Guatemala herself was doing against Cuba.

A prison camp was established in San Juan Acul in the jungle region of Petén for the detention of a small dissident element that had become disillusioned with the invasion plans. This was difficult to hide, especially when the camp was discovered by chicle harvesters and the newspapers reported that "500 armed guerrillas were in the area." When two U.S. pilots, who were flying the men in and out of the base were killed in a crash, it was impossible to hide the truth.[50] The government attempted to cover up by claiming that they had captured twelve Castroite guerrillas in the Petén area,[51] and that all was again normal in the region. Roberto Alejos repeated Ydígoras's invitation to the OAS to send an investigating team to his plantation to verify that the comings and goings of the huge Globemaster planes and the presence of U.S. military advisors were only to supply and train Guatemalan soldiers in counterinsurgency.[52]

NOTES

1 Ydígoras-Redención: 190,000; Cruz Salazar–MLN: 138,000; Mario Méndez Montenegro–Partido Revolucionario: 134,000. *El Imparcial,* February 6, 1958.
2 *El Imparcial,* September 24, 1959.
3 *Ibid.,* August 12, 1958.
4 *Ibid.,* Dec. 8, 1958.
5 *Ibid.,* July 8, 1958.
6 *Ibid.*
7 Ydígoras Fuentes, Miguel, *My War With Communism.* Englewood Cliffs, New Jersey: Prentice-Hall, 1963, p. 2.
8 *Prensa Libre,* March 3, 1969.
9 Ydígoras, *Op. Cit.,* p. 61.
10 *Ibid.,* p. 49–50.
11 *Ibid.,* p. 63.
12 *Ibid.*
13 *El Imparcial.* November 2, 1959.
14 *Ibid.,* February 1, 1960.
15 *Ibid.,* September 29, 1962.
16 *Ibid.,* October 17, 1962.
17 CIDA, *Op. Cit.,* p. 52.
18 *El Imparcial,* February 19, 1958.
19 *Ibid.,* April 28, 1958.
20 *Ibid.*
21 CIDA. *Op. Cit.,* p. 52.
22 *El Imparcial,* June 6, 1958 and October 31, 1958.
23 *Ibid.,* October 31, 1958.

24 *Ibid,* October 26, 1960.
25 *Ibid.,* September 9 and December 5, 1959.
26 The PR, political heirs of Arévalo and Arbenz.
27 *El Imparcial,* November 6, 1958.
28 *Ibid.,* December 22,1958.
29 *Ibid.,* March 25, 1959.
30 *Ibid.,* October 28, 1959.
31 *Ibid.,* December 9, 1959.
32 *Ibid.,* February 2, 1960.
33 *Ibid.,* February 13, 1960.
34 *Ibid.,* June 30, 1960.
35 *Ibid.,* September 7, 1960.
36 *Ibid.,* September 8, 1960.
37 *Ibid.,* November 2, 1960.
38 *Ibid.,* July 5, 1961.
39 *Ibid.,* April 5, 1962.
40 *Ibid.*
41 CIDA, *Op. Cit.,* p. 52–3.
42 On June 19, 1963, the Peralta government passed Law #52 which ordered a re-examination of all the transactions involving the National *Fincas* effected by the Ydígoras government, (*El Imparcial,* June 20, 1963). By July 7, 16 plantations had been reclaimed. (*El Imparcial,* June 22, 25 and July 7, 1963). In January of 1964, 89 *fincas* more were brought under investigation. Peralta ordered Ydígoras extradited from the United States, but the then ex-President left Miami and was welcomed in Costa Rica.
43 *El Imparcial,* June 28, 1958.
44 *Ibid.,* September 17, 1959.
45 *Ibid.,* November 11, 23 and 24, 1959.
46 *Ibid.,* October 30, 1959.
47 *La Hora,* March 3, 1966.
48 *El Imparcial,* April 25, 1960.
49 *Ibid.,* December 8, 1959.
50 *Ibid.,* September 23, 1960.
51 *Ibid.,* August 13, 1960.
52 *Ibid.,* January 1, 1961.

Once society becomes disorganized, military power becomes one of the few effective means for obtaining political goals.

Henry Bienen

9

a disorganized society

THE FATE of the national *fincas* is one measuring stick of the orientation of the Ydígoras government and the meaning of its agrarian program. Another frame of reference is the number of people who lost their lands (or what they thought were their lands), while the Redemption government was in power.

On June 2, 1958, less than three months after stepping into office as head of the DGAA, Colonel Enrique Peralta Azurdia announced that all people living on United Fruit Company land must get off. He denied the charge that he had already used violence against the peasants in Bananera and Tiquisate (the 2 areas of United Fruit Company operations) to accomplish this end. A few months later, "several peasants complained that they were expelled from the lands of a national *finca,* where their parents had been born while it was still under German ownership, for the "crime of Communism," in this case: voting for the Revolutionary Party.[1]

In May, 1959, two peasants were killed and another three were wounded when the owner of La Campana drove his tractor through the cornfields of eighty families, plowing the fields to sow cotton.[2] The owner himself received a machete cut on the hand and a bullet in the stomach. The lands had been given to these people by the government of Arbenz and though the Castillo Armas regime had decreed that the expropriation was invalid, for some reason, it was never enforced. The DGAA had warned the peasants they had no right there, and finally, the owner had taken matters into his own hands, with the results noted above.

On June 3, 1959, Col. Peralta Azurdia again denied that he was using soldiers to expel the Maya from the plantations Palmar, Aurora, Naranjo, Campana and Cadiz. He stated that the peasants were leaving willingly after receiving their indemnization. Two weeks earlier, referring to the expulsion of fifty families, a public letter written to the DGAA had been published in the newspapers:

My most sincere gratitude for the magnificent job done on my plantations, Bolivia and Aurora, located in Masagua, Escuintla, as regards the evaluations you made of the permanent crops and homes of those people who, aided by the calamitous Decree #900, have been occupying my above mentioned lands ever since, and now the whole affair has terminated with the removal of these invaders by means of the indemnization payment. Gonzalo Palma C., Owner.[3]

That same month, when the DGAA was accused of expelling people from lands in Navajoa and Santo Tomás in Izabal, both national *fincas,* it was claimed by DGAA that the people were "invaders" and had no right to the lands.

A few weeks later, when the Minister of the Interior was asked by a reporter why twenty-seven families had been expelled from the lands of the governent *finca,* San Andrés Osuna, he was told that only the police of Escuintla knew.[4]

In August, 1959, DGAA expelled 200 families from the lands of Ricardo Berger in San José where they had lived for twenty years.[5] The peasants maintained that when they had established their homesteads there, they were told that the lands belonged to the government and not to any private individual. No indemnization was made on this occasion.

That same month, 500 families invaded government lands on the outskirts of Guatemala City stating: "We cannot wait around with folded arms until the government takes care of us, since we know from experience that the colonies are given out to relatives and friends of government officials."[6] Police gave them three days to get out even though they had already constructed their shacks. When they marched en masse on the presidential palace, Ydígoras said that he would give them until December 31 to find some other place to live.

During 1960, the same type of incidents were reported from time to time in the press.

In early January, 1960, it was announced that 1000 families that had occupied United Fruit Company land in Izabal (Bananera) were to be expelled. They had been there since 1954 when Arbenz had given them the lands, and the Castillo Armas government paid rent to the company to avoid the implications of an expulsion.[7]

In February, the Judicial police moved into Los Angeles, Escuintla, where they captured one peasant while others escaped. "Their crime was trying to defend the 200 families that the DGAA was expelling from lands that they had received in 1954."[8] The police threatened to hold the wives as hostages until the other peasants gave themselves up.

In November, 1960, forty-eight families were expelled from another government *finca,* Bárcenas.[9] And then in June, 1962, the United Fruit Company expelled 200 peasant families from El Semillero, Escuintla. The Governor of the Department of Escuintla had received orders to remove them and to pursue the men. The Director of the DGAA later denied the report of this order as ridiculous: "The Governor is not a subordinate of the company." The peasants, he suggested, should take their case to court.[10]

In that same month, a group of approximately fifty young military officers decided that they had had enough of the Ydígoras government and tried a barracks revolt. The reason

for the attempted overthrow, according to Ydígoras, was international Communism:

The entire picture, starting with the urgent objective of destroying
the antiCuban bases in Guatemala; the seemingly pointless overpowering of a barracks in the capital to flee with arms to the
coast; the knowledge that Colonel Rafael Sesán Pereira was receiving money from Cuba that caused his dismissal; the intervention of the known Communist, Mario René Chávez García; the
admission in the revolutionary manifesto that "a free country,
which is truly sovereign" gave the movement support and cooperation; the intercepted message from Cuba; and the fact that the
movement was the culmination of months of political agitation, are
all powerful indications that the movement was not Guatemalan
in its essence.[11]

Ydígoras admits that the "local and international press
were incredulous as to the hand of international Communism
in the affair."[12] However, President Eisenhower did believe
the Guatemalan President and he sent the aircraft carrier
Shangri-La to wait off the Atlantic Coast so as to "discourage
any invasion attempt."[13] All participators in the original plot
were Guatemalan army men and they, along with many segments of the population, had plenty of reasons to find the
Ydígoras government intolerable.

Lt. Marco Antonio Yon Sosa, one of the leaders of the
revolt, differs from Ydígoras in his view of the incident, and he
relates it through Adolfo Gilly, an Argentinian writer who
spent several months with the guerrilla leader in the mountains of northeastern Guatemala:

The aim (of the coup) was to clean up the government, not to
destroy capitalism. The Ydígoras administration, which had risen
to power as a result of the electoral fraud of 1958, not only devoted
itself to the defense of imperialism and the *latifundistas* (owners of
large landholdings), but also lined its pockets with national treasury funds. . . . It was the movement's intention to prevent Guate-

mala's utilization as the base for aggression against Cuba, as planned by the U.S.[14]

When the plotters arrived in Zacapa and captured that military base, Gilly tells us:

Eight-hundred peasants presented themselves at the Zacapa barracks and asked for arms with which to fight against the government. This was not in the program, nor was it even anticipated by the rebels, who could not make up their minds to arm the peasants, . . . There were no facilities for holding organized discussions and making decisions; but in Guatemala, as in Honduras and in El Salvador (where many of the rebels fled), all the peasants helped and protected the rebels, tried to influence them and win them to their side. The peasants' motives were not only to offer solidarity but also to win allies and leaders in their struggle for the land . . . Many of the rebels did not respond but the effort was not in vain; the influence was felt by some, but not immediately. Yon Sosa and Alejandro de León and their *compañeros* did not jump to conclusions; but little by little, the peasants won them over.[15]

Ydígoras does admit that the rebels were able to "recruit over 300 civilians,"[16] but that their "ardor was cooled by the unappealing and unintelligible speech of a loyal government pilot who was obliged to address the meeting with a .45 revolver pressed to his ribs." Why the rebels would have a loyal officer address the crowd is not clear. In Zacapa, according to Ydígoras, "two light planes had dropped thousands of leaflets inciting the people to support a revolutionary movement."[17]

It is difficult to know how much peasant support the revolt of November 13, 1960, actually had, but that it had peasant support and that it still has peasant support is evidenced by the fact that Yon Sosa was still fighting and hiding in the mountains of Izabal ten years later—an impossibility without broad peasant cooperation.* That this support is based on the struggle for land, there can be no doubt. In February, 1962,

---

* Marco Antonio Yon Sosa was killed by a Mexican patrol on the Guatemalan border in June, 1970.

Yon Sosa's forces were fighting in the Sierra de las Minas mountains under the name "Guerrilla Movement, Alejandro de León, 13th of November," named for a dead leader of the revolt and the date of the uprising. By April, 1964, the name had been changed to "Revolutionary Movement, 13th of November"[18] to indicate the new orientation of the struggle, not just for a change of government but rather for a total change in the social, economic and political structures of the country.

The United States government recognized the threat to the stability of Guatemalan institutions that this movement represented and in May, 1962, established a counterinsurgency base in Mariscos, Izabal under the leadership of two officers and five enlisted men of the U.S. Special Forces, all trained in Laos and of Mexican or Puerto Rican descent.[19] Fifteen Guatemalan soldiers trained by the U.S. in Panama were also part of the teaching personnel. New jet airplanes (T-33's), transport planes (C-47's) and pilot training were given to the Guatemalan airforce.[20]

A pacification program was begun in the Zacapa area under the auspices of the United States Defense Department comprising the digging of wells, establishment of clinics and distribution of lunches to school children.[21] Generals Andrew O'Meara and Theodore Bogart of the United States Carribean Command flew in for a three-day look at the situation.[22] A C-47 without any markings on it had a forced landing in Guatemala City—the pilots were Guatemalans, and the passengers were U.S. paratroopers.[23]

No further reports of peasant expulsions from lands appear in the press during the years 1961, 1962, 1963, except for some difficulties on the United Fruit Company's land in Tiquisate, on the Pacific Coast. It is possible that either no actions of this kind were executed on the Atlantic Coast so as not to antagonize the people and guerrillas in the area, or else the publication of such actions was discouraged for obvious reasons.

An example of peasant struggles for land is the case of Huitzizil, Tiquisate. The first notice of the conflict there appeared in the press in January, 1961 when it was announced that "only 82 families, not 400," were to be put off the United Fruit Company's land.[24] In February, 1961, the AEU (Association of University Students) interceded for the families, stating their right to remain there after twenty years of occupation.[25] In May, 1961, Linwood Adams, a director of the United Fruit Company, was murdered in his office by one of the peasants.[26] The DGAA maintained that all the peasants wanted to move but that Communist agitators would not let them. Three days later the army moved in and escorted 105 families off the lands under heavy guard of machine guns and rifles.[27]

The peasants protested that they had paid over Q. 3,000 to Congressman Carlos Enrique Jiménez Peralta because he had promised that he would obtain for them legal title to their lands, having charged each family first Q. 10, then Q. 15 and finally Q. 8 for honorariums.[28] On May 29th, the DGAA announced that the problem in Huitzizil had been solved with the distribution of 108 new farms in the agrarian zones to the "invaders of the United Fruit Company's lands." Many others were said to have returned to "their place of origin," and all of them were advised that if they wanted compensation for their homes and crops, they would have to take their cases to court.

In August, 1961, an announcement was made that all was still not well with the peasants of Huitzizil. The United Fruit Company denied any responsibility, maintaining that it had given the government land in 1954 to resolve just such problems.[29] On August 27th, the Army moved in and burned the homes of the peasants.[30] In September, 1961, Ydígoras made a special appeal to the United Fruit Company to go slow until the legal position of the peasants could be clarified.[31] A week later, one of the peasant leaders was in jail at the request of the company.

In February, 1962, the peasants of Huitzizil hired a lawyer, Alfonso Bauer Paiz,[32] to defend their interests. He maintained that they had no place to live, no place to work.[33] A week later, the Minister of Agriculture said that the situation in Huitzizil was an exaggeration, and that everyone there had received farms in the agrarian zones. Nothing more was said of the matter in the press until five years later, in March, 1967, when the government of Méndez Montenegro offered to pay Q. 50,000 to García Salas for the Huitzizil lands that he had apparently bought from the United Fruit Company. The government planned then to sell the lands to the peasants, thus solving "the problem of thirteen years' duration, which had begun with Arbenz and Decree #900."[34] A month later, the MANO (National Organized Anticommunist Movement, a right-wing terrorist group) found a way of solving the problem. They "executed" Leopoldo Castillo and Arturo Schellenger in Huitzizil and announced their motive: "To stop their Communist demands to government agencies."[35]

Ydígoras did manage to give out some lands during his five-year administration and his policies were not exclusively negative in this field. He used the same propaganda ploy that the Castillo Armas government had used, that is, lumping all types of distributions together without regard to size or purpose, and thus effectively distorting the real picture. In mathematical terms his distributions consisted of 2,451 farms in the agrarian zones, 3,982 in communities, 371 microplots (*minifundios*) and 2,175 urban plots.[36] As with Castillo Armas, we again have to discount the latter two categories from a meaningful agrarian program. As regards the other two groups, the communities were lands distributed in cooperative holdings to peasant villages, but even here the ratio of land to people puts the extension in the *minifundia* class, for an average of 2.5 hectares (6.18 acres) per family.[37] The agrarian zones were sufficiently large family farms, averaging 19.5 hectares (48.17 acres) each; it must be noted, however, that all of these were not given out to landless and needy peasants, as the cancellations made by subsequent governments attest, and other revocations that should have been made but for political reasons never were effected. The situation of these agrarian zones, as was discovered during the Peralta government (1963–66), will demonstrate that they were and are not maintained as well as the government Secretary of Information would have us believe.

Ydígoras continued to alienate large segments of the population, due largely to the open corruption of his government. He had made an uneasy ally of the United States through his participation in the Bay of Pigs invasion. He attempted to gain the backing of the Catholic hierarchy and clergy and was only moderately successful, certainly never to the degree that Castillo Armas had been. The "Old Fox" began by giving the Archbishop, Mariano Rossell, Q. 5,000 for his birthday and was promptly "repaid" five days later when Pope Pius XII sent a special blessing to Castillo Armas's Liberation party.[38] But Ydígoras did not despair; he could not afford to and was able to push through Congress a number of laws favoring the Church, including the right to teach religion in public schools,[39] civil recognition for religious marriages[40] and finally, de jure recognition of the church,[41] which allowed it to own property for the first time in seventy-five years. Pope John XXIII responded by sending a special papal decoration to the President's wife.[42] Thereafter, Ydígoras felt enough confidence to demand that every Catholic, in fulfillment of his Christian duty, vote for his political party, "Redemption."[43]

But his difficulties multiplied, and according to many, their provocation was intentional, to distract the nation from more fundamental problems. He precipitated international incidents by ordering Mexican fishing boats strafed by his air force P51's and then severing diplomatic relations with that country in the resulting furor. Claiming British Honduras to be Guatemalan territory, he entered unannounced into that country, began an inspection tour and had to be requested to leave. He recommended that "every Guatemalan soldier should go to bed every night and get up every morning, thinking about Belice (British Honduras)," and even threatened to go to war with England over the matter. He fought with Salvador over the waters of

Lake Güija on their common border. He promised to use the powers of his office to obtain the canonization of Hermano Pedro Betancourt, a historical religious figure in Guatemala with a wide popular following.

The economy rapidly deteriorated due to his graft and incompetence but he steadfastly maintained that Guatemala's only salvation lay in the Central American Common Market; he wanted to be known as the "Great Unifier" even as Bolivar was known as the "Great Liberator." He tried to block Congress' criticisms of his underhanded dealings by accusing the Legislature itself of graft, then enjoyed the injured protests of outraged innocence that the public could compare to his own.[44] His police burned the ballots of the Congressional election[45] and the PR claimed electoral fraud and demanded that he resign.[46] He retaliated by imprisoning Mario Méndez Montenegro and other leaders of the Revolutionary Party on charges of Communism.[47]

Bombs were exploding all over the capital city and many people openly accused Ydígoras himself of responsibility for them. His intention, they claimed, was to excite the populace against his political opponents. He trucked in 7,000 workers from the national *fincas* for demonstrations in favor of his government and when 200 peasants refused to participate, he fired them.[48] University and high school students took to the streets demanding his resignation and protesting the fraudulent Congressional elections. The resulting military repression produced scores of deaths, several hundred wounded and hundreds more went to jail.[49]

The Church hierarchy showed only limited concern protesting that the chaos was weakening the nation and leaving the door open to Communism.[50] The Christian Democratic Party, basing its argument on the Bishops' Pastoral letter, demanded the immediate resignation of Ydígoras.[51] Then the Catholic Bishops finally came out with a strong Pastoral letter, on August 15, 1962, recognizing in its starkness the agony of the nation:

Large sectors, with just aspirations, now living in the most miserable and overworked state, aspire for their human dignification
and their institutional liberation. There is the problem of housing;
there is the economic plight of beggars, the lack of urbanization
and absence of schools. On the plantations, the peasant is frozen in
by customs hundreds of years old and submerged in conditions of
blatant inferiority, receiving salaries that hardly permit him to
avoid death by starvation. Also, these salaries are not paid with
regularity but rather are doled out weeks and months late, leaving
him without the hope of decently clothing his children and unable
to provide them with an education befitting human beings and free
citizens. Especially grave is the standard of living of thousands and
thousands of workers on state and privately owned plantations.
Besides the conditions of their work, they live collectively in
wooden shacks, without light, without windows, without interior
walls for privacy, generally without sufficient and adequate sanitary
systems, without the possibility of intimate family life nor morality,
in situations closely resembling concentration camps rather than
the homes of free human beings, upon whom rests precisely the
national wealth. It is here that infant mortality triumphs, reaching
astonishing ratios, as well as sickness and social disintegration.[52]

The Bishops went on to encourage the peasants and workers to form their labor unions, but to be on their guard that
they not be used for "political or atheistic purposes."

Meanwhile, Juan José Arévalo, living in exile in Mexico,
declared that he was ready to "assume the leadership of all
revolutionary forces in the country."[53] Ydígoras responded by
demanding his extradition from Mexico.[54] Early in 1963, Arévalo announced his intention of returning to Guatemala to
participate in the upcoming presidential elections. The Minister of the Interior then declared that Arévalo would be prose-
cuted for the assassination of Col. Francisco J. Arana.

Arévalo had often been castigated for not having conducted
a more thorough investigation of the murder, but he had never
before been so openly accused by right-wing forces of Arana's
death. That accusation had always been reserved for Arbenz.

Ydígoras then let it be known that he was prepared to allow

Arévalo to participate in the elections, though it was believed that the "Old Fox" was only trying to outflank some of his political opponents. Mario Rodríguez, a U.S. scholar who has written numerous books and articles on Central America, said that Arévalo would have been an easy victor if he had been allowed to run.[55]

Former interim president, Flores Avendaño, stated that Arévalo's entrance into the country would only mean civil war. The House of Representatives of the United States was quoted in the Guatemalan press as stating:

The basic position of the United States is that if any government requests aid to avoid being overthrown by Communists, they will receive help. We are militarily prepared, anticipating any government's request for this aid.[56]

Arévalo's feelings about the United States' role in the overthrow of Arbenz in particular and current interpretation of the Monroe Doctrine in general had not been in doubt since he had written his widely read book, *The Shark and the Sardines,* which characterized the United States as the shark swallowing up Latin American sardines.

Nor were the United States' feelings about Arévalo exactly a secret. United States Ambassador John O. Bell described the former president as "a Communist and thus unworthy of the presidency." Rodríguez describes the remark as "indiscreet" and says that it "made it appear that the United States government was officially opposed to the ex-president."[57] As official voice of the United States government in Guatemala, Bell's remarks would be considered more than indiscreet by Guatemalans, and no attempt was made by the Embassy to give a contrary impression.

On March 20, 1963, all the Central American presidents met with President John F. Kennedy in Costa Rica to discuss mutual interests. Ydígoras told Kennedy that:

The hour of armed invasion is passed (referring to Cuba). Now it remains for the U.S. to give effective and immediate help to the countries of Central America. Resolving our urgent economic problems of housing, education, sanitation and agriculture, we will be able to laugh at Communism and subversion; thus we will terminate once and for all the agitation that is used as a flag by national and international Communists to maintain our peoples in anxiety.[58]

Kennedy responded that their plans and projects would be studied, but a week later gave what is said to have been the green light for the overthrow of Ydígoras by his Minister of Defense, Col. Peralta Azurdia.[59]

NOTES

1 *El Imparcial*, October 15, 1958.
2 *Ibid.*, May 4, 1959.
3 *Ibid.*, May 16, 1959.
4 *Ibid.*, June 22, 1959.
5 *Ibid.*, August 27, 1959.
6 *Ibid.*, August 19, 1959.
7 *Ibid.*, January 5, 1960.
8 *Ibid.*, February 23, 1960.
9 *Ibid.*, November 25, 1960.
10 *Ibid.*, June 23, 1962.
11 Ydígoras, *Op. Cit.*, p. 169.
12 *Ibid.*
13 *Ibid.*, p. 167.
14 Gilly, Adolfo, "The Guerrilla Movement in Guatemala," *Monthly Review*, May 1965, p. 13.
15 *Ibid.*, pp. 14–16.
16 Ydígoras, *Op. Cit.*, p. 168.
17 *Ibid.*, p. 164.
18 Gilly, *Op. Cit.*, p. 20.
19 *El Imparcial*, May 17, 1962.

20 *Ibid.*, January 4, 1963.
21 *Ibid.*, January 4, 26 and 29, 1963.
22 *Ibid.*, January 26, 1963.
23 *Ibid.*, January 14, 1963.
24 *Ibid.*, January 18, 1961.
25 *Ibid.*, February 10, 1961.
26 *Ibid.*, May 17, 1961.
27 *Ibid.*, May 20, 1961.
28 *Ibid.*
29 *Ibid.*, August 24, 1961.
30 *Ibid.*, August 27, 1961.
31 *Ibid.*, September 3,1961.
32 A Congressman who survived assassination attempts by right-wing terrorists in 1968 and 1971. He is the author of a book citing United Fruit Company abuses in Guatemala.
33 *El Imparcial*, February 4, 1962.
34 *Ibid.*, March 29, 1967.
35 CIDOC, *Dossier #21*, Cuernavaca, Mexico, 1968, p. 4/282.
36 CIDA, *Op. Cit.*, p. 49.
37 *Ibid.*, p. 49.
38 *El Imparcial*, July 20 and 25, 1958.
39 *Ibid.*, November 3, 1958.
40 *Ibid.*, May 6, 1959.
41 *Ibid.*, July 11, 1959.
42 *Ibid.*, May 5, 1959.
43 *Ibid.*, December 5, 1959.
44 *Ibid.*, September 8, 1959.
45 *Ibid.*, December 11, 1961.
46 *Ibid.*, December 12, 1961.
47 *Ibid.*, January 25, 1962.
48 *Ibid.*, April 3, 1962.
49 *Ibid.*, April 13, 1962.
50 *Ibid.*, April 24, 1962.
51 *Ibid.*, April 27, 1962.
52 *Ibid.*, January 21-28, 1963.
53 *Ibid.*, January 3, 1962.
54 *Ibid.*, April 6 and May 25, 1962.
55 Rodríguez, Mario, "Guatemala in Perspective," *Current History*, December, 1966, p. 340.
56 *El Imparcial*, March 15, 1963.
57 Rodríguez, *Op. Cit.*, p. 339.
58 *El Imparcial*, March 23, 1963.
59 *The Miami Herald*, December 24, 1966.

Our aim in founding the commonwealth was not to make any one class especially happy, but to secure the greatest possible happiness for the community as a whole. We thought we should have the best chance of finding justice in a state so constituted, just as we should find injustice where the constitution was of the worst possible type.

Plato

10

a constitution of the worst possible type

WHEN Col. Enrique Peralta Azurdia decided that the country could no longer sustain the disaster of supporting a man such as Miguel Ydígoras Fuentes in the presidency, he took matters into his own hands. He did so knowing he would be applauded by the nation's politicized minority of almost every stripe and orientation. Ydígoras, in describing what happened on the night of March 30, 1963, tells us that he was "betrayed by the enemy within."[1] Nine-hundred soldiers and six tanks under the orders of Peralta Azurdia stormed his residence, guarded only by six loyal officers, but he did not surrender until a "tank crushed the weak doors of my home and aimed a cannon at my very face."[2] And so, "an emergent democracy was ruthlessly crushed."[3]

The ultimate event to trigger the military intervention was Arévalo's making good his threat to return to Guatemala from his Mexican exile to participate in the campaign for the presi-

dency. Ydígoras must have been in on the plot to have Arévalo
enter Guatemala, for he says in his incomprehensible way:

The situation was climaxed by the plans of the extreme Left, the
moderate Left, the Center and others, to use the figure of former
president Arévalo to unite all the extremists and to again impose
a Communist government on the country . . . They (Peralta
Azurdia and followers) had no faith in the people of Guatemala;
with no historic precedent, nor basis in fact, they assumed that
the entire country would rise up like one man to support the leftist
demagogue, Arévalo.[4]

To sort out the details of the various plots and counterplots
is next to impossible, nor perhaps is it necessary. Ydígoras
apparently arranged the return of Arévalo in the hopes of seeing him beaten in an "open" election. Whether Peralta Azurdia
ever agreed to this is not certain, but he could have done so
either for the purpose of capturing Arévalo on his arrival or to
afford himself the excuse he needed to topple Ydígoras. Many
people maintain that this last was the actual plan, executed
with Ydígoras's connivance, to give the old general an out—
what is known in Latin America as an *auto-coup* or an *auto-
golpe*.

There is no question that Ydígoras was an adroit political
schemer and a man who had survived many attempts against
his government. He had always managed to play one power
block off against another, and in times of political quakes,
when the dust settled, there he would stand in the middle,
straight as a rod, the rubble of political opponents spread
around his feet. It is this fact that prompted many to think
that he could have survived Peralta Azurdia's attempt if he
had so wished. It certainly did not take him by surprise since
the coup was talked about around the capital quite openly for
weeks in advance.

There is another ramification to this theory. It is believed
that Peralta received John Kennedy's go-ahead on the over-

throw without JFK's understanding that Ydígoras himself was
implicated.[5] This was an attempt to compromise the young
United States President as a responsible party to a coup and
thus to commit him to further financial aid to the new government.

Ydígoras did give Peralta his blessing a few days after the
latter was seated in the president's chair and even went so far
as to declare he was in voluntary exile and to name Peralta as
his "personal representative."[6] He says he did this to save the
country from "confusion and Communism" and not because
he agreed with the coup. The situation was one that demanded
clarification by Peralta Azurdia. His fellow countrymen could
understand much of the political dynamics, and were happy
that Ydígoras was gone, but it was also necessary for him to
justify his action to the world, to receive diplomatic recognition, especially that of the U.S., and to declare his political
creed. Everyone realized that the basic principle of any military government in Guatemala would be "antiCommunism,"
as Peralta Azurdia had stated in his "Fundamental Charter."
But this was not enough, since his predecessor had also been
rabidly "anti-Communist" and yet the country was in a very
sorry plight. Something more was needed, some virtue that had
not been practiced by Ydígoras, something that was anti-
Ydígoras even as Castillo Armas had been antiArbenz. It was
not difficult to decide what that virtue would have to be:
Honesty.

Peralta Azurdia was not seven days in power when
the new "Head of Government" decreed his "Fundamental
Charter,"[7] which was meant to temporarily replace the 1956
Constitution, abrogated by the very act of his coup. Herein lies
the basic rationale of the overthrow and the new government's
intentions: The army assumed control in an "absolutely disinterested way and without the slightest desire of perpetuating
itself in power"[8] and the sole object of its action was "to avoid
an imminent civil war and the establishment of a Communist
regime."[9] He promised, at the same time, "to prepare a favorable political climate that will permit the Guatemalan people a

free election of the person who will direct the destiny of our country without pressure of any kind."[10]

He followed this up two days later with the promulgation of his "Law for the Defense of Democratic Institutions," which reflected the first troubled days of Castillo Armas:

Communism denies God, the human personality and the highest values of the spirit, which is contrary to the traditions and aspirations of the great Guatemalan family . . . Communism is an international doctrine by means of which the minorities in power sell the national sovereignty and independence and give over their peoples to the most opprobrious slavery.[11]

He then decreed two years in prison as a penalty for passing out "Communist literature," five years for making explosives, ten years for belonging to the Communist party and fifteen years for terrorism. Execution was the penalty for anyone involved in an act of terrorism that resulted in the injury or death of anyone.[12] The application of this decree was extremely arbitrary and it was used to make it a crime even to speak out against unjust social conditions. It was also used to persecute "Communist" labor organizers and union members.

Peralta Azurdia adopted the name "Operación Honestidad," Operation Honesty, as the theme of his administration. He would attempt to bring "honesty" back to public life. To this purpose he took a reduction in his own salary, fired all "phantoms" on the government payrolls and quickly began looking into Ydígoras's financial transactions.

On June 20, 1963, Peralta Azurdia declared that all transactions of State properties that had been made by the "Redemption" government were illegal and subject to reversal. The Dictator immediately began a process of recuperation of these properties and tried unsuccessfully to bring Ydígoras back to the country to stand trial along with five of his cohorts, whom he had already jailed for malversion of public funds.

When we speak of Peralta Azurdia's agrarian reform, or rather what he characterizes as his agrarian reform, we must not lose sight of his declared orientation: antiCommunism and honesty. He maintained that his rule was only temporary, so it was understood that no long-range planning could be undertaken. His was a caretaker government. He stayed in office three years. Most observers believe that his government was relatively free from graft and corruption. He did prevent a "Communist takeover," if in fact one had been imminent. He therefore did fulfill the goals that he set for himself, and thus justified the rationale of his coup.

But what of the people? What of the great landless masses that every day were becoming more and more conscious of their misery, of the injustice of their situation? Was the new Dictator ignorant of their rights, their aspirations, their history and the social dynamics then at work in Guatemala?

On September 28, 1963, he announced what the agricultural policy of his government was to be. He said that Guatemala's fundamental problem was the low standard of living of the peasant population. The goal of his government would be "to raise this standard so that well-being might flow to the rural areas."[13] But this would be done gradually, by stages, with a socio-economic program that respected private property.

It would be a mistake to base our agrarian policy on a regime of massive expropriations of private lands, since this would produce inconvenient emotional reactions and have sterile effects, and are incompatible with the financial resources of the State.[14]

He announced that in order to demonstrate his government's sincerity, he had placed at the disposition of INTA "the extensive and magnificent State lands of Quiché and Izabal." Later, other measures regarding the national *fincas* would be announced.

Congressional elections were held to establish a "Constituent Assembly" that would draw up a "Magna Carta" to substitute for the abrogated constitution. The Christian Democrats refused to participate in the elections because they did not want to lend an air of legitimacy to a military government.

The Revolutionary Party did participate as did the Liberation Party, and a document was formulated that was meant to legitimatize and give permanence to the legislation issued by the government.

When Congress discussed agriculture, they suppressed the section of the "Magna Carta" that said: "The law shall determine the protection of family patrimony, the better use of the nation's natural resources, and the limitations of the right of private property that may be necessary for the transformation of idle lands."[15]

They did approve three articles that contained the basis for future agrarian legislation:

Article 63: Private property is guaranteed. The State has the obligation of assuring the proprietor the necessary conditions for the development and utilization of his goods. The law will determine the proprietor's obligations and rights.

Article 66: In concrete cases, private property can be expropriated. It will be paid for according to its actual value, within ten years, plus interest. To determine the value, all elements, circumstances and conditions will be considered instead of registrations or official documents.

Article 116: A program of agricultural reform will be based on: (1) No lands will be touched that are considered necessary by the proprietor for amplifying his enterprise; (2) While there are national lands that are not yet registered, private lands will not be touched unless they are legally declared to be idle; (3) Idle lands can be expropriated once the State has exhausted all national lands, has given the owner a reasonable amount of time and has paid for the lands in full; (4) Forest land will never be considered idle land.[16]

Even with the assurance of this constitutional protection, the National Agricultural Council was worried and wanted to make sure that the talk of land reform remained just that. They asked that the colonization of the northern region of the country be declared of public utility and national urgency.

They based their request on the fact that "all the attempts at reform since Arbenz have failed because they have always been accompanied by agitation and political explosions."[17] They went on to explain that the 27,000 (sic) beneficiaries of the different attempts at reform had not improved their lot due to a lack of understanding of the "idiosyncrasies of the peasants" on the part of the authorities. And they added:

The beneficiaries of lots of government distributions continue to be orphans in education, sanitary attention, live in housing that lacks comfort, without water, electricity or the hope of a prompt improvement of their standard of living in which they were placed at a given moment.[18]

If the expropriations and distribution of private lands were to follow the same pattern as before, they said, there could only come as a result "political convulsions which are negative to the development which Guatemala needs." This is the voice of the landowners and those who enjoy the comfort and luxury of a standard of living "in which *they* were placed at a given moment." They would like to see some of the landless peasants settled in the northern regions of the country, away from their own plantations where 60.7 percent of their lands are temptingly idle.[19] They criticized the lack of technical, sanitary and educational assistance to the holders of lots given them by the government, but they refused to face a raise in taxes—some of the lowest in the world[20]—and they maintained the workers on their own plantations in far worse conditions.

The National Agricultural Council warned the legislators that the expropriations and distributions of private lands would cause "political convulsions." These would come primarily from themselves, since they were the ones objecting to land reform. The question remains whether their plans for the development of Guatemala give the peasants a positive share in that development.

In the Economic Council of the United Nations, Michael George, the U.S. delegate, said that only if an agrarian reform has as its primary goal the increase of agricultural production, as well as social and political reform, will its results be socially and politically satisfactory. This statement produced the following remark in an editorial:

At last they (the U.S.) are beginning to realize the danger of the so-called peaceful revolution proposed by the Alliance for Progress. Rapid reform creates more political and social problems than it solves.[21]

This reference to the Alliance for Progress was becoming a hot point in Guatemala's Congressional discussions. Ydígoras's attempts to bring Guatemalan legislation into line with the demands of the Alliance had been political ploys not meant to effect social change. His Agrarian Reform Bill was a step backwards from that of Castillo Armas and his Income Tax Law, replacing other tax laws, amounted to an increase of tax revenues of from 11 to 13 million Quetzales, far too little to be meaningful. The Alliance for Progress had been set up a few months after the unsuccessful Bay of Pigs invasion and wisely recognized the popularity of Fidel Castro's agrarian reform. Title I.6 of the Alliance Chapter states:

To encourage, in accordance with the characteristics of each country, programs of comprehensive agrarian reform leading to the effective transformation, where required, of unjust structures and systems of land tenure and use, with a view to replacing latifundia and dwarf holdings by an equitable system of land tenure so that, with the help of timely and adequate credit, technical assistance and facilities for marketing and distribution of products, the land will become for the man who works it the basis of his economic stability, the foundation of his increasing welfare and the guarantee of his freedom and dignity.[22]

In December, 1964, in Lima, Peru, the Third Annual Meeting of the Inter-American Economic and Social Council was held at the Ministerial level and it clarified what was meant by "Agrarian Reform" in the Alliance Charter. It recognized that "the majority of Latin American countries have established legal instruments aimed at bringing about agrarian reform,"[23] but stressed that to be effective such a reform had to produce structural changes. These changes included "giving the land its social function" and "modernizing rural life," as well as "changing the power structure of the nation."[24]

The concept that land could have a "social function" became the subject of an acrimonious debate in the Guatemalan Congress.[25] The Congressmen were being pressured by the Chamber of Industry which maintained that:

Social justice is a dangerous ambiguity. For the Communists and socialists, social justice is administered by the State; for Catholics, social justice is left to the conscience of every individual."[26]

El Imparcial, the leading daily, published editorials against the concept of social justice every day[27] and the Coordinating Committee of the Association of Landowners, Businessmen, Industrialists and Bankers demanded that all references to social justice be stricken from the constitution:

We are not against social justice but rather against the demagogic way this term is used. Private enterprise might collapse if we augment the burdens of the owners.[28]

By the end of June, 1965, only one Congressman out of 80 was arguing for the rights of the little man:

It seems that you people need a "cacique"* in order to tell you what it is that you should approve; nothing for the benefit of the worker has been approved by this Assembly.[29]

The Congressman, Mauro Monterroso, complained that he was accused of Communism every time he presented one of his motions.[30]

* cacique—strong leader

Finally the "Magna Carta" was approved and it was signed by all the deputies minus one, his objection being not to the fact that all mention of social justice had been excluded but rather that the Archbishop's representative, Monsignor Girón Perrone, did not like the text and had said, "No special rights have been democratically conceded that correspond to the Church."[31] He was answered by José Calderón Salazar of the Liberation Party, who had led the fight for the rights of the Church:

Seven months we fought over this Magna Carta and not a word out of the Church; even when we discussed the topic of social justice, the Catholic Hierarchy could be found toasting at a reception, turning their backs on the religious reality of Guatemala.[32]

The justification for the exclusion of such concepts had been given by Congressman Menéndez Sandoval of the Liberation Party:

The evil phrase, "the social function of property," gave birth precisely to Decree #900 which was on the point of carrying Guatemala to the greatest disaster in its history, this both in practice and in theory, because the real agrarian problem of Guatemala is not the scarcity of lands but rather that the lands be made to produce more.[33]

In view of the fact that the Alliance recognized the need for changes in the power structure that were based on the ownership of land, the Lima Meeting specified that "expansion of agricultural production and colonization are not acceptable substitutes for agrarian reform."[34] Yet colonization was the program that Castillo Armas had begun with his agrarian zones; the one that was continued by Ydígoras; and it seemed now that it would be the line of least resistance that would be followed by the Peralta Azurdia government.

On June 11, 1965, an agrarian decree (#354) was promulgated. Its preamble stated its purpose:

Considering that it is the fundamental obligation of the State to dictate the measures necessary to bring about the greatest possible good for the inhabitants of the nation and that among these measures, one that is urgent is the provision of lands to be dedicated to the production of foodstuffs, in order to satisfy the demands of a minimum diet for the inhabitants;

Considering that the lands of Guatemala that are actually dedicated to the production of foodstuffs will not be sufficient in the immediate future to produce what is necessary for the inhabitants;

Considering that it is urgent to foresee what the consumption of foodstuffs in Guatemala will be, and that this makes it necessary to prepare and colonize new lands, such as those along the banks of the Usumacinta River and its tributaries, which, for ecological reasons are the most appropriate for this purpose; . . .

Article one then stated what would be done:

The fixed goal of greatest priority is to obtain, in a time period no greater than 10 years, the intensification of the colonization and the rational utilization of the lands of the Department of Petén, and of all the rest that constitute the banks of the Usumacinta River and its tributaries.[35]

The notice of the shortage of primary foodstuffs was something Peralta could not continue to ignore. During the Ydígoras administration, the yearly shortage of corn necessitated the importation of hundreds of thousands of *quintales* from the United States and Mexico, and now rice too, another peasant staple, was being imported. If for no other reason than to maintain a more favorable trade balance, more lands had to be brought into production. However, the banks of the Usumacinta River and its tributaries were not the most appropriate for this purpose, as will be discussed later.

The colonization of Petén had been seen as a partial solution to Guatemala's land difficulties seventeen years earlier and had even been attempted by Arévalo without much success. When Ydígoras had come to power, he proclaimed, as one of the primary goals of his government, the development of Petén, which comprises one-third of the national territory and is covered largely by rain forests. Shortly after Ydígoras had taken office, a law (#1286) was issued declaring the economic development of Petén to be of "national urgency." This was to be accomplished by the "scientific exploitation and preservation of its forests and other natural resources, a program of public health, its colonization and industrialization."[36] It can be seen, though, from article #6 that this colonization was not directed for the benefit of the landless and illiterate masses, but rather was aimed:

To stimulate an increase in the population of Petén, organizing industrial, agricultural and cattle raising colonies and to establish new urban communities and tourist centers, looking to the needs that a gradual development of Petén demands. To accomplish this, FYDEP (Institute for the Economic Progress and Development of Petén) will study the conveniences of bringing in immigrants, preferably those who are specialized in particular crops, techniques of forestry, animal husbandry or industry. . . .[37]

The program never seriously got underway with Ydígoras and now Peralta Azurdia also decided that the colonization of the Petén could be the solution to the agrarian problem after all.

There are a number of reasons why the Alliance for Progress technicians would not accept colonization as a substitute for land reform. Colonization means the opening up of virgin lands that are in the hands of the State. Colonization is meant to avoid touching those unused lands that are in private hands. Where political, economic and social power are very intimately linked to the possession of lands, the unwillingness to expropriate excessive lands in private hands in reality represents an unwillingness or inability to change the archaic political, economic and social structures. Furthermore, the mere fact that virgin lands are still in the hands of the State after more than 400 years of domination by the Spanish tradition of land ownership, says much about the condition of these lands, either as regards their inaccessibility and/or their physical worthlessness. In addition, to substitute colonization for the expropriation of large, idle, private holdings means a far greater expense in both economic and social terms while still not directly affecting the political system, and therefore can be nothing more than tokenism.

When Castillo Armas began his program of agrarian zones in 1956, CIDA stated that:

The spirit of the law, nevertheless, gave the new program all the characteristics of a colonization, rather than a reform.[38]

The reason for qualifying it as such were that the two main projects of the program were on virgin lands that had been purchased from private owners: United Fruit turned over Nueva Concepción in a special agreement with the government and La Máquina was purchased for half a million Quetzales. The implications are that State lands are largely worthless for colonization and that to obtain suitable lands is a very expensive project. Such an expense puts a very real limit on the amount of help that can be provided by such a solution, as Castillo Armas and Ydígoras well understood. Peralta Azurdia could not have been blind to the limitations of such a program.

In August, 1964, a precursory notice appeared in the newspapers to the effect that the Ministry of Public Health was fighting a malaria epidemic in the Agrarian Zone of Nueva Concepción. Doctor Ponce Archila, the Minister of Public Health, had to utilize emergency methods to aid the "more than 10,000 homes in which live more than 38,000 people."[39] A month later, Col. Pedro Rodríguez Valenzuela, head of INTA, ordered an investigation of Nueva Concepción, in view of the fact that there were supposed to be only 1150 farms in the area, "because there are people living there illegally, others are renting their farms, and others have sold theirs, contrary to Decree #1551."[40]

Part of the difficulty was that many farms had been given out to undeserving recipients and they in turn had gotten *colonos* to work the lands for them. But the real reason that Nueva Concepción had turned into another project of *minifundismo* was that the effort was too modest in view of the gigantic needs. People flowed into any area where lands were distributed by the government and it was difficult for the beneficiaries to refuse entrance to their relatives and *compadres* who were in the same miserable conditions as the fortunate beneficiary.

The same thing happened to La Máquina. In October, 1967, it was observed that the "floating population of the zone had reached between 17,000 and 18,000 people."[41] This figure plus the legitimate population put the total somewhere near 24,000 people on 1,147 farms—another rampant case of *minifundismo*. This should have been some indication of the difficulties Arbenz had experienced in holding back the peasants from illegal invasions once distributions had begun.

That Peralta Azurdia really believed that the colonization of the northern jungles would solve the agrarian problem may legitimately be doubted. He was not an ignorant man and his interest in the Petén region dated from his term of office as head of the DGAA. In June, 1963, only two months after his coup, he attended a meeting with the directors of the government bank and members of the National Economic Planning Commission to study the proposal of F. M. Warren of Coastal Timber and Pulp Company to invest $100 million in Petén's lumber industry. The project was named "Showcase for Democracy" and the Company wanted timber rights for the entire area.[42] In July, another group of United States investors went to Guatemala and made counterproposals of huge investments, one of which was a plywood factory. FYDEP officials were also busy showing Guatemalan cattlemen the treeless savannahs, excellent for their livestock, that they could purchase for a song.[43]

In December, 1964, FYDEP announced the creation of its new department of colonization with Colonel Romeo Samayoa as its director. His first declaration stated the intention to create 125 farms of 22.5 *caballerías* (2,470 acres) each for cattle raising—not meant for small family farms. He mentioned that he already had 2,400 requests for land in Petén and that within eight years the population of the Department would be 70,000 people, or an increase of 45,000 over the existing population. He said that selection of those who would receive lands would be made by lottery so that no second guessing would occur.[44]

A month later, the first official word was given that Petén was being considered as the solution to the agrarian problem. The economic development plan for 1965–69 stated:

The government contemplates a massive colonization of the government lands situated in the northern portion of the country, by means of a system that will take care of the great needs of the western population, dispossessed of lands, as well as the manner of exploiting the same.[45]

The first farm of 22.5 *caballerías* (2,470 acres) was given to Pompeyo del Valle Cano, a native of Petén. He was promised that title would be given later.

In June, 1965, J. Philip Murphy, President of Murphy Pacific Corporation of California, went to Guatemala to "finalize the investment of $30 million in the colonization of the northern part of the country, forming CIAINSA (Compañía Impulsadora del Norte, S.A.) for Petén and Alta Verapaz."[46] A week later, the Secretary of Information of the government announced:

Our goal is the intensification of the colonization and rational exploitation of the lands of Petén and all the others that constitute the Usumacinta River basin and tributaries within ten years. These lands are very suitable due to ecological conditions. The government will stimulate private enterprise to aid in the project.[47]

In October, 1965, the National Council of Agriculture, a private organization composed of the various lobbying groups, gave this measure its wholehearted support declaring:

The colonization of the Petén is of national emergency and public necessity in order to increase the production of basic foods, to relieve the congestion of overpopulation in certain regions, to combat crime and decrease unemployment, to maintain the sovereignty of our territory in the North, to stop the invasions of national lands and to guarantee the respect and inviolability of private property.[48]

A few days later, Colonel Peralta Azurdia anounced to the landowners that they should not fear expropriations of their properties since the government had no money to pay them. He also announced that in view of his new agrarian law, 590,000 hectares (1,457,300 acres) of Petén would be incorporated into the national economy: 330,000 hectares (815,100 acres) for cattle and 260,000 (642,200 acres) for agriculture.[49] That same month, the first two groups of landless peasants went to the banks of the Pasión River in Sayaxché: ninety families formed the cooperative Felicidad from the floating population now grown huge in the government's agrarian zone of Nueva Concepción; another fifteen families formed the cooperative, Manos Unidas from Cabricán, Quezaltenango, a parish cooperative founded by the Maryknoll Fathers.[50] In March, 1966, the National Council of Catholic Bishops announced its backing of the colonization program represented by the Cabricán parish cooperative, and promised that it would lend moral support to the effort to transfer 5,000 families to Petén.[52] AID stated its willingness to lend money to the cooperatives for the cultivation of rubber, but when their technicians analyzed the soil, they found that the land given to the peasants had a very high water table and that the top soil was only a few inches deep. Doctor James Walker of the University of North Carolina, a leading expert in the field, predicted that the land would be swamp within five years if it were given over to agriculture. No money would therefore be given for rubber or any other crop to be sown on the lands along the banks of the Pasión and Usumacinta Rivers. This, despite the fact that the government was still maintaining that "these lands are very suitable due to ecological conditions."

Sebol-Chinajá was another creation of the Peralta Azurdia government, planned along the lines of the agrarian zones and meant to correct the errors of Nueva Concepción and La Máquina. It was organized to settle 25,000 families in the forests of northern Alta Verapaz at a cost of Q. 64 million. Since the project was to be developed by INTA, and the lands ran into the Petén, which was FYDEP territory, it was not certain how the obvious conflict was to be resolved. The first public information about the project came in July, 1963 with the formation of the agrarian zone, Fray Bartolomé de las Casas, in which 1,000 families would receive 2 *caballerías* (219.6 acres) each and 552 families 1 *caballería* (109.8 acres) each.[52]

In May, 1964, the announcement was made that 100,000 families would receive lands "in the north," that AID would give two million dollars toward the study and that the Guatemalan government would give eight million for the same purpose. A loan was being made from AID for seven million dollars to start settling 1,000 families in the Sebol-Chinajá area.[53]

Just as it had happened in Nueva Concepción and in La Máquina, as soon as people heard that lands were to be given out, they began moving into the area so as to receive preference. In July, 1964, INTA warned that those who, without INTA's authorization, moved onto the lands to be distributed, would be considered invaders and would never receive lands. INTA claimed that unscrupulous people were organizing landless peasants to invade the area.[54] In 1965, a UN report on the colonization zone, Fray Bartolomé de las Casas, stated that there were already 475 single-room houses of rustic poles and palm roofs with damp dirt floors, housing approximately 3,000 people.[55] The majority of these homes had no latrines or baths and all were getting their water from open streams. Control of malaria was most difficult.

In May, 1967, when FYDEP and INTA were arguing over which institution would control the colonization of Petén, the head of FYDEP charged:

The impotency of INTA during these past four years in the land distributions of Sebol, Fray Bartolomé de las Casas, and Puerto Sebol-Chinajá, constitutes an irrefutable case of that paralysis that appears in the distribution of lands suitable to their purposes and it will be much more grave in lands that are not so suitable.[56]

If INTA's purpose was land reform, the suitability of the lands can be legitimately questioned. But when these lands are compared to those of the Petén, the point was well-taken. By July, 1967, 530 farms had been distributed and already 7,000 people were living on them.[57] The process continued.

The total land distributions made by the Peralta Azurdia government were: forty-five titles to farms (extension unknown),[58] 200 urban lots[59] and 530 provisional titles in the Sebol-Chinajá project.

NOTES

1 Ydígoras, *Op. Cit.*, p. 2.
2 *Ibid.*
3 *Ibid.*, p. 3.
4 *Ibid.*, p. 5.
5 *The Miami Herald,* December 24, 1966.
6 Ydígoras, *Op. Cit.*, p. 6.
7 Azurdia, Vol. 82, p. 21.
8 *Ibid.*

9 *Ibid.*
10 *Ibid.*
11 *Ibid.*, p. 24.
12 *Ibid.*, p. 25.
13 *El Imparcial*, September 28, 1963.
14 *Ibid.*
15 *Ibid.*, March 25, 1965.
16 *Ibid.*, March 26, 1965.
17 *El Imparcial*, April 1, 1965.
18 *Ibid.*
19 CIDA, *Op. Cit.*, p. 20.
20 *El Imparcial*, January 5, 1968: Out of the 64 countries listed,
    Guatemala rated 63rd with taxes comprising 7.7 per cent of the
    gross national product.
21 *Ibid.*, July 16, 1965.
22 CIDA, *The Agrarian-Reform and the Alliance for Progress,*
    Washington: CIDA, 1965, p. 2.
23 *Ibid.*, p. 3.
24 *Ibid.*, pp. 3–4.
25 *El Imparcial*, March 12–16, 1965.
26 *Ibid.*, February 2, 1965.
27 *Ibid.*, March 12–16, 1965.
28 *Ibid.*, May 27, 1965.
29 *Ibid.*, June 30, 1965.
30 *Ibid.*
31 *Ibid.*, September 14, 1965.
32 *Ibid.*
33 *Ibid.*, October 30, 1964.
34 CIDA, *The Agrarian Reform . . .* , p. 4.
35 *Diario Oficial, El Guatemalteco,* Vol. CLXIII, No. 85, June 11,
    1965.
36 Azurdia, Vol. LXXVIII, p. 12.
37 *Ibid.*
38 CIDA, *Tenencia . . .* , p. 47.
39 *El Imparcial,* August 29, 1964.
40 *Ibid.*, October 2, 1964.
41 *Ibid.*, October 11, 1967.
42 *Ibid.*, June 11, 1963.
43 *Ibid.*, June 4, 1964.
44 *Ibid.*, December 17, 1965.
45 *Ibid.*, January 9, 1965.
46 *Ibid.*, June 9, 1965.
47 *Ibid.*, June 14, 1965.
48 *Ibid.*, October 9, 1965.
49 *Ibid.*, October 15, 1965.
50 Maryknoll is a North American Catholic missionary society of

which the authors were members. Manos Unidas is one of the cooperatives founded by the author.

51 *El Imparcial*, March 2, 1966.
52 *Ibid.*, July 17, 1963.
53 *Ibid.*, May 16, 1964.
54 *Ibid.*, July 18, 1964.
55 Oficina Internacional del Trabajo, *Informe al Gobierno de Guatemala sobre Colonización*, Ginebra, 1965 (mimeo), p. 89.
56 *El Imparcial*, May 24, 1967.
57 *Ibid.*, July 17, 1967.
58 *Ibid.*, May 4, 1965.
59 *Ibid.*, February 16, 1965.

An aristocratic government has an inherent vigor, unknown to democracy. The nobles form a body, who by their prerogative, and for their particular interest, restrain the people; it is sufficient that there are laws in being to see them executed.

Montesquieu

11

an aristocratic government

SINCE THIS interim military regime had no other social goal than honesty in the conduct of its business, perhaps it should not be expected that it would do anything about the outstanding social problems of the nation. Still, this cannot mean that it was completely indifferent to what was going on in the country. There are some indications of Peralta Azurdia's concern with his government's prestige in the rural area. One effort was the construction of 191 small but very visible schools, financed by his government, the AID and the local communities. No attempt was made, however, to upgrade the quality of education, where in many areas *Ladino* teachers often refuse to instruct the Maya pupils.

The reported expulsions of peasants from lands they had possessed for many years were not as numerous as those effected by the Ydígoras government. However, the constant "state of siege" declared by the military government extensively limited the freedom of the press. And it can also be recalled that the individual in charge of the expulsions under the Ydígoras government had been the then head of the

DGAA, Col. Peralta Azurdia himself. On January 29, 1964, the newspapers record what might have been the first expulsion order under the military government:

Twenty-five families in El Manchón were told by the governor of Retalhuleu[1] to leave their homes and burn them, or go to jail. They have lived for 30 years on the lands of the *finca* Buenos Aires and the former owner had left them alone. Two months ago the *finca* was bought by Juan Samayoa whose son was named military commissioner of the area.[2]

The other reports are more terse: "Several families were expelled from their homes by the municipal government in zone 8 of Guatemala City;"[3] "Fifteen families expelled from their lands in Zone 12. Women and children crying in the streets. The men demand to see the president. They have lived there twenty years now and they have no place to go."[4] "Ten families expelled from municipal property in Guatemala City."[5] "The AEU appeals to INTA to investigate the expulsion of thirty families from their lands in Gualán where they have legitimate ownership papers dating back to 1928. The man who claims ownership, Ricardo Miralles, is the brother-in-law of the judge of the Zacapa area who is accused of falsifying the papers of ownership."[6] Indigenous people in Chipacatox, Baja Verapaz, claim that Fernández Isaguirre has stolen three *caballerías* from them. Fifteen years before he tried the same thing and the Arbenz government declared that the lands belonged to the Indians. Now he has built a fence around the land."[7]

A more serious indictment of the military government arises from the situation it permitted to exist on the cotton plantations. Ydígoras had been quite generous in extending credits and encouraging the large landowners to devote more lands to cotton, in order to diversify the country's exports. He was successful in this, but just as the *latifundistas* became wealthier on their cotton, the peasants' lives became more miserable on the plantations. On October 15, 1963, the Inspector General of Labor under Peralta Azurdia "energetically warned the cotton growers to build houses for their workers since a great number are obliged to sleep exposed to the weather. There has been much sickness and often this results in the deaths of entire families."[8]

Warnings such as these, however, do not carry much force in Guatemala. Indeed they are not meant to, since the government itself backs up the plantation owners' attempts to secure unwilling laborers.

In 1965, the army went into some villages in the Department of San Marcos and rounded up peasants at gun point to work on the cotton plantations.[9] The army was also used in at least two other departments.[10] In all three cases, this action had been taken by the departmental governors at the request of the Minister of the Interior.[11] These men responded to the pressures of the National Cotton Council.

In 1966, when enough migrant workers could not be found to pick the cotton (it was estimated that between 300,000 to 400,000 are needed to harvest the crop),[12] the government was roundly condemned by the landowners for scheduling an election that interfered with their labor-seeking campaign.[13]

Since conditions on the cotton plantations are even worse than those on the coffee *fincas,* obtaining workers for the harvest is not easy. Much of the difficulty can be ascribed to the use of deadly insecticides. The Institute of Social Security announced that there had been five cases of deaths and 151 cases of intoxication reported during the months of July, August, and September, 1963, all due to insecticide poisonings.[14] Cases such as these are not often reported so the figures available can be considered to be conservative. The director of the Social Security Institute maintained that 325 *fincas* had secured authorization for spraying without the necessary legal inspection. He himself had denied authorization to many other owners only to have the permission granted by the Minister of Agriculture.[15] Nowhere is there mention of any landowners being taken to court for the poisonings and deaths of their workers. Nor is there apt to be.

The treatment that the migrant workers receive from the landowners is consistent, if not just. They work for eleven hours a day and are paid sixty cents, as in Cotzumalguapa.[16] Sixty-three peasants from Cobán working in Tiquisate were not paid at all and managed to escape from the farm and get a ride to Guatemala City. There, the Red Cross found them all sick from not having eaten for several days. They were fed and sent home—nothing happened to the plantation owner.[17] Another thirty peasants were dumped on the highway after having worked on a cotton plantation without pay. Of the thirty, "twenty-seven were sick with malaria, malnutrition and bronchial infections." The Red Cross got to them after they had gone forty-eight hours without food. They were fed and sent home. Nothing was done to the plantation owner except that he was made to promise to pay their salaries, probably because the incident made the newspapers.[18] How many similar incidents occurred that never appeared in the press can only be conjectured.

Peralta Azurdia dedicated himself to the persecution of plantation labor unions, seeing them as a Communist threat. He imprisoned many of the movement's leaders as a "preventive measure." He sent secret police to work among the peasants in order to identify and capture the leaders of these organizations. When the secret police found the field work too difficult, he promulgated a decree (#332) which ordered the army to take over the obligations of the national police on the plantations.[19] This law declared that whatever aid needed by the plantation owners or their administrators was to be given and that "those who get the peasants excited" were to be reported to the army. The law was rather open-ended as regards punishment.

A projected law, reminiscent of Ubico, was submitted to Congress by the Minister of Interior. Fortunately, because of the outcry against it, the law was not passed. It was to have been a law against vagrancy:

Any individual detained for what is classified as dangerous vagrancy will be sent to a work camp where he will be obligated to work for a period of not less than six months nor more than six years.[20]

It was meant to apply to anyone between the ages of 16 and 60 years.

As the situation of the peasants deteriorated, the guerrilla movements got more backing in the Escuintla, Zacapa and Izabal areas. Encounters between the army and the guerrilla forces became more frequent, and the government had a difficult time determining where they were picking up their support. On March 8, 1966, the police moved into Rio Hondo, Zacapa and took prisoner every adult male in a village of over 100 men:

It is not known where they are . . . they were detained by members of the police, and until this time it is not known where they are or why they were detained.[21]

Actually it was very well known why they were detained. The guerrilla movement of Luis Turcios Lima was very active in the area and the government was desperately trying to find out what peasants and villages were supplying the combatants with food and information.

Turcios Lima had participated with Yon Sosa in the November 13, 1960, uprising and had continued the struggle with him. But as the two of them studied the politics of armed revolution, they had a parting of ways, Yon Sosa following a Trotskyist orientation and Turcios Lima, under the name of FAR (Armed Forces of Rebellion), a stricter Leninist Philosophy. FAR aligned itself with the PGT (Partido Guatemalteco del Trabajo) * but subsequently broke that relationship, reunited with Yon Sosa and his MR-13 (13 of November Movement), then broke off again. The difficulties seemed to

---

* PGT—Guatemala Labor Party—Communist Party established at the end of the Arévalo presidency but outlawed since the counter revolution of 1954; now operates underground.

revolve more around the tactics of the revolution than about its objectives, because all three groups maintain that the principal aim of the revolution is to give land to the peasants. FAR declared:

The fact is that we fight for a democratic and nationalistic program; we fight to effect an agrarian and anti-imperialist revolution . . . We are after an agrarian revolution, the rapid expropriation of the large *latifundios* by the peasants themselves and by this means to restructure our whole national economy, all our industrial planification . . . The replacement of the large landowner by the peasant is not done by slaps on the back and loving embraces. It is done by force . . . [22]

As the battles between the army and the guerrillas became more frequent, often with the army coming out on the losing end, the government became more desperate in trying to gain control over the situation. In Quirigüá the military commissioners forcibly entered into peasant homes and nine men were reported missing and not consigned to any tribunal.[23] Two days before the peasant roundup in Rio Hondo, the government had also captured twenty-eight other persons, leaders of the PGT, union organizers and guerrilla sympathizers, taking them from their homes. Víctor Manuel Gutiérrez and Leonardo Castillo Flores, labor organizers under Arbenz, were among them.[24] As the government claimed no knowledge of these captures, the guerrillas of the FAR staged a daring daylight kidnapping of the Secretary of Information of the government and the head of the Supreme Court. They followed this up with the capture of the President of Congress, who was also head of the Institutional Democratic Party (PID), the political party set up by the military government to participate in the upcoming elections. FAR offered to exchange these three men for the twenty-eight persons still presumed to be in the custody of the government. The head of the Red Cross, the head of the National University and the new Archbishop of Guatemala City, Mario Casariego, all offered to be intermediaries in the exchange but the government continued to deny knowledge of "the 28's" whereabouts.

It became known months later, when the military government was no longer in power, that "the 28" had been murdered by the government's number two strongman, Col. Rafael Arriaga Bosque[25] and so no exchange could be made. Upon learning of the execution of their twenty-eight companions and judging it to be politically wise, the FAR released two of their prisoners. The President of Congress, Menéndez de la Riva, had already managed to escape from his captors and had gone to the U.S. to live. The hostilities were becoming more pronounced and the government did not seem capable of handling the situation.

The United States' Military Mission in the country, as well as other sectors of the AID program being offered to Peralta Azurdia, were being ignored. For one thing, the Dictator was trying to put his balance of payments in order and he couldn't accept help that would cost him money. It was common during the last days of Peralta's rule to hear expressions of despair in the corridors and offices of the Cruz Azul building (AID headquarters) in Guatemala City from the directors of the Alliance for Progress. Their chagrin was matched only by Peralta Azurdia's stubbornness in refusing offers of loans for every conceivable (or ill-conceived) project. This also included his unwillingness to allow MAP (U.S. Military Assistance Program) to expand its activities; however, this refusal was apparently due to a military and nationalistic pride, rather than the U.S. price-tag. It was in such an atmosphere that the guerrilla revolutionary bands were able to expand their activities and that the Army was unable to control them. The landed aristocracy and the business sectors of the populace were becoming quite upset and very outspoken about Peralta Azurdia's refusal to cooperate with the United States.

When a United States senator was quoted in the Guatemalan press as stating that the United States would intervene in Guatemala if the situation did not improve, Peralta was furious and his government responded: "We are not the

Dominican Republic. The Guatemalan government can handle any internal subversives by itself."[26] But Peralta was not surprised by such an attitude. Six months earlier, the local press had reported similar sentiments expressed in a resolution that had been passed overwhelmingly by the United States House of Representatives:

In any such situation, any one or more of the high contracting parties to the Inter-American Treaty of Reciprocal Assistance may, in the exercise of individual or collective self defense, which could go as far as to resort to armed force, and in accordance with the declarations and principles above stated, take steps to forestall or combat intervention, domination, control and colonization in whatever form, by the subversive forces known as international Communism and its agencies in the Western Hemisphere.[27]

The vote had been 312 to 52 in favor of the resolution and was intended to give the United States President "liberty of action." It was seen as a grave threat by many in Latin America, especially the proud Peralta. It was condemned as a "stupid attitude" by the Chilean Congress and Mexican labor leaders condemned it as the "worst threat ever faced by the peoples of Latin America."[28] The declaration never became known to the majority of landless peasants of Guatemala, but the landowners breathed a sigh of relief.

It was in opposition to this stubborn stance of Peralta that Colonel Miguel Angel Ponciano and the MLN built their election campaign, promising closer cooperation with the United States in suppressing Guatemalan insurgents.

This time, however, the United States could not be accused of trying to defend the lands of the United Fruit Company. Ever since the antitrust case had gone against them in a New Orleans Court on February 4, 1958, the banana company had been trying to unload its lands. The court had ordered the company to sell 30 percent of its assets to competitors, since it had been functioning as a monopoly in the U.S.[29] Lands seemed to be the most vulnerable asset the company owned, as President Sunderland had stated in April of 1960:

The United Fruit company has decided to sell or rent or negotiate, up to a reasonable point, the lands that it owns in Latin America. The Company will buy the production of the new owners or renters. The times are changing in Latin America and consequently we ought to change also. There exists a completely natural and understandable desire on the part of the citizens of the countries in which we operate, to own their own lands and to cultivate their own crops in order to sell them in international markets. We will try to change according to the rhythm of the times and to negotiate with them in a manner they find acceptable.[30]

By early 1964, Guatemala understood what these words meant. Twenty-five hundred workers were fired by the company as it closed down operations[31] in Tiquisate. The workers' union made a vain attempt to try to buy the lands from the company, but Ted Holcombe, manager of United Fruit Company in Guatemala, said that the lands had already been sold to "twelve former employees of the company."[32] These "former employees" of the company included Holcombe himself, his son and his son-in-law, who were in the process of becoming large cotton farmers. The workers protested the sale and threatened to go to court in the United States to demand that the lands be sold to them because they had applied as soon as the offer of sale had become public knowledge.[33] The threat of appealing to a United States court was impossible for them to carry out. The company refused and the sale went through to the "twelve former employees of the United Fruit Company."[34]

It was a profitable arrangement: the United Fruit Company now dealt with these former employees, having sold off its lands to "competitors" as the New Orleans court had ordered; they no longer looked like a big bad wolf; they no longer had to deal with a solid union, since the workers were split among several owners; most of these owners were native Guatemalans, consequently denying the workers the cry of imperialism that had formerly united them; and the company could discontinue expensive educational and health services.

But the new deal did not discourage the guerrilla movement from continuing its blasts at the United States as the backbone of the oppressive social, economic and political structure of the country; the former United Fruit Company workers did not feel that the antitrust decision of the New Orleans court had been particularly in their favor; nor did the resolution of the House of Representatives convince the politicized segments of Guatemala that the United States was seeking the best interests of the people of that Central American nation.

The Peralta Azurdia government did say that it backed the workers' petition to purchase the United Fruit Company lands.[35] No one paid much attention to the statement however. It was recognized that the government was concentrating on demonstrating its honesty and its antiCommunism.

The government's suppression of peasant leagues and union activities as well as its attempts to stamp out the guerrilla movements were its antiCommunist banners. Its honesty was demonstrated by its reclamation of the national *fincas,* its withdrawal from other questionable commercial enterprises, and its fulfillment of the promise to be only a transitory government.

It was this proud banner of *Operación Honestidad* that finally spelled Peralta's political demise. He was determined to prove to the people that he was all that he claimed to be and this included holding to his word that he would "prepare a favorable political climate that would permit the Guatemalan people a free election of the person who will direct the destiny of our country without pressure of any kind."[36] He realized than an honest victory at the polls was impossible for himself. Rather than be accused of the electoral legerdemain that made Ydígoras so hated, he preferred to establish a political party

headed by a candidate other than himself, who would per-
petuate the firm hand that he had brought to the nation. So the
PID was formed and a colleague of Peralta Azurdia, Col.
Juan de Dios Aguilar, was chosen as its candidate.

NOTES

1 All governors of the Departments under the military government as
   well as under Méndez Montenegro were Army officers.
2 *El Imparcial*, January 29, 1964.
3 *Ibid.*, February 25, 1964.
4 *Ibid.*, February 13, 1965.
5 *Ibid.*, May 17, 1965.
6 *Ibid.*, January 6, 1966.
7 *Ibid.*, April 16, 1966.
8 *Ibid.*, October 15, 1963.
9 *Ibid.*, April 21, 1964.
10 *Ibid.*, April 15, 1964.
11 *Ibid.*, April 23, 1964.
12 *Ibid.*, June 10, 1966.
13 *Ibid.*, February 16, 1966.
14 *Ibid.*, September 18, 1963.
15 *Ibid.*
16 *Ibid.*, August 16, 1965.
17 *Ibid.*, October 11, 1965.
18 *Ibid.*, May 27, 1966.
19 *Ibid.*, February 24, 1965.
20 *Ibid.*, July 7, 1965.
21 *El Gráfico,* March 8, 1966.
22 *Prensa Libre,* August 26, 1966.
23 *El Imparcial*, February 28, 1966.
24 *El Gráfico*, March 6, 1966. (Among "the 28" were two women, one
    was Yon Sosa's cousin.)
25 *Ibid.*, July 17, 1966.
26 *Ibid.*, March 3, 1966.

27 *Congressional Record*, Vol. III, Part 18, p. 24347.
28 *El Imparcial*, September 21, 1965.
29 *Ibid.*, February 5, 1958.
30 *Ibid.*, March 24, 1960.
31 *Ibid.*, January 4, 1964.
32 *Ibid.*, January 31, 1964.
33 *Ibid.*, February 5, 1964.
34 *Ibid.*, February 24, 1964.
35 *Ibid.*
36 Azurdia, Vol. 82, p. 21.

Thus society is in a perpetual state of war. Lacking moral and rational resources to organize its life, without coercion, except in the most immediate and intimate social groups, men remain the victims of the individuals, classes and nations by whose force a momentary coerced unity is achieved, and further conflicts are as certainly created.

Reinhold Niebuhr

12

a momentary coerced unity

AFTER HAVING PROMISED to turn the country over to democratic rule, Peralta Azurdia led the nation to the polls on March 6, 1966. The chance that the election would terminate the military government was slim indeed, since two of the three candidates were army colonels: Col. Juan de Dios Aguilar was the candidate of the PID set up by the military government to represent its interests; Col. Miguel Angel Ponciano was the candidate of the MLN, the Liberation Party, and ran on the Castillo Armas platform of antiCommunism, private property (big business and large landholdings), increased counter-insurgency warfare and Church rights; Julio César Méndez Montenegro was the civilian candidate for the PR and ran on a platform of social justice, the mystique of the 1944 Revolution, an anti-military government and sympathy for his dead brother, Mario Méndez Montenegro.

Mario Méndez Montenegro had become the head of the revolutionary elements in the country after the Arbenz overthrow. He had opposed Ydígoras Fuentes for the presidency in 1957 and 1958 and was thought to be making a deal with Arévalo when Peralta Azurdia overthrew Ydígoras. But Mario Méndez Montenegro caused much confusion among his followers when he gave his blessing to the rightwing dictatorship of Peralta Azurdia stating that he "supported the coup against Ydígoras in order to avoid allowing the country to fall into chaos."[1] He allowed his party to join the Dictator's rubber stamp congress even while the Christian Democrats refused to participate in this political farce. Finally, he seemed to give himself a *coup de grace* as far as the political Left was concerned by stating: "Arévalism is something of the past."[2]

On October 31, 1965, Mario Méndez Montenegro was discovered by his wife and son, shot to death in his own home. The government claimed it was suicide, and his brother, Julio César Méndez Montenegro, ex-dean of the University's Law School, maintained that it was murder. The Secretary of Information of the Presidency stated:

The government does not have the slightest interest in interfering in the investigation of this painful incident which is being carried out by the tribunals of justice. It will not permit, however, that baseless speculations be made that give birth to even more painful situations. The paraffin tests are positive and the bullet corresponds to Mario Méndez Montenegro's own gun.[3]

Julio César Méndez Montenegro maintained that the paraffin tests were negative and that the bullet was not from his dead brother's gun.[4]

But the death of Mario Méndez Montenegro remains in doubt to this day and is listed with the murders of Col. Francisco J. Arana and Col. Carlos Castillo Armas as murky political events of primary magnitude in a murky political environment.

The campaign was a bitter one and full of acrimonious and exaggerated charges. The Liberation Party wanted to make some kind of agreement with the government party to run only one candidate, Col. Miguel Angel Ponciano, under their dual banner. But the PID turned down the proposition.[5] The government also refused to allow the DCG, the Christian Democrats, to run their candidate, with the excuse that they had not fulfilled the stipulation of presenting a list of 50,000 bona-fide party members before the legal deadline.[6] The real reason was probably the fall from grace suffered by the DCG when they had refused to participate in Peralta Azurdia's congress. When the DCG declared that they would tell their adherents to deposit blank ballots to show their lack of support for the elections, the directors of the Electoral Register (the authorizing commission) said that the party would be sanctioned for attempting "to obstruct the right of the free exercise of voting."[7]

The accusations reached a high pitch in early February when the Revolutionary candidate accused the military government of trying to assassinate him, of having burned the seven small airplanes being used by the PR for propaganda purposes, and of imprisoning a number of his body guards without benefit of legal charges or court trials.[8] The PID (the government party) denied all the accusations and responded that it would take Julio César Méndez Montenegro to court for his calumnies.[9]

The following day the government followed up with a broadside of its own, calling Méndez Montenegro guilty of "excessive flights of the imagination or a sneaky spirit" and his denunciation of attempted assassination a "theatrical statement incessantly repeated in every tone of voice as a part of his political campaign."[10] It further guaranteed that the electoral process would develop normally "under the protection of the Armed Forces."

The PID charged that the PR was Communist-controlled, which in turn prompted a vehement denial by its candidate.[11]

The vice-presidential candidate for the PR was Clemente Marroquín Rojas, chosen not for his political ideology (he was not even a member of the PR) but rather because of his fearlessness in attacking every and all institutions in his own

newspaper *La Hora*. The choice was a good one and his newspaper was a valuable vehicle for mounting attacks against the
government and the Liberation Party. A typical editorial of his
consisted in enumerating the faults and failures of the Peralta
Azurdia government and even questioning the dictator's
masculinity, following it up with abuse for the MLN:

As for the Liberationists: Is it heroism to be at the service of the
Yankee Police, the dictators of the Americas, in order to invade
Guatemala with Honduran troops? . . . Castillo Armas didn't do
anything even though his opposition was scattered, he had high
prices for coffee, and was the spoiled brat of the gringos and their
money. Ydígoras had low coffee prices, the gringos didn't like him
and he did nothing. Peralta didn't try to do anything . . . Why does
the MLN complain about Castro intervening? They invited the
gringos to intervene. When they win from intervention it is good;
if they lose, it is bad.[12]

There is no question about Marroquín Rojas's pen playing a big role in the Méndez Montenegro campaign, and there
is justification for speculating that the PR could not have
made it without him. Nevertheless, there were many occasions when Méndez Montenegro wondered whether the sharp-
tongued right-wing newspaperman was more of a liability
than an asset.

The MLN and the PR did line up against the PID on one
issue: they wanted observers from the OAS to oversee the
legitimacy of the elections. Col. Juan de Dios Aguilar, however, as the hand-picked successor to Peralta Azurdia, was
confident that the government machinery would guarantee his
election and publicly stated that outside observers would be
an insult to the political maturity of the Guatemalan people.[13]

A few days before the casting of ballots, the issue of religion came up. The Church hierarchy had maintained a
prudent silence even when Col. Ponciano had said that all the
lands confiscated from the Church 75 years earlier should be
given back to it. Col. Aguilar apparently felt he did not need

the help of the Church, and neither the presidential nor the vice-presidential candidate of the PR was known as *muy católico*, very Catholic. When a group of Catholic women paid for an advertisement in the newspapers saying that they were voting for the PR, they were assailed by another group of 500 women in another advertisement saying that no Catholic could vote for the PR because of its anti-Catholic vice-presidential candidate.[14]

But it was too late, the die had been cast. Julio César Méndez Montenegro closed off his campaign the night of March 5, 1966, with a blast at the government for the imminent fraud it was about to perpetrate on the country, while Peralta Azurdia assured everyone of his intention to maintain calm throughout the nation during the following day's activities.

March 6th came and went. It was followed by days of speculation in the press as to who had won. Most agreed that the PR seemed to be pulling a majority. The turnout had not been as large as expected—little more than fifty percent of the registered voters. This was an even smaller numerical turnout than for Ydígoras's election in 1958, and just a few more than for Castillo Armas's plebiscite in 1954. By March 10th, the MLN was demanding a new election alleging fraud and the PID declared that it had knowledge of "grave anomalies."[15] Both charges seemed an admission of defeat even though the results were still not published.

Then the MLN declared that Peralta was to blame for the defeat of the "antiCommunists" since he had split them into the MLN and the PID, while on the other hand uniting the "Communists" into the PR by not letting the Christian Democrats run.[16] Two days later the results were made official, more than a week after the polls had closed. The PR had a plurality of 60,000 votes over the PID, but since it lacked an absolute majority, the election would be thrown into Congress.[17]

During this week, while the results were withheld, there was a lot of movement evident among the candidates. There were rumors that Col. Ponciano had been the object of an at-

tempted assassination and that Méndez was in jail.[18] Talk
flowed freely as to what the United States government would
do about the elections, and many people even believed that
Méndez Montenegro had the Embassy's support. The Liberation Party considered United States support as its birthright,
and Ponciano had gone to the United States during the campaign and had come back declaring that he had obtained more
United States military aid to defeat the "Communist guerrillas." Finally, two days after the results were published, the
Embassy felt constrained to issue a statement:

The Embassy of the United States has received information to the
effect that one of the political parties is not satisfied with the election results, and is trying to get backing from certain elements of
the military in order to effect a coup against the government, while
claiming that it has the backing of the U.S. Embassy. The Embassy
categorically denies that it favors or supports any attempt against
the government or any effort of any party that would result in the
annulment of the elections.[19]

This served as a warning to both the public and the MLN that
the Embassy actually did support Julio César Méndez Montenegro and wanted to see him in the presidency. It surprised
many, especially the MLN.

But this was not enough. Méndez still needed the Guatemalan army's backing, or at least the approval of the segment
from which Peralta Azurdia drew his support. Peralta was
now in a difficult position. He obviously had not expected the
PR to win the election, especially after throwing the government apparatus and treasury behind Col. Juan de Dios
Aguilar. However, he had made "honesty" the watch-word
of his government and had taken great pride in the cleanup
campaign he had carried out. Now that the election results
were in and Julio César Méndez Montenegro was the winner,
he was in a quandary. He had to go through with his pledge of
honest elections and let the PR take over. But not before
eliciting promises to guarantee that the orientation of the new

government would be very similar to that of the military government itself. On March 19, the Secretary of Public Relations of the PR said that their attitude toward the army was "one of respect," and they accused the MLN of printing up handbills criticizing the army and signing the PR's name to them.[20] The following day, Méndez Montenegro himself said, "I will respect the organic structure of the army"—quite a switch from his campaign when he said that some army colonels had to be retired.

But the secondary election by Congress was still a hurdle to be jumped. If the election of deputies to Congress was allowed to stand, the PR would have a plurality of four members over a coalition between the MLN and PID and would guarantee the election for Méndez Montenegro.[21] The MLN proceeded to label a number of PR congressmen as "Communists" and maintained that their election was illegal under the "Law of Defense of Democratic Institutions."[22] The matter was taken to the Supreme Court and a week later the court handed down its decision: none of the PR congressmen had been convicted under the law, although some had been arrested under its application, and thus they could not legally be prevented from taking their congressional seats.[23] Since the military government's "Constituent Assembly" was still in session, and was to remain so until the new congress could take over on May 5th, the entire block of MLN deputies and some of the PID members of Congress refused to attend the meetings designed to set up commissions for the transferral of powers.[24] The PR deputies maintained that they would take their new seats on May 5, regardless.

Finally, as the inevitable approached, the Constituent Assembly, as its last act of legislative duty, passed a bill granting "amnesty to all members of the army, all policemen and all their superiors for those acts committed in the repression of subversive activities."[25] All congressmen, including members of the PR, voted for the law making its passage unanimous, thereby healing some of the wounds that had been opened up in the preceding days' debates over Congressional seats.

On May 10, 1966, Julio César Méndez Montenegro and Clemente Marroquín Rojas were elected by Congress to be the new president and vice-president of Guatemala. Congress, immediately before adjourning, appointed a commission to search for the twenty-eight members of the Guatemalan Labor Party (PGT) who had been captured by the previous government.

Being elected President of the Republic of Guatemala by the Congress of that country was the end of one series of difficulties for Méndez Montenegro, but the beginning of another far more complex. If he ever hoped to rule, it was necessary for him to line up solid support among the political powers of the nation. With less than one-half of the adult population registered to vote, and few more than half of those registered participating, the ex-Dean of the University Law School had managed to poll only 40 percent of the ballots cast.[26] The popular vote in his favor was numerically less than that received by Juan José Arévalo twenty-two years earlier when the population was just over fifty percent of what it was in 1966. His popular support, nevertheless, was impressive and surprised everyone, including the candidate himself. But it was not sufficient to give him the small lever of power he needed to bargain with other political groups. Even his control over the PR was very tenuous, since his entrance as its head was more a tribute to his "martyred brother" than acknowledgement of his leadership capabilities. He was in a very weak position.

One of the first blocs he courted was that of the Catholic hierarchy. He went to the archbishop of Guatemala City, Mario Casariego, and begged him for public support. The archbishop, an astute politician himself who had taken over after the death of Mariano Rossell, was not about to allow the opportunity to strike a blow for God and Church to slip by. He protested that he could not publicly support the president-elect since the latter was not a practicing Catholic, having never been married in the Church. Méndez Montenegro replied that he had always wanted such a marriage but never had had the time; he requested that the archbishop perform the marriage himself in his private chapel. This was done within the week without any public announcement. Very soon afterwards the bishops were requesting prayers for the new president and his government from all the faithful.

The United States government had already shown its support through the Embassy statement. Méndez Montenegro had previously conferred with Ambassador John Gordon Mein and had promised to seek more United States counterinsurgency aid to stop the guerrilla movements as soon as he took office, offsetting in this way the stubborn and proud resistance to such help from the Peralta Azurdia government.[27]

Statements were also made by the President-elect that he supported private property—(big business and big landholdings)—in a meeting with the Chamber of Industry and the AGA.[28] He went so far as to denounce the invasion of lands by peasants as a trick to make things difficult for his government. He maintained that he had become president legally and that he would not tolerate the "danger of bringing violence to Guatemalan agriculture by taking advantage of insatisfaction or by means of unrealizable promises."[29] It was beginning to look as if his government was not going to be so very different from that of his predecessor.

But there was only one real power in the country and it was imperative that Méndez Montenegro cultivate and develop its favor: the military. The armed forces had established themselves too firmly to be seriously challenged and they constituted the most significant political power.

When the families of "the 28" charged the Peralta Azurdia government with murdering their relatives, the now PR-controlled Congress called the case "very delicate"[30] and later, by a secret vote, unanimously rejected the claim (see pp. 177–178), thus covering up for the Peralta government's mass murder. "Even if it were true, the amnesty granted for such acts by the Constituent Assembly covers this case."[31]

When the army picked up another 125 peasants in Zacapa and no further trace could be found of them, no outcry came from the president-elect.[32] But when some guerrillas returned the compliment and ambushed an army patrol, Méndez Montenegro went personally to the Mariscal Zavala Brigade and expressed his condolences for the captain and the ten soldiers killed in the encounter.[33] He told all the assembled military brass that "the government and the army must stand together."[34]

A few days before Peralta was to turn over the staff of office to his successor, he made a public speech to the army but directed it to the nation, and specifically to the new president. He told his companions in arms: "You will be responsible before the nation for what happens to the future of Guatemala."[35] Méndez Montenegro could not miss the message, and he did not.

On July 1st, Méndez Montenegro took over as the first civilian president in sixteen years. He wasted no time in naming Col. Rafael Arriaga Bosque, Peralta's right arm, as his Minister of Defense. United States Ambassador Gordon Mein and Peter Costello, AID director for internal security matters, visited the new Minister of the Interior a few days later to offer their help in stabilizing the situation of the country.[36] On the 11th, the new president began a trip to visit all the important military bases in the country, accompanied by Col. Arriaga Bosque. The first stop was Zacapa: "I hope that you will interpret my conduct as a friend of the army, a friend who recognizes and esteems the true worth of the armed forces."[37]

When the chief of the secret police of the former government admitted that "the 28" had been murdered, nothing was said.[38] Then at the army base in Poptún, Petén: "The Army can be sure that my attitude is one of respect and esteem."[39] The following day's papers headlined: "The Army is united against the threat of subversion." Arriaga Bosque, in the company of the military high command, stated: "We only await orders from our Commander-in-Chief, our President."[40]

At the base in Jutiapa, the President declared: "We hope for and count on the loyalty of the army of Guatemala and I can assure you that there will be no obstacle in our common road."[41] When he went to the Retalhuleu Air Base and the Quezaltenango western command he said: "My first duty consists in presenting myself at all the military centers in the Republic, in order to personally present my cordial best wishes and express my personal regards. This duty has been doubly gratifying because of the promises of loyalty that I have received from the armed forces."[42] He even found it propitious to give homes to twelve Colonels "in gratitude for the protection they have given the nation."[43]

Then Clare H. Timberlake and William L. S. Williams of the United States State Department came to Guatemala to accompany Ambassador Mein on a visit to the Minister of Interior in order to make "an evaluation of the programs of internal security conducted with the collaboration of the United States Military Assistance Program and the United States Agency for International Development."[44] Although the President had offered amnesty to "all who had borne arms from November 1, 1960, to July 26, 1966, with the exception of those guilty of the murder of Mario Méndez Montenegro,"[45] he was obviously preparing to crush the guerrilla movements in a way that Peralta Azurdia never had been able to do alone. It was undeniable that for his political survival he had to demonstrate quickly and decisively that he would not tolerate the actions of the extreme left. His offer of amnesty was seen as a political ploy and was rejected as such. The guerrillas stated that they were not fighting for amnesty.

In order to comprehend the policies of the Méndez Montenegro government, it is necessary to understand the basis of his power, or rather, this lack of a true base. He called his administration "the Third Government of the Revolution" and there is every reason to believe that ideologically he could be identified with most of the principles of the Arévalo and the Arbenz governments. It is worthy of note that he was one of the major participants in the October, 1944, revolution and he periodically made statements to show that his heart still belonged to the movement. But the forces at work in Guatemala in 1966 were different from those of 1944, and Julio César

Méndez Montenegro obviously did not have the support that was given to both Arévalo and Arbenz. This forced him to align himself with all the *status quo* power blocs in the country and to deal with crying social needs only peripherally.

NOTES

1 *El Imparcial*, August 8, 1965.
2 *Ibid.*
3 *Ibid.*, November 2, 1965.
4 *Ibid.*
5 *Ibid.*, January 25, 1966.
6 *Ibid.*, January 26, 1966.
7 *Ibid.*, February 7, 1966.
8 *Ibid.*, February 9, 1966.
9 *Ibid.*
10 *Ibid.*, February 6, 1966.
11 *Ibid.*, February 18, 1966.
12 *Ibid.*, February 19, 1966.
13 *Ibid.*
14 *Ibid.*, March 4, 1966.
15 *Ibid.*, March 10, 1966.
16 *Ibid.*, March 12, 1966.
17 Johnson, *Op. Cit.*, p. 19: PR–191,000 votes; PID–136,000 votes; MLN–103,000 votes.
18 *El Imparcial*, March 11, 1966.
19 *Ibid.*, March 15, 1966.
20 *Ibid.*, March 19, 1966.
21 *Ibid.*, March 31, 1966.
22 *Ibid.*, April 13, 1966.
23 *Ibid.*, April 19, 1966.
24 *Ibid.*, April 22, 1966.
25 *Ibid.*, April 28, 1966.
26 *Ibid.*, March 31, 1966.
27 That such a deal was made has been denied. The facts indicate

otherwise. The authors heard from reliable sources on various occasions, even before Julio César Méndez Montenegro took office, that the price of United States backing was his suppression of the guerrilla movements. On June 16, two weeks before Méndez Montenegro took office, word was sent to Col. Carlos Arana Osorio, Guatemalan military attaché in Washington, that he was to head the new counterinsurgency program. This the latter admitted to in his own electoral campaign of 1970.

28 *El Imparcial*, May 27, 1966.
29 *Ibid.*
30 *Ibid.*, May 21, 1966.
31 *Ibid.*, June 1, 1966.
32 *Ibid.*, May 25, 1966.
33 *Ibid.*, May 28, 1966.
34 *Ibid.*
35 *Ibid.*, June 25, 1966.
36 *Ibid.*, July 6, 1966.
37 *Ibid.*, July 11, 1966.
38 *Ibid.*, July 16, 1966.
39 *Ibid.*, July 18, 1966.
40 *Ibid.*, July 19, 1966.
41 *Ibid.*, July 25, 1966.
42 *Ibid.*, August 1, 1966.
43 *Ibid.*, November 22, 1966.
44 *Ibid.*
45 *Ibid.*, July 27, 1966.

The problem of the indigenous peoples arises from our economy. It has its roots in the pattern of landownership. Any attempt to resolve this problem by administrative or police action, by agricultural education or road construction, while the feudalism of the landowners still exists, constitutes a superficial attempt.

José Carlos Mariátegui

13

a superficial attempt

THE AGRARIAN POLICY of the Third Government of the Revolution was expressed in a three-part program officially adopted as of "national urgency" at a Cabinet meeting on August 19, 1966.[1] It included the distribution of the remaining national *fincas* to the workers living on them; the restructuring of the existing agrarian zones; and the use of the unexploited government lands in Izabal, Quiché, Petén, Alta Verapaz and Huehuetenango. Although this was announced as a new plan of agrarian reform, it can hardly be considered as such. None of the three aspects of the plan were new. The colonization of the unexploited lands to the north had been planned since 1945 and initial attempts had already been made by Arévalo and Peralta Azurdia. The agrarian zones that had been started during the Castillo Armas government were in grave need of reorganization. They needed principally to have their undue growth of population reduced. More im-

portantly neither of these two aspects of the program represented a true agrarian reform.

The national *fincas* had gone through a long history of
changing government policy. This new proposed distribution
could be an authentic gesture of agrarian reform but it now
represented such a small extension of land as to be negligible in
the national context.

In less than a month after the "new plan" was announced,
the INTA office had received 2,000 new requests for land and
by October 10, 1966, they had 20,000 requests from the south
coast (Pacific) alone, in what the newspapers termed an
"agrarian explosion."[2] Most of the peasants, however, either
did not hear of the government's proposed plans or were still
too intimidated after their experience with the promises broken
and the threats fulfilled of the three previous governments.

The agrarian reform program had been declared of "national urgency" and on December 22, 1966, Méndez Montenegro signed his first agrarian decree (#1653). It ordered
that the national *fincas,* the least controversial object of the
three-pronged program, which were still under the control of
the Liquidating Commission of the ex-Department of National
Fincas, be turned over to INTA to be distributed to the peasants who were working on them. The stated goal of this distribution was to give impulse to the socio-economic development of those families. The land was to be given free of charge
to the cooperatives that would be established there. If INTA
determined that a given *finca* could sustain more than the
workers already living there, provision was made so that other
peasants could receive land.[3]

The free distribution was subject to two provisions: (a)
that the lands could not be sold nor exchanged within 30 years,
and (b) that if within this length of time INTA judged that the
lands were not being used for agricultural production or if they
were being exploited below a predetermined level, the lands
could be taken back from the recipient.

Ninety days were given as the deadline for the transferral
of the national *fincas* into INTA's jurisdiction. In March,

1967, when the deadline was almost up and nothing had been done yet, a Presidential Order commissioned the Minister of Agriculture to intervene in the transferral of the *fincas*. Those *fincas* that were under court injunction to determine ownership due to Ydígoras's manipulations were exempted until the matter was settled. INTA's budget had not been drawn up with the new item of the *fincas'* administration in mind, however, and this constituted a veritable impediment. The new decree (#1653) was too vague to be applicable and INTA demanded a revision of the legislation.

The law covering cooperatives had already been amended on September 10, 1966, to include the projected establishment of a federation of cooperatives of the distributed national *fincas* to be supervised by INTA.

Two more plantations were claimed by the government after a long legal process and this brought the number of national *fincas* owned by the State to 26. The Banco Nacional Agrario and INFOP were in control of a number of fincas, approximately seventeen, that they had received as payment for uncollected loans from the Department of National Fincas as well as from beneficiaries of the Arbenz Agrarian Reform who had been dispossessed and were unable to pay their debts. Both the BNA and INFOP tried to sell some of these at auction in order to avoid being deprived of them. Other government agencies had *fincas* which were administered to provide operating funds for the agency.

Finally on June 7, 1967, another decree (#1679) was passed amending and clarifying the original law (#1653) and on June 27th INTA at last received the twenty-six fincas, valued at Q.10 million plus Q.400,000 in the treasury of the Department.[4]

It was announced on June 28, 1968, that Juan Mini was returning to the government the thirteen *fincas* he had received from Ydígoras. But their number has not officially been added to the total received by INTA.

The first distribution took place on July 8, 1967: Cacahuito in Santa Rosa, twenty-two *caballerías* (2,416 acres), valued at Q.115,000 to 203 families. Las Cabezas, 4.3 *caballerías* (472 acres), also in Santa Rosa, was given out in October of the same year to 173 families. The third *finca* to be given out was Güiscoyol in Escuintla on March 4, 1969, to eighty-five families; however the proceedings for this distribution had begun many years earlier under the auspices of CONTRAGUA (Confederation of Workers of Guatemala) and under the new legislation they were finally successful in obtaining it.

At the distribution in October, President Méndez Montenegro spoke, "visibly moved":

The Third Government of the Revolution is for social justice. It is giving land to the landless. We have given out hundreds of titles. The revolution of 1944 is in full march ahead because it is the one that vindicated the rights of the people that had been trampled on by tyranny.[5]

The "hundreds of titles" mentioned in his talk was a reference to several minor distributions of lands, most of which were of insignificant extension. He was attempting the ploy used by his three predecessors of lumping all distribution totals together.

The President had not been able to wait for the passage of the law for the distribution of the national *fincas* because pressures were building up too quickly. Peasants continued to invade lands, and the director of INTA claimed that "unscrupulous leaders" were advising the people to do so.[6] The head of the Instituto Politécnico (Guatemala's West Point) said: "The army will not long tolerate what is going on outside this institution's walls."[7] Marroquín Rojas, the vice president, argued that no peasant leagues should be created "until the peasants have a cultural level that is indispensable to act with liberty."[8] Méndez Montenegro declared, "Things better get peaceful fast in the rural areas."[9] A Q. 216,000 allotment was made to the Minister of the Interior to hire more rural police,[10] even as the head of the National Police announced that: "This institution will cooperate with INTA to bring order to the rural zones . . . 500 new special police jobs are being created."[11]

But the new President had another image to protect and he spoke with apparent sincerity:

I speak of liberty that will permit us to resolve the great social, economic and cultural problems of the people of Guatemala. The liberty to die of hunger or to die of misery is not liberty but a fallacy.[12]

However, it did not look as if he would have time to even face these "great problems," let alone solve them. The Armed Forces of Rebellion demanded that he do something about the murders of "the 28,"[13] and the Liberation Party demanded an end to FAR's activity.[14] Vice-president Marroquín Rojas did not help matters by publicly denouncing three congressmen of the government's own party (PR) for "agitating the workers on the plantations."[15] Then the Liberationists decided that they had had enough of the government's toleration and warned: "The government should not consider it strange that the citizenry organize to take justice into their own hands."[16] It was from here that the development of the right-wing terrorist organizations was openly noticeable and Méndez Montenegro had less and less to say about the conduct of his own government.

By early October, the President was desperate and he promised that his agrarian reform would give lands to 150,000 peasants,[17] while the President of Congress assured the nation that the reform made by the Third Government of the Revolution would be "based on the constitution, that is, with respect for private property."[18] Then on October 11, Méndez gave out his first 534 titles in ten different zones for a total of 7,483 hectares (18,484 acres).[19]

Loans for 16 million dollars from AID were announced[20] as well as a new tax law that would bring in 10 million quetzales to be used mostly for internal security.[21] Forty members of the Interamerican Defense Pact, under the direction of

Vice-Admiral Bernard L. Austin, came to Guatemala to check on the "security of the hemisphere."[22]

By early November, the MLN had carried out its threat of developing right-wing vigilante groups and was engaged in terrorist activities. Twenty-five of the top members of that party were jailed for the possession of "war materiel,"[23] held for almost a month and released in early December.[24]

There were other land distributions, but these were smaller and their purpose was obviously more propagandistic than anything else. At such a distribution in December, 1966, to fifty-two peasants in Los Amates, Izabal, a focal point of guerrilla activity, the President begged the peasants to back him and the army in the struggle against the guerrillas.[25] A week later, Alberto Méndez Martínez, the Secretary General of the PR and oldest son of the deceased party leader, Mario Méndez Montenegro, gave out sixty-four titles for lands in Champerico on the Pacific Coast, stating: "The guerrillas say that this government is not revolutionary. With the assignment of these land titles, we give them the lie."[26]

These references to the guerrillas were backhanded compliments acknowledging the effectiveness of the guerrilla movement and an indication of the cause they were constantly emphasizing to the landless peasants. The army had been staging numerous demonstrations of support around the country, trucking peasants to and fro in military vehicles in an obvious orchestration of peasant backing for the armed forces and repudiation of guerrilla activities. Even in Rio Hondo, where the army had kidnapped and apparently murdered over one hundred men as guerrilla supporters only eight months before, it was publicized that the people there "were asking for guns to fight the guerrillas."[27] Then the government decided to designate all plantation owners and their administrators as its special police, allowing them to carry guns, make arrests and "to shoot those who tried to evade justice."[28] The President himself had already survived two attempts by right-wing factions in the army to topple his government, and he could not afford to allow any one to doubt his loyalties:

The Revolutionary Party has decided to support the army in those determinations that it takes in order to maintain peace and tranquility, to strengthen our mutual relationship, in view of the fact that the army is our guarantee of national sovereignty.[29]

A few days later, on a visit to the Permanent Commission of the Council of Defense of Central America, the President announced that "popular support for the army and government is increasing" and that in view of this he would augment its services of internal security, health and education.[30]

On December 13, the press announced that a Chicago newspaperwoman had talked with the Guatemalan Chief of Police and he had confirmed rumors that there were United States Green Berets in the country.[31] The writer, Georgie Anne Geyer, quoting a guerrilla source, set the figure at 1,000. She was the object of a death threat made by a right-wing terrorist organization for establishing contact with the guerrilla organization. Washington immediately denied the report and said that the United States had only four members of its Special Forces in the country and that they were working with the Guatemalan army's Civic Action Program.[32] Arriaga Bosque, Minister of Defense, also denied the allegation as well as the reports that his army was working hand in glove with the right-wing terrorist organizations, "Because," he said, "this is against the Constitution."[33] Meanwhile, the director of the National Police solicited funds for the creation of 561 more police jobs.[34] The squeeze was obviously increasing on all sides and Méndez Montenegro acted like a wind-tossed boat on a stormy sea. He continued the lesser distributions and the drum-thumping propaganda: in January, 1967, thirty-three titles were given out in Escuintla;[35] in February, it was announced that 1,000 families would receive lands within four months in Izabal;[36] in March, it was declared that the national finca, Las Cabezas, would be given to 200 families as soon as the new law passed Congress;[37] the acknowledgement that a half-million-dollar contract had been signed with AID for the development of the areas of Izabal (where Yon Sosa's 13 of

November Revolutionary Movement was active) and of Zacapa (where the Armed Forces of Rebellion functioned) came
in April.[38] Finally in June, a new law (#1679) was passed
transferring the national *fincas* to INTA and it was announced
that the Third Government of the Revolution was finally going
to begin its land reform.

Méndez Montenegro was thinking principally of Nueva
Concepción and La Máquina when he stated that the second
basic aim of his agrarian reform would be "to restructure the
agrarian zones" started by Castillo Armas. Shortly before he
had taken office, it became public knowledge that the Peralta
Azurdia government had been transferring people out of these
zones to the banks of the Pasión River in the Petén jungles.
This news item in the press was accompanied by a discouraging
description of conditions in the Nueva Concepción zone:

These people have been in a calamitous situation that any
Guatemalan can see for himself if he visits the zone; especially in
the area of Palo Blanco where thousands of families live jammed
together without lands, without work, in a desperate situation of
misery and in the worst possible hygienic conditions.[39]

But the task loomed too big for INTA's resources and in
September, 1967, the President called for a meeting of all
the interested national and international organizations in the
country to discuss the manner for strengthening these zones.
The urgency of the matter increased when several individuals
were found murdered in Nueva Concepción.[40]

The settlers' principal crop was corn and it was suffering
tremendous price depressions because of difficulties in getting
the produce to market. Priority in INTA's meager budget was
given to the construction of four bridges which were finished
by the following December. But the basic problem remained:
an excessive population influx, nearly 40,000 people instead
of the 6,000 planned for at the project's initiation.

Finally, it was announced that the Organization of American States (OAS) and other international institutions were providing a $3 million dollar loan in an attempt to salvage Nueva Concepción.[41] The need became even more obvious when two months later it was revealed that thirteen bodies of murdered individuals were discovered in the zone in a three-day period.[42] This was typical of news items that were being repeated with frightening persistence throughout the nation.

In September, 1968, Méndez Montenegro decided to visit the area.[43] He was met by 5,000 chanting peasants who carried signs: "We demand new legislation that conforms to reality" and "We demand that uncultivated lands be expropriated." Not all the signs were threatening, however: "We will defend the constitutional government" and "We will defend the Revolutionary Party." The President responded with one of his impassioned discourses of self-defense:

The efforts generated by my government are for the people and we are in power thanks to the popular will, especially the will of you, the peasants, who make up the vast majority of our people . . . Despite the enemies of the people and the problems we have, I will finish my term with accomplishments and not with promises. Especially will we progress in the matter of agrarian reform which we have already planned because I am and I always will be, a sincere friend of the peasants.[44]

His promise to finish his term of office with real accomplishments and not just promises seemed to be an answer to the accusation that his only preoccupation since reaching the half-way mark of his four year tenure was to remain in office and finish his constitutional term. Such a feat would automatically guarantee Méndez Montenegro his place in Guatemalan history books—he and Arévalo would be the only men to accomplish that in 100 years. Nevertheless, it looked as if the accomplishment would have to be made at the expense of real progress. Still, the difficulties continued. When the administrator of a plantation in Escuintla was killed and two others were shot in March, 1969, the plantation owners announced that they were forming their own vigilante group. This was followed by four more murders in Nueva Concepción and the protest of the inhabitants of the area that a list of unknown origin had been published containing sixty names of peasants marked for execution.[45] The army and police did their part to spread terror by sweeping through the whole project and arresting "over 100 people."[46]

A source of the trouble is discernible in a letter, written by an inhabitant of the Pacific Coast area in which the zone is located, directed to the authorities and published in the press. The writer charged that the people living in La Máquina and Nueva Concepción were delinquents, since in their majority, "they are persons who fled before the Liberation Movement (driven off their lands by Castillo Armas) from the east to the Pacific coast."[47] The author of the letter goes on to describe the illegal activity of gun smuggling from Mexico into the agrarian zones, but leaves the impression that its object is simple delinquency. The government, however, had maintained on many occasions that these zones were fertile fields for guerrilla activities.

La Máquina did not receive the same attention as Nueva Concepción, yet its problems seem not much different. It too had a population of nearly 25,000 instead of the original quota of 6,000. The two projects together represented one half the total land distributions made in the category of agrarian zones, the heart and soul of the "agrarian reform" begun by Castillo Armas and continued by all his successors.

In February, 1965, eight years after the founding of La Máquina project, a road 27 kilometers long was finally built to facilitate the marketing of the corn production of the zone. But it had not been built by the government; rather it was the product of the labor of the people themselves.[48] By October, 1967, these same inhabitants had managed to build themselves a "modest dispensary" and had purchased an ambulance in an attempt to provide themselves with the much needed medical care.[49] The Red Cross, finally acquiescing to the pleas of the local populace, took charge of the vehicle and stocked the dispensary with medicines.

The excess population of La Máquina was dealt with by transferring people to the jungles of Petén much as was done in Nueva Concepción. Two-hundred people had already left,[50] when in December, 1968, ninety families were taken out, but this time they were not given land in any other area. The secretary general of the regional peasant organization wrote an open letter to the President describing conditions in the zone, requesting the much needed technical help that was supposed to be the basis of the original program and denouncing the injustice of the government authorities in expelling the ninety families.[51]

It is obvious from these two examples that the agrarian zones did indeed need "restructuring." But what that restructuring could have been remains to be seen, since the government never admitted that the basic flaw in the program was too little land for too many people. The 3 million dollars that were now earmarked for Nueva Concepción may or may not resolve the crises of that particular area. But what of the rest? Would the international organizations continue to foot the bill for other programs or projects of restructure? Given that the basic premise or orientation of the agrarian zone is colonization, the expense can only be astronomical. One of the problems from the beginning has been that only massive infusions of money can make the agrarian zone concept work. And money is one thing the DGAA and now INTA have never had in sufficient amounts despite the international helping hand.

Méndez Montenegro's attempts to pass tax legislation that would enable him to fund some of his programs had met with solid resistance. It came from the same socio-political structure that has obliged a succession of governments to turn to colonization in lieu of land reform. This structure has never permitted meaningful tax legislation that would cut the profits of the wealthy, and so the government had few resources for dealing with the basic problems of the nation. Internal security was about the only battle cry that would carry tax legislation through Congress,[52] and even then it was very inconsequential, since Congress took advantage of the United States' propensity to pay for such expenses.

When the Archbishop of Guatemala blessed fifty-four new radio police cars in March, 1967, he congratulated his countrymen on their efforts for internal security and he said to the police, "It is important that you take good care of these vehicles since they were purchased with the money of the people."[53] Actually, much of the cost had been borne by the Alliance for Progress.[54] Nevertheless, the local contribution had been significant.

Even though Méndez Montenegro declared his first attempt at new tax legislation to be necessary for internal security, it was met by AGA and other landowning and business lobbies with the cry: "The government wants equality of poverty for all Guatemalans."[55] In order to get it passed, the President responded with the promise that the tax would only be in effect one year.[56] The proposed tax law called for an increase in the land taxes raising the rates from a miniscule .3 percent on land evaluations made in the early 1930's to a progressive tax that would go to two percent on properties valued at Q. 600,000. "Opponents denounced the progressive property tax as confiscatory and Communistic."[57]

In its attempts to rectify its fiscal deficit, the government admitted in December, 1967, that the country was in a "terrible financial crisis"[58] and followed this up with the statement that Guatemala was sixty-third out of sixty-four countries surveyed as regards the percentage of income taxed.[59] These declarations were the culmination of the regime's struggle to maintain in effect a five percent general sales tax with levies up to twenty percent on some luxury goods. "Tax collection machinery was inadequate, but some officials believe businessmen deliberately sabotaged the new measure by exploiting the initial confusion and by price gouging."[60]

The consequent uproar over the tax resulted in demands

for the resignation of the minister of finance and shook the Méndez Montenegro government to its foundations.[61] The President decided the issue was not worth the effort and so he rescinded the tax and the Chamber of Commerce immediately expressed its support of the enlightened President.[62]

In December, when new tax legislation was being discussed for 1969, the association of coffee growers had their "eight year fight for justice"[63] crowned with victory when Congress began to discuss a bill that would eliminate all taxes to be paid on coffee exports.[64] The rationale was that this "would make the income tax burden much lighter."[65] And so the struggle to obtain the same dispensation for the cotton growers was taken up with renewed vigor. By late 1969, its passage looked certain.[66]

It is no wonder then that one of the government programs hardest hit by the financial squeeze was INTA. By September, 1967, INTA had to fire 300 employees.[67] Five months later, another 520 technicians and employees were discharged by the institute,[68] all while Méndez Montenegro was talking about "restructuring the agrarian zones." But the dismissals did not go unnoticed. The peasants in La Máquina protested that they would be left without the schools and roads promised by the new government.[69] Two weeks later, the inhabitants of Nueva Concepción also raised their voices in protest as the inconsistency became apparent.[70] Four congressmen qualified the firings as the "beginning of the end of INTA."[71] The accuracy of their prophecy was seen by February, 1969, when thirteen Congressmen appealed to the Minister of Finance to resolve INTA's budgetary problems. Fuentes Pieruccini deftly shifted the blame right back where it at least partially belonged, on the legislative body: "The difficulty resides in the fact that the tax laws of last year were never enacted."[72]

Leopoldo Sandoval, INTA's first director under the Revolutionary government, did what he could to fulfill his President's promises, even though with scarce funds. One of the aspects of his program was to continue the cleanup campaign, begun by the military government, of revoking titles that had been issued to undeserving beneficiaries. In January, 1967, he denounced one of the frauds of the Ydígoras government. It had given thirty caballerías (3,294 acres) to fifteen people, among them military officers, members of the DGAA (INTA's predecessor), an Ydígoras aide and others, who had joined together to form a cooperative called "Sacred Heart of Jesus." This cooperative had borrowed Q. 30,000 from the BNA and had gone into the lumber business. As the land was cleared of forest, it was rented out to peasants.[73] A month later, another five complete agrarian zones were cancelled for 234 *caballerías* (25,693 acres) in Izabal because "the recipients had not fulfilled the requirements that the law demanded" of the beneficiaries of the program.[74] Sandoval promised that these lands would be given to 1,000 peasant families "in the near future."

Shortly thereafter another 263 lots were cancelled, also in the department of Izabal, "because their owners were not using them."[75] When it was revealed almost a year later that one of these farms had been given to Fuentes Mohr, Minister of Foreign Relations in the Méndez Montenegro government, who had also been Ydígoras's finance minister, it caused only a slight flap.[76] Fuentes Mohr defended himself by claiming that he had previously notified INTA himself that he did not want the farm. No notice was taken of the fact that the law stipulates that beneficiaries be landless peasants.

These illegal apportionments of land perhaps do not represent a significant percentage of the total distributions, but neither do they represent all the recipients who were not qualified as beneficiaries. Among them can be counted the bishop of Quezaltenango, the number two man in the country's Catholic hierarchy. However, it cannot be expected that Méndez Montenegro's limited political power was sufficient for him to right the wrongs that even Peralta had felt constrained to ignore.

There have also been claims and counterclaims that the same farm has been awarded to several recipients and that the same individual has received more than one farm. These failures may not always be intentional, but they contribute to the suspicion that the agrarian zone phase of the land programs has never been as the DGAA or INTA propagandists have painted it. This was even more evident when, in November, 1968, there was a meeting of the inhabitants of the south (Pacific) coast zones in an attempt to federate themselves for their own protection.[77] The necessity of the move became obvious a month later when the peasants of three zones all protested that the BNA was forcing them to pay an unjust debt that went back to the days of the Castillo Armas government. At that time, they had been obliged to mechanize their crops and the contract was given to a company, Agrimec, established precisely for this purpose. Agrimec charged them from Q. 75 to Q. 96 each for work that was calculated to be worth Q. 15, and then the company had never finished the job. They were billed at the same time for homes that had never been built.[78] They insisted that they could not pay what was being charged them.

So went the second of the three-pronged agrarian effort of the Revolutionary government's program. It was not a successful effort, partly because there were no financial resources to strengthen the program. As Colom Argueta, a recent director of INTA, admitted in late 1968 when talking to the peasant leaders on the south coast: "The narrow economic situation of INTA is a reality, but we have plenty of good will. Money without good will is worthless."[79] He failed to observe how valuable is good will without money.

NOTES

1 *El Imparcial*, August 20, 1966.
2 *Ibid.*, October 10, 1966.
3 *El Guatemalteco, Diario Oficial,* Tomo CLXXVIII, No. 61, January 12, 1967.
4 *El Imparcial*, July 11, 1967.
5 *Ibid.*, October 17, 1967.
6 *Ibid.*, September 7, 1966.
7 *Ibid.*, September 1, 1966.
8 *Ibid.*, September 5, 1966.
9 *Ibid.*, September 8, 1966.
10 *Ibid.*, September 9, 1966.
11 *Ibid.*, September 8, 1966.
12 *Ibid.*, September 16, 1966.
13 *Ibid.*, September 10, 1966.
14 *Ibid.*, September 14, 1966.
15 *Ibid.*, September 24, 1966.
16 *Ibid.*, September 27, 1966.
17 *Ibid.*, October 10, 1966.
18 *Ibid.*, September 21, 1966.
19 *Ibid.*, October 11, 1966.
20 *Ibid.*
21 *Ibid.*, October 17, 1966.
22 *Ibid.*, October 29, 1966.
23 *Ibid.*, November 3, 1966.
24 *Ibid.*, December 2, 1966.
25 *Ibid.*, December 20, 1966.
26 *Ibid.*, December 30, 1966.
27 *Ibid.*, November 24, 1966.
28 *Ibid.*, December 6, 1966.
29 *Ibid.*, December 7, 1966.
30 *Ibid.*, December 10, 1966.
31 *Ibid.*, December 13, 1966.
32 *Ibid.*
33 *Ibid.*, December 12, 1966.
34 *Ibid.*
35 *Ibid.*, January 23, 1967.
36 *Ibid.*, February 24, 1967.
37 *Ibid.*, March 14, 1967.
38 *Ibid.*, April 7, 1967.
39 *Ibid.*, March 14, 1966.

40 *Ibid.*, September 8 and 28, 1967.
41 *Ibid.*, May 21, 1968.
42 *Ibid.*, July 29, 1968.
43 *Ibid.*, September 20, 1968.
44 *Ibid.*
45 *Prensa Libre*, March 31, 1969.
46 *Ibid.*
47 *Ibid.*, April 28, 1969.
48 *El Imparcial*, February 5, 1965.
49 *Ibid.*, October 11, 1967.
50 *Ibid.*, September 27, 1967.
51 *Ibid.*, December 24, 1968.
52 *Ibid.*, October 17 and December 9, 1966.
53 *Ibid.*, March 14, 1967.
54 *Ibid.*
55 *Ibid.*, November 25, 1966.
56 *Ibid.*
57 *The New York Times,* December 3, 1966.
58 *Ibid.*, December 22, 1967.
59 *Ibid.*, January 5, 1968.
60 *The New York Times*, January 27, 1968.
61 *El Imparcial*, January 6, 1968.
62 *Ibid.*
63 *Ibid.*, December 18, 1968.
64 *Ibid.*, December 13, 1968.
65 *Ibid.*
66 *Prensa Libre*, May 16, 1969.
67 *El Imparcial*, September 12, 1967.
68 *Ibid.*, February 2, 1968.
69 *Ibid.*, February 8, 1968.
70 *Ibid.*, February 21, 1968.
71 *Ibid.*, February 2, 1968.
72 *Prensa Libre*, February, 1969.
73 *El Imparcial*, January 13, 1967.
74 *Ibid.*, February 24, 1967.
75 *Ibid.*
76 *Ibid.*, January 31, 1968.
77 *Ibid.*, November 22, 1968.
78 *Ibid.*, December 12, 1968.
79 *Ibid.*, November 11, 1968.

And when a group of men controls the commonwealth by virtue of their wealth, their birth, or any advantages they happen to possess, they form an oligarchy but they call themselves leading citizens.

Cicero

14

by virtue of wealth

THE THIRD and most important part of the Méndez government's "new program of national emergency" was the colonization of the unexploited, state-owned lands in Izabal, Alta Verapaz, Petén, Quiché and Huehuetenango. There were three main colonization projects in this area: Ixcán-Grande in northern Quiché and Huehuetenango; Sebol-Chinajá in Alta Verapaz; and the cooperative-colonies of Petén. Since the government has continually made the differentiation between the colonization and agrarian zone programs, we treat them here as distinct, even though, as has been noted previously, the agrarian zone approach is also essentially colonization: "The spirit of the law for the agrarian zones gave the new program all the characteristics of a colonization rather than a reform."[1]

In the case of what has been done in the jungles of Petén, there is no confusion because this is clearly labelled colonization by all parties. The Ixcán-Grande project has always been designated as colonization although there is not the slightest difference between it and the plans for Nueva Concepción and La Máquina. It could easily be referred to as an agrarian zone.

The major project in Alta Verapaz is alternately denominated "the agrarian zone of Fray Bartolomé de las Casas" and "the colonization project of Sebol-Chinajá." We have chosen to include it as colonization because it represents an even smaller public investment of money on communal facilities than those executed in Nueva Concepción or La Máquina, even though the original plans drawn up by the military government foresaw a cost of Q. 64 million. This leaves the major portion of the task of settlement to the individuals concerned and is obviously colonization rather than even rhetorical reform.

The Ixcán-Grande project was initiated by the Maryknoll Fathers[2] in January, 1966, in northern Huehuetenango and Quiché, in an area that was being colonized spontaneously by the Maya from the western altiplano. By March, 1967, INTA claimed that it had located 170 *caballerías* (18,666 acres) of state lands that could be used for the settlement of 240 families and that they would localize more lands so as to expand the project to include 2,000 families.[3] By March, 1970, 184 families had received their lots of 20 *manzanas* (34 acres) each[4] but none had received their legal titles. There were arguments over whether the state really owned these lands because many conflicting claims are still being made by *latifundistas* of Huehuetenango, as well as those resulting from a few confusing grants made earlier in the century to people's militias for defending Guatemala's borders against the Mexicans.[5] Many of the original settlers left because of the arbitrary conditions established by the first priest-director, one of which was that the recipient had to be a practicing Catholic. He has since been replaced by another priest, much more understanding of the Mayan culture and needs, who has received renewed promises from INTA for further extensions of colonizable lands. INTA has given no aid other than technical help for the localization and measurement of the lands as well as sundry promises to push a road into the area. Meanwhile, the official interest in developing the area is attracting more and more attention from the *latifundistas* and, consequently, their claims of ownership to lands in the zone are becoming more concrete, more determined and more expansive.

The Sebol-Chinajá project does not seem to find itself in any better situation than the Maryknoll project in Huehuetenango. Much of the difficulty, as has already been noted, is the veritable impossibility of controlling the influx of land-hungry people. By May, 1967, Col. Oliverio Casasola, director of all the projects in Petén, was accusing INTA of a "4-year paralysis in the land programs of Sebol."[6] Only 530 farms had been given out in the area and already by July, 1967, more than 7,000 people were living on them.[7] The total project called for a settlement of 6,000 families in the area and roads were being built to facilitate the colonization. By September, 1967, INTA had spent a quarter of a million dollars on the main road[8] and with its completion the perennial disputes over landownership began.

The road to Sebol-Chinajá, which is planned to go into Petén, has opened up many of those lands previously inaccessible and so the historical pattern of land tenure has begun to take over. On November 26, 1968, a meeting was held in Cobán with the director of INTA, the governor of Alta Verapaz, the head of the military zone and the mayors of the department. The meeting was called to deal with a "serious problem": people from outside the department, thirty in number, had filed claims to 409 *caballerías* (44,798 acres) which the Mayan settlers had occupied for years in the Sebol-Raxuha area.[9] The peasants had been given the choice of vacating the lands or working for the new owners as *colonos*. The accusation was being made that the outsiders had obtained the titles surreptitiously with "the aid of the authorities" and by using "the law of supplementary title." These were the same lands that INTA thought were available for their colonization projects.

Regardless of these projects, when one speaks these days of colonization in Guatemala, one automatically thinks of Petén. Not to downgrade the efforts being made in Ixcán-Grande or

Sebol-Chinajá by INTA with its parsimonious budget, but rather because Petén represents such a huge and unexploited area. Also, the government has been able to provide a greater amount of money for FYDEP, even though this is principally destined for the creation of a serviceable infrastructure.

The Department of Petén represents one third the national territory, and practically everything that goes on there falls under the direction and control of FYDEP, giving its director far more power than the Petén governor. Col. Oliverio Casasola, the FYDEP director until August, 1969, had managed to survive the change of governments from military to civilian, as did many other military men. Ingeniero Leopoldo Sandoval, head of INTA, insisted that his department be given the job of colonizing the Petén region and that FYDEP limit itself to building roads, bridges, schools and hospitals.[10] He was only echoing the opinion of a 1965 UN study that had stated:

There are two organisms that have jurisdiction for colonization, FYDEP and INTA. Both are planning colonization programs with totally different criteria . . . it is not possible to think of structuring a national program of colonization when there are two institutions working with different criteria and motivations.[11]

The United Nations Commission opted for INTA to handle the whole program because of its experience in the field.

The Council of State went to Petén in February, 1967, to see for itself what FYDEP was doing and were told of Colonel Romeo Samayoa's success in colonizing the banks of the Pasión and Usumacinta Rivers. They were not shown the colonies, going only to Sayaxché, and part of the reason was the terrible state the colonies were in. About nine cooperatives existed at this time, having been literally dumped at various points along the river with no means of communication with the outside world, no living quarters, very little food and less medicine. Sickness and hunger plagued all the cooperatives except that of

Cabricán[12] and people began leaving as fast as new colonizers were coming in. FYDEP's desire for rapid and haphazard colonization was creating more problems than solutions.

The Council of State returned to Guatemala City very pleased with what little they had seen, stating that the banks of the rivers "possessed one of the areas most suitable for colonization since the fertility of the banks of the Pasión River could not be better."[13] This was just one year after the AID technicians had told the Cabricán cooperative that the land along the rivers was useless for agriculture. The FAO study revealed the same information.

In March, 1967, FYDEP admitted to the mayors of Petén just what their criteria for colonization were: Mexico was making a study in preparation for building a dam on the lower Usumacinta River which would flood these Petén lands; therefore, it was necessary to place people along the banks of the rivers in order to thwart the Mexican plan. The urgency of the situation demanded prompt colonization, the mayors were told. They had been upset by the class of people being brought in to colonize.[14] At the end of March, Méndez Montenegro visited Mexico and it was reported that he was going to sign an agreement with that country for the construction of the Usumacinta dam.[15] The President denied this report and declared that he would not compromise the lands of the Usumacinta basin.[16] In the 1970 presidential campaign, however, the Christian Democratic candidate said that the plans to build the dam were still in effect.

In May, 1967, FYDEP said that Caritas (Program of U.S. Catholic Bishops) was aiding it to feed 536 persons in three cooperatives along the Usumacinta: Cabricán, San Bernardino and Felicidad.[17] The latter had experienced a number of infant deaths, other families had abandoned the project and discontent was general and open due to the lack of food and the bad administration by the cooperative's inexperienced president.

The internal fight over FYDEP's control continued. Some members in Congress wanted to remove Colonel Casasola for running the enterprise as if Petén were his private empire;[18]

others wanted the department transferred from the Ministry of Defense to the Ministry of Agriculture; and Leopoldo Sandoval wanted the colonization, at least, under INTA. In May, the Council of State returned to Petén to look over the situation and it reported, still without having visited the colonies, that the colonization should be in the hands of FYDEP. INTA should "help but not interfere."[19] At the end of May, 1967, eighty-seven heads of families went to form two more cooperatives on the Pasión River under FYDEP's auspices.[20]

Colonel Casasola, now concerned about the possibility of INTA taking over the colonization of Petén, appealed to the public through the newspapers:

Now the hour for giving our lands in Petén has arrived, the prized colonization. There cannot be an agrarian reform in the Petén because you cannot reform what does not exist. If FYDEP turns over its banner to some other entity, hundreds of thousands of Guatemalans, attracted by the false siren of reform, will leave their lands in other areas of the country to hurl themselves into a massive migration, disordered and anarchical, with no possibility of progress.[21]

He went on to state that FYDEP was doing a good job of colonization and was thereby preventing Mexico from flooding the "best lands that Petén has in this region." He told of his plans to establish sixty-three cooperatives along the rivers in this area with over 15,700 people, with each family possessing one *caballería* (110 acres). He maintained that eleven of the sixty-three were already functioning. "FYDEP is going to colonize the banks of the Usumacinta River as fast as it can, establishing an army of farmers that will be an obstacle to the Mexican plans for flooding these lands."[22] These colonization plans of Colonel Casasola were not aimed at solving the agrarian problems of the landless masses.

In July, the President himself went to Petén to see the FYDEP colonization program. He was able to visit only two cooperatives, Cabricán and Felicidad, the two oldest in the area.[23] He gave a speech in the former, promising the peasants titles to their cleared lands when the Mayan leader of the cooperative voiced his fear that some day the lands would be stolen from them if they had no titles. In Felicidad he also heard the same complaints as well as one about an onerous debt on the shoulders of the cooperative, placed there by *La Fundación del Centavo* (The Penny Foundation) run by an American businessman. He promised to see what he could do. Both cooperatives were the best in the area and he was not shown the miserable living conditions of the others.

In September, ninety-one colonizers left for Petén to join the cooperatives Buena Fé, Canaán and Sinaí on the Pasión and Usumacinta Rivers. They were from the floating population of the agrarian zones of Nueva Concepción and La Máquina, having been preceded by 600 other colonizers from these same zones who had worked there as peons for the owners.[24]

In October, FYDEP announced that it was firing 150 workers "because of the Q. 100,000 cut in its budget that was being used for the internal security of the country."[25] That same month, Colonel Casasola, in an interview, talked about Petén, saying:

Poptún (Arévalo's project) has shown that planned colonization does not attract true colonizers and it is absurd to attempt to place men on lands not their own when subsidies and State paternalism intrude. Fifty thousand peasants will be the tolerable maximum after a very slow process of careful selection. Decades will pass before Petén will be able to absorb 150,000 inhabitants.[26]

He blamed the American anthropologist, Sylvanus Morley, for the excessive estimates that were being made as to the maximum number of inhabitants that Petén could support. He stated that "it is a false idea that Petén once housed from six to twenty-six million Maya."[27]

In April, 1968, FYDEP announced that it had trained thirty teachers for twenty-two cooperatives who were going to teach 321 peasants to read and write.[28] This would put the number of colonizers in the Usumacinta Basin at that time at approximately 1,600 people, few enough for the clamorous propaganda the government insisted on making for itself. In June, 1968, 250 families that were in Guatemala City, preparing to go to Petén, were refused transportation by Col. Casasola, who thus managed to bring the trickle of immigrants to a halt. That same month Casasola announced that the saw mill built by FYDEP near Sayaxché would be sold with lumber rights for 470,000 hectares for Q. 40 million with the explanation that:

Petén is an economic experiment, not a political one. The government must give out the lands to capitalist enterprises so that the lands are developed and populated progressively. Therefore, it is necessary that Congress pass the law they now have in their hands so that this dangerous and anomalous situation of provisional land settling can be terminated. It is like giving out clouds.[29]

When the Rosario saw mill was inaugurated a week later, he stated that "Petén has to stimulate great capitalist enterprises."[30]

The "dangerous and anomalous situation of provisional land settling" referred to by the director of FYDEP represented an interesting situation. There exist few legal titles of direct ownership to the lands in the Petén region and most of these go back to colonial days. None of the successive governments, up until the government of Peralta Azurdia, had ever bothered to officially inscribe this huge territory as national land. This was probably due to the fact that no one was ever sure of what the country owned there, and besides, myriad problems revolved around the boundaries with both Mexico and Belice. Without roads in the area, everyone tended to forget Petén until it was time to draw up a map. This led to the "anomalous situation" that contemporaneous governments were not the "owners" of Petén and therefore could not grant legal titles in the area. Peralta Azurdia had begun the process of rectifying the situation when he published an "Internal Resolution" (#57) on November 4, 1964: "All natural persons or *de jure* entities are prohibited from taking possession of uncultivated lands in Petén. These will be under the jurisdiction of FYDEP until the regulations for such a purpose are adopted." Later, a new law (#266), was also passed by Peralta Azurdia and this gave FYDEP the powers already delegated to INTA for other areas of the country; that is, "to survey and register"[31] all uncultivated lands in Petén. Finally, the military government also promulgated another law (#354) which granted FYDEP the power to colonize, especially the Usumacinta Basin. But none of this legislation authorized the distribution of land titles.[32]

Many lawyers maintained that all that had ever been needed was a presidential decree permitting FYDEP to distribute ownership rights. Others believed that only Congress could pass the law that would make such distributions legal. The dispute seemed to be more political than legal. Peralta certainly would not have had any difficulty in passing such a law through his rubber-stamp congress. In August, 1969, three years after Méndez Montenegro had taken over the government, his Congress finally passed such a law.

The underlying problem has been the wealth that is at stake. It is speculated that fabulous treasures exist in the Petén, contained in the recently discovered oil and ore deposits. The precious lumber content of its forests has been recognized for decades. Now that roads are finally being pushed through the area, dreams of agricultural and cattle production multiply geometrically. Today, there are concrete reasons for the government to give out legal land titles, and Congress has activated itself to meet such needs. It only remains to be seen who gets how much.

Meanwhile, FYDEP continued to give out provisional contracts of settlement that Col. Oliverio Casasola compared to "giving out clouds." Some of the biggest landowners in the country have thereby gotten their foot in the door: Ralda and Berger are already operating in Petén but FYDEP refuses to say how large the extentions of their lands are. Also, there are a number of U.S. businessmen who have gotten 22.5 caballerías (2,471 acres) in the Santa Ana area. Their lands are situated along the roads that FYDEP is constructing in that zone. The amount of land given President Mendez's nephew, son of his dead brother and General Secretary of the PR, is not known. But a large area was reserved for him and "other relatives" along the main road from Flores, capital of Petén, to the Belice border.

By December, 1969, there were approximately 600 peasant families on the almost inaccessible lands along the banks of the Usumacinta and Pasión Rivers. Father Mario García Rodríguez, the Catholic priest in charge of the spiritual welfare of these colonists, made a public appeal for help through the press in early December, 1969, claiming that the "600 families are in an anguished and dramatic situation, since they lack the tools to work their lands, they have neither food, medical attention nor medicines, and it is difficult for them to take care of other basic needs such as clothes, since they have been placed in areas very far from any urban center."[33] It is doubtful that any more peasants will be allowed to settle lands in the area unless it is to provide peon labor for capitalist enterprises, feudalistic landholdings, or to further block Mexican plans for flooding the area. Colonel Oliverio Casasola explains this in his book, *Grandezas y Miserias del Petén* (Greatness and Misery of Petén):

Let us speak clearly. It is not a question of settling Petén at any price and thus contaminating from its birth an organism that must remain imperatively healthy in order to communicate its health to the whole country. An example: the illiteracy rate in Petén had been one of the lowest in Guatemala and Central America, but in the last few years it has gone up 22%. The cause? The Kekchí Maya immigrations to the municipality of San Luis, due to the economic and agricultural failure of Alta Verapaz . . .We would also clarify that of the 2,849 immigrants to Petén, 1,908 were Indians and 941 nonIndians, coefficient of regression, since no matter how much sympathy we may have for the Indian problem, they are not the human contingent that Petén needs to progress.[34]

In November, 1968, Méndez Montenegro named a commission to study the situation and to draw up a law that would govern the distribution of land titles in Petén.[35] The commission decided that 10 *caballerías* (1,098 acres) should be the limit given to any one individual and that no one should be given even that amount if he already owned land valued at more than Q. 20,000 as a private individual, or over Q. 50,000 as a legal entity. After observing that FYDEP had already given out many farms far surpassing that limit, it was decided that such restrictions would be too constricting and that extensions of 1,000 hectares (2,470 acres) could be given out. It was also decided that it was not relevant how much land the beneficiary already possessed, thus assuring that *latifundistas* would be eligible. The only limitation would be that one person (not one family) could receive no more than one lot of 1,000 hectares (2,470 acres) in Petén. This was approved unanimously by the commission[36] and an audience was sought with the President to explain the new changes and to obtain his backing in pushing the law through Congress. A few days later, the Christian Democratic Party sent a telegram to the President asking him to reject the commission's projected law in view of the fact that it was obviously designed to continue a state of *latifundismo*.[37]

The Maya peoples of Guatemala are not the "human contingent that Petén needs to progress," according to Col. Oliverio Casasola, but if we can judge from the nature of the law that was finally passed on August 21, 1969, after weeks of acrimonious debate, it can be foreseen that as the *latifundistas* take possession of the lands, and their need for cheap and often slave labor develops, the "coefficient of regression" will climb as the landless and illiterate peasants are brought in to perform their historical tasks.

Brief but valiant attempts were made to incorporate a note

of "social sensibility" into the new law that was meant to regulate the distribution of idle lands that comprise almost one-third of Guatemala's national territory. Congressman Lionel López Rivera of the PID party proved to be an unexpected opponent of the law:

The proposed law does not benefit the peasants of Guatemala in any way, nor is it aimed at developing Petén. There is no trace of social sensibility in it since there is not one single article of the law that is going to benefit the poor peasants. The agrarian development of Petén is not even contemplated by the law since the thousands of *caballerías* of land there will be occupied by huge business, and for this reason I repeat that the law lacks social sensibility.[38]

The charge was met with outraged cries of wounded pride by the congressmen of the PR whose members had composed the commission that drew up the law. They could not afford to allow the accusation of a lack of "social sensibility" to go unchallenged. Congressman Antonio Morales Baños of the Revolutionary Party took up the standard and sarcastically declared: "I suppose the only thing this Congress needs now is another Father Bartolomé de las Casas to defend the Indians."[39] The reference was to the celebrated priest who almost singlehandedly fought the colonial government to procure humane treatment for the Maya from the *Conquistadores*. The blast was continued by a confrere of Morales Baños, Congressman Pedro Díaz Marroquín:

Let us be practical when it comes to legislating and not proceed with absurd sentimentality that is prejudicial for making laws. If we wish to look for the solution to the problems of the thousands of poor peasants, then let us reform the agrarian law and there we will find the solution.[40]

The criticism was correct of course, since colonization could not replace agrarian reform. But the blast was made, not from a profound desire to protect the rights of the Maya or to alleviate their needs, but rather to block even this feeble effort to give them some future in the Petén under the laws of the nation.

The debate continued for weeks as the argument raged back and forth, but all attempts to amend the law were beaten back by the wholesale exodus of numerous congressmen depriving the legislative assembly of the necessary quorum and rendering further debate devoid of any legality. When it was suggested that the land titles be given out by the FYDEP office in the Petén to ensure that all the beneficiaries would have had to live in that Department, Congressman Morales Baños, with his usual dry sense of humor, stated that: "According to my criterion, there is no necessity to sign the contracts for the acquisition of lands on some tree trunk in Petén." The office for land distribution would remain in Guatemala City, to be of no assistance to those who had already migrated into the area; rather it was meant to insure easy acquisition of lands by absentee landlords in the capital.

Finally, tired and disgusted after weeks of haggling, Congress passed the bill on August 21, 1969, in what the newspapers described as "a marathon."[41] Four and one half hours of uninterrupted reading produced the desired result: confirmation. Only one article provoked any discussion and that was the one limiting the distributions to Guatemalans by birth. This seemed to exclude some of the United States citizens and other foreigners who had already received large extensions of land from FYDEP in the Petén, but the article stood. It would not be difficult for such people to form some kind of holding company with willing Guatemalans to avoid this precept of the law.

Strangely enough, nothing was heard from outspoken Col. Oliverio Casasola during the weeks of prolonged debate. Perhaps his position had been publicized so often before that no clarification was needed. The mystery was compounded when a week after the new law's passage, Col. Casasola resigned as director of FYDEP, a job he had held with distinction since his appointment by Ydígoras Fuentes. The announcement of

his resignation was accompanied by the parallel announcement of a shift in INTA. Its director Colom Argueta, was
named head of the nation's registry of real estate, an extremely
important job in view of the implications of the new law.
Colom Argueta was replaced as head of INTA by Col. Elías
Herrera Ayala.

Some light may have been thrown on these developments
by a letter that appeared in the press two weeks after the new
appointments, written by a consultor to Petén's Catholic
Bishop and an old opponent of Col. Casasola's, Francisco
Sagastume Ortíz, an outspoken critic of FYDEP's neglect of
the needs of the peasants:

Now that the electoral campaign is beginning to heat up, Casasola
has resigned, knowing that the electoral strategy of the government
requires that it have all key posts in the hands of members of its
own party (PR) so that it may exercise coercion in its favor on
government employees, notwithstanding constitutional precepts to
the contrary. Casasola never did this nor would he ever allow such
a thing, and this in part accounts for his resignation.[42]

The author of this letter, reading the handwriting on the wall
as contained in the new law, goes on to give a few words of
approval to the retired colonel:

Casasola has retired precisely at the moment when the law for
the distribution of lands in Petén goes into effect. He should be
very happy for this, because now history will not be able to
condemn him for giving these lands to the new and old *latifundistas*, both Guatemalan and foreign, who, with their greed, take
away the opportunity to work, (and thereby dignify themselves),
from the great majority of Guatemalans who will have to continue
as their eternal servants, condemned to die of hunger in the greatest misery, crowned with ignorance and sickness.[43]

Is it any wonder then that a full year earlier, at about the
same time that Méndez Montenegro was naming his commission to draw up this law, a meeting was held in Guatemala of

all the agrarian reform executives of the Central American countries, and agrarian reform in the area was admitted to be "a myth." The director of the Interamerican Institute of Agricultural Sciences of the OAS, Enrique Torres Llosa, stated:

It seems to me that the common denominator of this meeting has been the frank and sincere admittance that, in spite of the efforts made by the different organizations that you direct, action for the true transformation of agrarian structures is not and has not been an object of your activities . . . The definition and realization of an authentic policy of integral agrarian reform can no longer be put off.[44]

The director of INTA, Colom Argueta, agreed and added:

The importance given by the government to braking the accelerated demographic increase is well known . . . What was an apparently good solution in years past is no longer so. We have two Americas separated by a huge abyss: On one side, the America of deliberations, meetings, resolutions and agreements, but without concrete accomplishments; and on the other side, the America of the disinherited, the great America.[45]

He went on to add, almost as an afterthought, that seventy percent of the Guatemalan population lived on less than $100 a year.

The Petén legislation was not meant to do anything about this situation. Integral or even partial agrarian reform continued to be deferred and opposed and Guatemala remains an integral part of the "America of the disinherited." This conclusion is no harsher than the facts themselves, as can be seen when they are separated from the soothing rhetoric of governmental agencies and the political propaganda of Méndez Montenegro. A common ploy was to announce a number of distributions months in advance, juggling the numbers of beneficiaries, the members of their families and the titles to be distributed. It works as follows: On June 26, 1969, Colom

Argueta announced that INTA was to give out 402 land titles, without stating where the land was nor its extension;[46] at a press conference two weeks later, July 11, INTA announced that it would give out land titles to 5,000 peasants during the month in progress; upon reading the article it is seen that the 5,000 peasants consist of 917 heads of families and the rest are their dependents; among the 917 titles, 402 will go to beneficiaries in Ocós, San Marcos; also mentioned are thirty-two titles in Champerico as well as other listings; almost three weeks later, July 29, INTA again proclaims that it will give out thirty-two titles in Champerico on the following Saturday; on August 6th, a big ceremony was held to which the press was invited for the distribution of thirty-two titles in Champerico; on August 13th, the newspapers carried a picture of the Vice-President of INTA giving a land title to a peasant, one of nineteen titles, to the "microplots" in El Coco, Jutiapa; this same distribution was one of those mentioned in the July 11 press conference; finally, on August 26th, another big ceremony was held with much press coverage at which the 402 titles in Ocós, San Marcos were given out by the Minister of Labor "in representation of President Méndez Montenegro;" no more of these 917 titles were given out during the remainder of the year even though only 453 titles of those originally promised in July had been distributed. The amount of land distributed was not noted in any of these cases, though those in Champerico and Jutiapa were called "microplots."

During the last few days of the electoral campaign for the presidency in February, 1970, more than 1,300 other titles were given out in what was viewed as a last ditch propaganda ploy aimed at shoring up the sagging fortunes of the PR's uninspiring presidential candidate. 745 titles were given out in the agrarian zone of La Máquina and 138 more in Cuyuta, Escuintla.[47] Another 326 were distributed in several different areas of Izabal, even while the head of INTA, Elías Herrera Ayala, reminded his listeners of Méndez Montenegro's great dedication to land reform.[48] Here, too, no mention was made of the amount of land in the plots distributed.

Approximately 3,450 land plots had been distributed in the three categories of agrarian zones, communities and "microplots," with more than one-half of these classified as microfarms or *minifundios*. Some of those not classified as such, the community distributions, for example, have land extensions that place them also in the category of *minifundios*.

As of February 28, 1970, 530 provisional titles had been given out in the Fray Bartolomé de las Casas project. It is not clear whether or not these are the same 530 provisional titles distributed by Peralta Azurdia. INTA had another 600 titles ready to distribute if the legal complications of the land claims to 409 *caballerías* (45,560 acres) made by "thirty outsiders" could be cleared up. In Ixcán Grande, 184 families had land and no titles and the same situation existed for almost 600 families allowed into Petén by FYDEP. Thus, the grand total of families aided by the Méndez Montenegro "agrarian reform program" was 4,764 families as of February 28, 1970, many of whom were not even given provisional titles, and many others were the beneficiaries of programs that did not owe their existence to government efforts.

The annual increase of peasant families living on subsistence agriculture or less averages 20,000 a year.[49] And so we have the Third Government of the Revolution receiving the dubious distinction of facilitating lands of insufficient acreage to fewer than 5,000 out of the 80,000 landless families that had proliferated during its four-year regime. It was a record in keeping with the standards of Castillo Armas, Ydígoras and Peralta, not with those of Arévalo and Arbenz.

NOTES

1 CIDA, *Op. Cit.*, p. 47.
2 See Chapter 10, note 50.
3 *El Imparcial*, March 28, 1967.
4 *Prensa Libre*, February 28, 1970.
5 *El Imparcial*, May 4, 1964.
6 *Ibid.*, May 24, 1967.
7 *Ibid.*, July 17, 1967.
8 *Ibid.*, September 11, 1967.
9 *Ibid.*, November 26, 1968.
10 *Ibid.*, December 12, 1966.
11 OIT, *Op. Cit.*, p. 105.
12 Part of the reason was the money provided by the Maryknoll Fathers and another was the Defense Department's permission to use the abandoned training base of the Cuban invaders at San Juan Acul.
13 *El Imparcial*, February 22, 1967.
14 *Ibid.*, March 17, 1967.
15 *Ibid.*, March 21, 1967.
16 *Ibid.*, March 22, 1967.
17 *Ibid.*, April 11, 1967.
18 *Ibid.*, April 18, 1967.
19 *Ibid.*, May 16, 1967.
20 *Ibid.*, May 24, 1967.
21 *Ibid.*
22 *Ibid.*
23 *Ibid.*, July 14, 1967.
24 *Ibid.*, September 27, 1967.
25 *Ibid.*, October 31, 1967.
26 *Ibid.*, November 18, 1967.
27 *Ibid.*
28 *Ibid.*, April 5, 1968.
29 *Ibid.*, June 1, 1968.
30 *Ibid.*, June 8, 1968.
31 OIT, *Op. Cit.*, p. 35.
32 *El Guatemalteco, Diario Oficial,* Tomo CLXXIII, No. 85, June 11, 1965.
33 *Prensa Libre*, December 4, 1969.
34 Casasola, Oliverio, *Grandezas y Miserias del Petén.* Guatemala: Indiana, Ltd., 1968, pp. 44–46.
35 *Prensa Libre,* April 29, 1969.

36 *Ibid.,* May 22, 1969.
37 *Ibid.,* May 27, 1969.
38 *Ibid.,* August 7, 1969.
39 *Ibid.*
40 *Ibid.*
41 *Ibid.,* August 22, 1969.
42 *Ibid.,* September 18, 1969.
43 *Ibid.*
44 *El Imparcial,* September 11, 1968.
45 *Ibid.*
46 *Prensa Libre,* June 26, 1969.
47 *Ibid.,* February 25, 1970.
48 *Ibid.,* February 28, 1970.
49 CIDA, *Op. Cit.,* p. 200.

> With mere good intentions, hell is proverbially paved.
>
> **William James**

15

mere good intentions

WHEN COMPARED WITH the three men who preceded him in the president's chair, Julio César Méndez Montenegro can be characterized as a man with a developed social conscience. That he was not able to translate this conscience into a realistic program of social development cannot be blamed on the president alone. Nevertheless, the same negative policies aimed at the peasants did continue during his regime as they did during those of his three predecessors, though far fewer in number and fury. Méndez Montenegro's protestations have been limited to a lame defense of his government's activities in the face of Guatemala's enormous social ills. The peasants continue to live in the tenuous situation of never knowing when they will be expelled from lands on which they have lived for years, but to which someone else repeatedly acquires the "legal" title.

On January 21, 1967, sixty families in Jacaltenango, Huehuetenango complained that they were being expelled from communal lands by the mayor so that he could share these lands with two other large landowners. The peasants declared that they did not have the money needed to hire lawyers to defend their claims.[1]

Two months later, another anguished cry rose from the throats of a group of peasants. It is worth repeating in full for

233

it tells succinctly the story of the ever recurring dynamic of Guatemalan social life:

We demand that the President of the Republic, who himself is a revolutionary and has said that his government will support the peasants, intervene immediately in order to bring to an end our anguish of 42 years duration by giving us titles to our own lands which we purchased as members of our community of Monjas, Jalapa. In 1923, we bought 54 *cabellerías* for 40 thousand pesos for 623 peasant families from Lawyer Antonio Godoy, General David Barrientos and Engineer Benedicto Cárcamo, who had obtained them from President Orellana. The lands were measured then and in 1943 they were measured again, but we were never given titles. Now we are collaborating with the Institute of Community Development and still nothing. We suffer from this insecurity.[2]

On May 16, 1967, the Maya of Cahaboncito in Alta Verapaz claimed that Oscar Lemus had stolen land that they had owned for over 100 years, the burial place of their ancestors. They stated that he had done so by means of a fraudulent bill of sale.[3]

Three hundred peasant families in Santiago, Sacatepéquez denounced their mayor in January, 1968 for underhanded dealings in his attempts to give the lands on which they lived to his political friends.[4] By June of the same year, an even bigger problem had arisen: "Several hundred families abandoned without lands or roof in Taxisco."[5] Two days later, on June 20th, the Red Cross reported that it was feeding the 1,700 people in Candelaria, Taxisco where they were without lands and "living exposed to the elements."[6] INTA sent a commission to resolve the conflicting claims between what was said to be two peasant groups of fifteen and 392 families, respectively, and published the following information:

The problem is not new; it began in 1954 when the peasants were violently expelled from the lands of the *finca* Chiquibuitán in Taxisco, where they had been settled by the previous government.

From among the expelled families, many dispersed and fled while others took refuge in the area between the Pacific Ocean and the Chiquimulilla Canal. . . . There are now 15 families there on state lands employing 115 families as *colonos*. We are going to divide that land equally among all.[7]

By the end of August, it became clearer who was behind these difficulties, when Manuel Ralda Ochoa demanded that INTA expel the "hundreds of peasant families" from his finca Chiquihuitán in Taxisco.[8] His view of the problem was different: "INTA says that this finca was expropriated in 1953. But this is not true. It was invaded and then everything was straightened out later under Castillo Armas."[9] INTA responded two days later saying that when the peasants were expelled in 1954, the owner, who later sold out to Ralda Ochoa, also laid claim illegally to state lands nearby and it was these state lands that INTA was going to give to the campesinos.[10] A year later, in late 1969, the peasants still did not have title to the lands in Taxisco, nor is it likely that they will ever get them, though INTA put up an unusually spirited defense of the peasants. Ralda Ochoa's own final public word in the affair was to show how important the land was to him: "I have 20,000 workers on the *finca* Chiquihuitán and a weekly payroll of Q. 40,000. It produces 2,500 calves annually."[11] He goes on to denounce the trouble as the work of agitators and does not even advert to his public admission of paying his workers an illegal salary averaging less than thirty cents a day.

In the meantime, slight notice is taken of the fact that the mayor, the municipal secretary and the municipal authority in charge of measuring lands in San Juan Ixcoy, Huehuetenango have murdered a peasant and his wife because of a land dispute. There is speculation about the mayor's immunity from prosecution.[12] At the writing of this book, neither man has been charged with the crime.

On November 27, 1968, 300 indigenous families were put off their lands in Palín and their coffee was confiscated as indemnization. The action was taken by the municipal authorities who belonged to the Revolutionary Party. "The people had been given the lands by Arbenz and had lived there since 1954."[13] In February, 1969, some of these same Maya held a news conference, a novel event in the history of Guatemala's fourth estate, to which two reporters went: "Some were barefoot; some spoke Spanish with difficulty. But all of them knew with precision what they wanted to say . . . that the press publicize the truth about their situation: the abuse of authority and the open robbery of which they are victims."[14]

The day following the expulsions in Palín, sixteen families were put off the *finca* Acapalón in Champerico.[15] The news item noted that this was the second group thrown off this particular *finca*. And in December, INTA itself began getting into the swing of things by ejecting ninety families from La Máquina, an action which was protested by the regional peasant organization. Three months later, the *Prensa Libre* published a letter from Silvino Sánchez, representing forty families from Acasaguastlán, El Progreso, who had lost "their lands, corn, fruit trees and coffee" to INTA in 1964. They had been appealing to INTA since that time to give the lands back and grant them their rightful titles.[16]

By May, 1969, INTA was situating 400 families in Los Angeles and Sehilá and another 250 families in Rio Negro, all in the department of Izabal. "All of these people had been expelled for diverse reasons from lands that they had been cultivating."[17] There is no mention of their receiving titles for their new lands. Izabal is the area in which Yon Sosa and his guerrilla movement were having such success in educating the people to the dynamics of the Guatemalan land tenure pattern.

A good example of the process can be seen in the story of the small village of La Esperanza in Izabal, where 200 families had cleared a section of the jungle for themselves. In mid 1963, the military commissioner of the area told them that they had to move out since the land was owned by a wealthy family by the name of Padilla. When the peasants refused, soldiers were brought in, their homes burned and tractors were used to plow up their crops. They complained to the governor of Izabal but he did nothing about the case since "he and the Padilla brothers used to drink together; the orders of investigation were filed away while our small children died of hunger because we then had to live in the jungle like animals."[18] Finally, these same people were able to clear another section of the jungle for themselves but again the Padilla brothers moved them off, backed up by another newly acquired title. "It seems like those evil men had decided not to let us live and we were losing all hope when we met the guerrillas and they told us that they would kill the Padillas and give us back our land."[19]

In the early part of 1964, the Padilla brothers were killed in an ambush near Quiriguá Viejo. The army immediately sent out a patrol looking for the guerrillas and the lieutenant colonel in charge was killed in another ambush. The military was furious and then arrested the ten outstanding peasant leaders in the area, including the peasant leader of the Christian Democrats, throwing them all in jail where they remained until Peralta Azurdia turned the government over to Méndez Montenegro. The wife of one of the arrested men said:

A few nights ago the guerrillas came to see me. They told me that the government was after them for defending the poor and that the only solution left was for everyone to join them in order to defeat the soldiers and put in a government of the working people.[20]

Another situation in the same area may provide the setting for a similar dynamic. We refer to the small town of Chichipate on Lake Izabal, where the population grew from zero in 1950 to 346 inhabitants in 1964. All these migrants were Kekchí-Maya from Alta Verapaz who moved to Chichipate in an attempt to obtain land to sustain themselves. "The greatest sense of disappointment has come, though, from the fact that private absentee owners suddenly appeared after the Chichipateños had cleared the land."[21] When the absentee owners established their claim, they sold the lands to the International Nickel

Company and an adjacent *finca*. The company allowed the settlers to remain where they were but insisted that no more be allowed into the area so as not to interfere with their extensive mining operations. The owner of the Yuscarán *finca* was also more generous than is usually the case, for he "entered into an agreement whereby Chichipateños living on his property would work for him at their discretion, in return for which they could make *milpa* on Chichipate land and would receive cash payment of fifty cents per man-day of labor."[22] Such an arrangement was very generous in view of the common practice in Izabal to oblige a *colono* to "give two weeks of free labor per month during the periods of planting and harvest. Another custom is to require him to clear and cultivate approximately 60 percent as much for the landowner as he clears and cultivates for himself."[23] Perhaps this favorable treatment was indirect recognition of the guerrilla activity that existed in the area. But expulsions in other areas did and do continue.

On June 6, 1969, "a group of military police came into Montufar, Jutiapa, interrupting the tranquility of the neighbors with several bursts from their machine guns, followed up with insults and threats while ordering six peasant families to abandon their homes under threat of death."[24] The aforegoing accusation was made by Emilio Gómez Galicia in the name of the other families and he produced documents from INTA demonstrating their legal ownership of the lands from which they had been expelled. The secretary of public relations of INTA immediately protested that the accusation was false, since the agrarian authorities in the region had informed the institution that Gómez Galicia possessed "large extensions of land" and that he was a *persona non grata* in the area.[25] On June 24th, a suit was brought against INTA by Gómez Galicia in the name of "nine families" that had lived on the lands since 1905, stating that they had first tried to get their titles legitimized by DGAA and then by INTA, having been successful with the latter institution.[26] No more was heard of the incident.

The following month another problem came up in the same area, Jutiapa, that again landed INTA in the courts. This time the government was on the side of the peasants, though not for long. The owner of the *finca* Armenia, Francisco de Jesús Valenzuela Reyes, had thirteen families expelled from his lands on April 16, 1969. INTA subsequently intervened and returned the dispossessed *campesinos* to the lands, and this action resulted in the suit.[27] INTA won the day by maintaining that it had already cancelled its former resolution in favor of the peasants even before the suit was filed.[28]

Toward the end of July, 1969, seventeen peasant families that had been expelled from national lands in Sebol-Raxuha, Alta Verapaz, were allowed to settle in the agrarian zone Fray Bartolomé de las Casas "until their juridical situation is resolved."[29] INTA threatened legal action against those responsible for the expulsions, "who, in this case, have violated the law of supplementary title."[30] The threat was never carried out.

In September of the same year, 1969, a delegation representing 1,000 people who were being expelled from their homes in zones 5 and 8 of Guatemala City, protested to the Vice-Minister of the Interior that they had lived on their lands for thirty years and were now being put off by two lawyers who had taken over the lands from a German company.[31]

At the end of this same month of September, another group of fifty men tried to construct "cardboard houses" in the ravine El Tuerto in zone 1 of the Capital but were driven off by the people who lived there.[32] The former had lived in other ravines around the city but their homes had been washed away by a heavy rain storm and El Tuerto looked drier and safer to them. The occupants, no better off than the "invaders," refused to share their refuge with the newcomers.

On October 8, 1969, a family with fifteen members had to abandon its home in Chiquimula because the military commissioner in the area claimed that the land belonged to him, and he threatened them with death if they did not pack up and leave. He had already shot and wounded one 19-year-old member of the family.[33]

Two indigenous inhabitants of Itzapa, Chimaltenango, Cornelio Tahul and Victor Xiquinajay, announced on October

23, 1969, that INTA was expelling them and 211 other
peasant families from their lands to which they had title.[34]
INTA defended itself by maintaining that the lands had been
given to these families in 1956 by the government of Castillo
Armas for which they were to pay Q. 422 for each lot. Since
the money had never been paid, INTA claimed they were ex-
ecuting their right to expel the peasants and turn over the
land to other families.[35]

A look at other fields of social concern reinforces the picture already painted and shows, if nothing else, at least a con-
sistency in governmental policy.

On December 8, 1966, the AEU asked the Méndez Montenegro government to set up a special commission to work
with the Ministers of Labor and Public Health to investigate
the cotton plantations and sanction those cotton growers responsible for the sickness and death of their workers.[36] The
plantation owners often do not provide the simple education
and equipment needed by the peasant for protection against
insecticides. When the subdirector of the Social Security Institute of the government in 1967 complained publicly that the
cotton growers were not abiding by the legal recommendations
for insecticides, a campaign of villification was mounted
against him in the newspapers by the National Cotton Council
that resulted in his losing his job.[37]

Often a plantation owner will order his field sprayed and
will not pull the workers out while the operation is effected.[38]
The result of this is sickness or death for the workers. In late
1967, in one thirty-day period, over one-hundred cases of
insecticide intoxication were reported, "many of whom died."[39]
The author has heard spray pilots talk about how they would
swoop down and spray an unsuspecting group of laborers in
the field to be met by the protest of a few hurled sticks, stones
or even hats. There is no recorded punishment either for them
or for the plantation owners.[40]

Once in a while some of these conditions will come to the
notice of the Minister of Labor or the Institute of Social Se-

curity and a well-publicized trip will be made to one or another part of the country, and after a "heart to heart talk" with a few plantation owners, the official comes back with the encouraging news that the landowners will see that something is done to eliminate the problem.[41]

In November, 1968, the National Cotton Council thanked the Institute of Social Security and the Minister of Agriculture for their help in the campaign against poisoning. They congratulated those cotton growers who had had no cases of intoxication and requested those that did have to try "twice" as hard in the future to avoid them.[42] The campaign consisted of flying over the plantations and dropping leaflets on the illiterate peasants explaining that they should not drink, eat or smoke, unless they first wash with soap and water; that they should bathe and have a change of clothes after being sprayed themselves; and not to enter the plantations for forty-eight hours after the spraying. The fact that few plantations have adequate washing or bathing facilities for the workers, that most peasants do not have a change of working clothes, and that it is not their decision when to enter the fields, does not seem to have occurred to the National Cotton Council.

Only two days before this campaign began, it was headline news that Salvadorean workers were being "smuggled" across the border with the help of immigration authorities, having been promised "fabulous salaries." When they finished picking the crop, they were made to sign onerous contracts or were released without wages and threatened with exposure for illegal entry if they complained.[43] This has never been a difficult operation for the landowners to effect as long as the authorities cooperate since Salvador's land problems are even worse than those of Guatemala. In 1969, the insecticide intoxications continued, still with no evidence of any legal sanctions against those responsible.[44]

In one twenty-four hour period in November, 1969, forty-eight persons were interned in the Social Security (IGSS) hospital in Escuintla because of insecticide poisoning.[45] Many were confined to the intensive care units because of their serious condition. It was reported that alarm had swept over the peasants who work on the cotton plantations in the south (Pacific) coast. They feared that the poisonings would continue to occur and get worse if preventive measures were not taken. This was the highest number of people poisoned in one day; during the previous week, thirty cases had been admitted to the hospital.

When the National Cotton Council changed its board of directors during that same month, the Vice-Minister of Agriculture was on hand to congratulate the cotton growers for their contribution to the national economy: "Cotton is the second most important crop as regards foreign earnings and is first in the number of people it employs."[46] No mention was made of the problem of worker poisonings.

In January, 1970, the Social Security Institute (IGSS) carried on a campaign against the poisonings by visiting 265 plantations and "encouraging the owners to provide the necessary protective equipment for those workers engaged in spraying."[47] The public relations director of the IGSS noted the success of the campaign: a 45.6 percent drop in poisonings since 1968. He said: "Last year, 1,374 accidents were recorded, while in 1969, we recorded only 748."[48]

On October 9, 1969, the press contained a little-observed notice tucked away on an inner page: "4,000 people affected by the grippe. An average of five to six people a day are dying from the grippe on the finca Oná, in El Quetzal and San Marcos. . . . The attempts that have been made to combat the sickness have been useless, since the grippe has been propagated enormously and many workers and their families are sick."[49]

The epidemic spread and intensified to the point that the Minister of Public Health ordered an investigation. It was reported that the "epidemic is strongest in rural areas, and although the infant mortality rate in the areas affected is generally about five percent, in some areas it goes as high as thirteen percent. The percentages in adults are lower."[50] On

December 4, 1969, the Secretary General of the PR, in Guaza-
capán announced that over 200 people had died from "dysentery and the grippe" in his village alone, and that it was not a
"small outbreak" as was being publicly claimed.[51] On February
13, 1970, Pueblo Viejo, Iztapa, announced that it had had
"more than 300 deaths in these last months from dysentery"
and they requested that "urgent action" be taken by the authorities.[52]

In these cases no official notice was taken of the terrible living conditions that allow sickness to spread so deva-
statingly. No mention was made of the fact that according to
the Nutritional Institute of Central America and Panama
(INCAP), "ninety-eight percent of the total Guatemalan population suffers from worms."[53] The news of these epidemics
did provoke some reaction. A newspaper article on the subject
stated:

Our Indians live in such a precarious state that they seem like
beings completely alienated from the society in which we live—exploited, mistreated and humiliated. They live and die like animals
in the rural areas without any medical attention . . .[54]

The relationship existing between the large landholdings
on one hand and the need for landless peasants to work them
on the other, continued to manifest itself under Méndez Montenegro. This balanced equation between *latifundismo* and
minifundismo can be maintained as long as the peasants are
not allowed to effectively organize. Méndez Montenegro had
"come to power by the will of the people, the peasant people,"
as he constantly reminded everyone, and had to show himself
a friend of organized labor. So it was that during his presidency the number of labor unions and rural cooperatives increased impressively. The President made it a point to appear
at most of the important national meetings of the labor movement and reiterate his support for the working man. On May 1,
1969, International Labor Day, such a meeting was held.
Méndez Montenegro assisted and spoke. He was followed by a

labor leader who roundly criticized the army for interfering in politics.[55] A few days later, the army issued a hot denial of the charge and the President had to do some fast backpedaling to demonstrate that the speaker had represented only his personal point of view.

Méndez Montenegro's inability to give the labor movement the strength that it needed to work effectively was consistent with every other aspect of his attempts to make effective his programs for social change. He could not give what he himself did not have, political power, and any attempts by labor leaders to wield political power were met with harassment, imprisonment and death.

The labor movement has always been considered a haven for Communists and Marxist-oriented agitators and as such it is the recognized target of antiCommunist activities. There is no question that Marxists and socialist thinkers have been instrumental in both the development and, at times, as under Arbenz, the control of large segments of the movement. This has not been true since the advent of the Liberation regime. Since that time the Christian labor movement has increased its activity under the auspices of the Christian Democrats. Nevertheless, the battle cry for the control and suppression of the movement since the Castillo Armas government has been in the name of freedom and private enterprise as interpreted by the antiCommunist landowners.

Méndez Montenegro had a problem relating to this situation because he could not withstand the charge of being soft on Communism. The landowners, the army, the Church and the United States government were the principal institutions that kept him in power, and all consider a vaguely defined Communism as their chief enemy. The labor movement suffered as a result.

Walter Widmann's feud with the union in his sugar plantation is an example. Widmann, a prominent Catholic layman,[56] is part owner of Concepción, a large sugar plantation in the country. Under the Ydígoras regime, he tried to destroy the union, alleging Communism, by firing hundreds of families on several occasions. The union appealed to the Labor Court for protection and in fact did manage to have labor inspectors come to the plantation and demand that the fired workers be restored. Then, with the help of Col. Pedro Cardona, the *finca* administrator who was also the local military commissioner, a second union was sponsored by Widmann and the workers were forced to join.[57] In order to gain government support, it was publicized that this second union was "Ydigorista" while the first one was "Communist." The law specifies that only one union can be legalized on a plantation and there is chronological preference. A Ministry of Labor official supported the first union and insisted that the fired laborers be rehired. He was then overruled by one of his superiors.

In February, 1963, three peasant leaders on the plantation were jailed as Communists. The union secretary protested that it was a false accusation.[58] When Peralta Azurdia became president there was no longer any political lever in an "Ydigorista" union, so the plantation was forced to rehire the men. They continued, nevertheless, to be persecuted[59] and imprisoned. When Méndez Montenegro came to the presidency, the peasant labor federation of that zone dared to raise its head and in August, 1966, threatened a strike.[60] They were blocked from organizing it and, as a result, Col. P. Cardona, the administrator, was assassinated. Later the Armed Forces of Rebellion attempted the assassination of Widmann himself but were unsuccessful. On September 11, 1967, Pedro Fajardo Ajín, the secretary general of the worker's union, was kidnapped and murdered, along with two other union members. It was never discovered who did the killings. After that a military guard was based permanently on the plantation, and even the clergy were prevented from talking to the workers.[61]

Neither the landowners nor the peasants could rest easily. It was impossible to unravel the murders from the executions, the personal vendettas from self-defense. The papers carried daily the pictures of those who have disappeared and the descriptions of unidentified and mutilated bodies found around the country. The right-wing terrorist groups functioned in the city as well as in the rural zones, paid by the wealthy and actively assisted by the army and police. It was hard to distinguish organized guerrilla activity from isolated peasant action in the countryside. This is what Méndez Montenegro had to face. Late in September, 1966, the plantation owners demanded that the government step up policing activities in the country districts and the chief of police promised squads of patrolmen to protect all threatened landowners.[62] By December, 1966, the owners and administrators of plantations were commissioned as members of the national police.[63] In February, 1967, 20,000 tons of sugar cane were burned on fifteen different *fincas*.[64] Other fires were followed with the landowners' insistent demand for further protection.[65]

The government requested that the workers' right to organize be respected but the landowners usually replied with violence. In August, the government sponsored a campaign to teach the peasants to read and write. One-hundred landowners cooperated by allowing teachers onto their plantations and granting them facilities for the activities. It was requested of all of them at this time that they allow union organizing to be carried out among their workers.[66] Two months later, Méndez Montenegro attended a meeting of 2,000 delegates to CONTRAGUA and assured his listeners that his government supported them.[67] A month later the undersecretary of peasant affairs for the Christian Democrats in Izabal was jailed.[68] He had already spent two years in jail under Peralta Azurdia for his "Communism." Archbishop Mario Casariego did not help matters for the government when, on December 14, 1967, he requested that it produce the 273 people that had been arrested and never consigned to any tribunal.[69] The police and the Minister of Interior maintained that they knew nothing of the whereabouts of the individuals named on the list.

But peasants continued to disappear. In March, 1968, the two leaders of the labor union in the plantation Cerro Redondo, Santa Rosa, were abducted, never to be seen again.[70] By the end of the same month, lists were published naming twenty-five leaders of Central Worker organizations that had been marked for execution by right-wing terrorist organizations.[71] The same day, 15,000 tons of sugar cane burned on the largest plantation in the country, El Salto, in Escuintla. Another 41,000 tons went up on three other plantations in the same area.[72] In July, nine peasants were kidnapped and murdered in Chiquimula.[73] In September, when 300 coffee harvesters protested the intolerable conditions on a plantation in Quezaltenango, the police were called in and they arrested the ten leaders.[74]

The government party itself was the target of antiCommunist activities. Two congressmen, three regional party heads and a number of other notable members of the PR, all active in the labor movement, were assassinated.

On October 12, 1969, the secretary general of the Confederation of Workers of Guatemala, Hugo Vásquez Barrientos, was wounded by unknown assailants in Jutiapa.[75] Two days later, Reinero Zan Hurtarte, a director of the Confederation of Syndicates (Unions) of Guatemala, was also shot, but this effort was more successful and the labor leader died as a result of his wounds. He had been threatened many times previous to his execution.[76] The newspapers reported a few days later that the leaders of the labor movement had been "threatened by masked men with machine guns not to insist that the assassination of Zan Hurtarte be cleared up."[77] The dead man was a leader of the PR in the area of Escuintla and it is interesting to note that the government's interest in clarifying the crime was not sufficient by itself but had to be prodded by the insistence of the labor movement.

It is impossible to ascertain the number of murders, killings, assassinations and executions that occurred during the time Méndez Montenegro was president. In an editorial written in April, 1967, the director of *Prensa Libre* calculated that the country was averaging over 100 political murders a month at that time.[78] His figures were based on the number of deaths reported, an elusive criterion at best. Lucas Caballeros, the Christian Democratic presidential candidate, claimed in February 1970 that 6,000 political murders had occurred under Méndez Montenegro.

The situation progressively worsened during 1967 and the first months of 1968. But the incident that sent reverberations throughout the country was the kidnapping of Archbishop Mario Casariego, in March, 1968, in broad daylight, a block and a half from the presidential palace. For a city armed to the teeth, and under martial law, with two machine gun-toting soldiers on every corner, and pairs of police radio cars patroling every street with two or three bullet-proofed officers pointing guns out of the windows, such a derring-do was clearly impossible without official police and army connivance. These connections had been known publicly for more than a year and it was impossible to deny them any longer. The government swiftly relieved three top men of their posts: Col. Arriaga Bosque, the Minister of Defense; Col. Manuel Sosa Avila, the head of the national police; and Col. Carlos Arana Osorio, commander of the Zapaca army base. The police also managed to murder Raúl Lorenzana, right-wing terrorist leader and scapegoat, after he had been taken into custody. An unofficial truce seemed to have been called.

The respite was not long-lasting and it flared up again when the police captured Camilo Sánchez, the FAR's second-in-command. The FAR's reaction was swift: the attempted kidnapping of U.S. Ambassador, John Gordon Mein. When the ambassador broke from his captors and began to run, they panicked and shot him. The government's response was predictable: they murdered Camilo Sánchez in jail. These were mutual signals to intensify the conflict.

The following months were bloody and Méndez Montenegro's political longevity did nothing to ameliorate the situation.

NOTES

1 *El Imparcial,* January 21, 1967.
2 *Ibid.,* March 9, 1967.
3 *Ibid.,* May 16, 1967.
4 *Ibid.,* January 2, 1968.
5 *Ibid.,* June 18, 1968.
6 *Ibid.,* June 20, 1968.
7 *Ibid.,* July 12, 1968.
8 *Ibid.,* August 31, 1968.
9 *Ibid.,* September 7, 1968.
10 *Ibid.,* September 9, 1968.
11 *Ibid.,* September 16, 1968.
12 *Ibid.,* July 31, 1968.
13 *Ibid.,* November 27, 1968.
14 *Prensa Libre*, February 26, 1969.
15 *El Imparcial*, November 28, 1968.
16 *Prensa Libre*, March, 1969.
17 *Ibid.,* May 10, 1969.
18 CIDOC, *Dossier #21,* p. 4/104.
19 *Ibid.*
20 *Ibid.,* p. 4/105.
21 Carter, William E., *New Lands and Old Traditions.* Gainesville: University of Florida Press, 1969, p. 3.
22 *Ibid.,* p. 5.
23 *Ibid.,* p. 4.
24 *Prensa Libre*, June 12, 1969.
25 *Ibid.,* June 13, 1969.
26 *Ibid.,* June 25, 1969.
27 *Ibid.,* June 12, 1969.
28 *Ibid.,* July 30, 1969.
29 *Ibid.,* July 23, 1969.
30 *Ibid.*
31 *Ibid.,* September 4, 1969.
32 *Ibid.,* September 29, 1969.
33 *Ibid.,* October 8, 1969.
34 *Ibid.,* October 23, 1969.
35 *Ibid.,* October 25, 1969.
36 *El Imparcial*, December 8, 1966.
37 *Ibid.,* January 9, 1967.
38 *Ibid.,* October 5 and 17, 1967.
39 *Ibid.,* November 11, 1967.

40 *Ibid.*, October 17, 1967.
41 *Ibid.*, January 19, 1967.
42 *Ibid.*, November 21, 1968.
43 *Ibid.*, November 19, 1968.
44 *Ibid.*, October 27 and November 4, 1969.
45 *Prensa Libre,* November 29, 1969.
46 *Ibid.,* November 19, 1969.
47 *Ibid.,* January 28, 1970.
48 *Ibid.*
49 *Ibid.*, October 9, 1969.
50 *Ibid.*, November 13, 1969.
51 *Ibid.*, December 4, 1969.
52 *Ibid.*, February 13, 1970.
53 *Ibid.*, November 17, 1970.
54 *Ibid.*, January 6, 1970.
55 *Ibid.*, May 2, 1969.
56 He is a lay member of the Opus Dei, a conservative Catholic
   association.
57 *El Imparcial,* January 12, 1963.
58 *Ibid.*, March 4, 1963.
59 *Ibid.*, June 26, 1963.
60 *Ibid.*, August 12, 1966.
61 Recounted to the authors from the personal experience of a fellow
   Maryknoller.
62 *El Imparcial,* September 20, 1966.
63 *Ibid.*, December 6, 1966.
64 *Ibid.*, February 27, 1967.
65 *Ibid.,* April 3, 1967.
66 *Ibid.,* August 12, 1967.
67 *Ibid.,* October 16, 1967.
68 *Ibid.,* November 25, 1967.
69 *Ibid.,* December 14, 1967.
70 *Ibid.*, March 4, 1968.
71 *Ibid.*, March 27, 1968.
72 *Ibid.*
73 *Ibid.*, July 20, 1968.
74 *Ibid.*, October 5 and 9, 1968.
75 *Ibid.*, October 13, 1969.
76 *Ibid.*, October 15, 1969.
77 *Ibid.*, October 17, 1969.
78 *Prensa Libre,* April 5, 1967.

Of itself no election resolves anything, least of all problems of misery, hunger, unemployment, illiteracy, which are faced by the Latin American countries. What can be solved by the ballot if it is known beforehand that the popular will is not respected, that it is always subject to what high Army officialdom determines? If elections are the road to solutions, that road is already closed to these nations, who are being pushed to the foot of the wall, without another road open but that of arms. This is the origin of the guerrillas.

Miguel Angel Asturias
(Guatemalan, Nobel prize for literature, 1967)

16

at the foot of the wall

THERE IS only one door to justice and progress in Guatemala: an integral agrarian reform. It was for this reason that the Alliance for Progress Charter stipulated certain conditions for Latin American countries to receive continued United States aid, primary among them: an integral agrarian reform and a reform of tax structures (both closely related). Guatemala has so far been unwilling to effect either of these reforms and it is doubtful that she will do so in the foreseeable future for reasons that will be underscored here.

The problem rests basically on the mentality of the landowners themselves. Their religio-cultural heritage does not permit them to admit that there exists a problem, let alone take effective measures to deal with it. Catholicism, especially

Latin American Catholicism, is imbued with a spirit of resignation that preaches "everyone in his place" and that one's
life condition is the result of God's Will. Not that the landowners are exceptionally religious people, but rather, that
Catholicism appears to give them, on a religious level, the
justification they need for the dehumanizing socio-economic
system that is Guatemala's. "Thou shalt not covet thy neighbor's goods" is effectively used by the landowners and the
wealthy in addressing themselves to the destitute to keep them
from becoming dissatisfied with their lot. Thus it was that the
Archbishop of Guatemala City could say to the poverty-
stricken people of La Limonada, one of Guatemala City's cardboard and tin barrios:

You, the humble ones of this colony, are the most cherished by me;
I was poor like you; you live in shacks like that of Bethlehem that
housed the Infant God, but you are happy because where there is
poverty, there is happiness.[1]

La Limonada is one of the numerous colonies that have sprung
up around Guatemala City in the ravines that encircle it. They
are called the "Crown of Thorns" and house the tens of thousands of landless peasants who have left the countryside and
have come to the city hoping for work, for a livelihood. Often
they have to turn to a life of crime or begging to stay alive,
and almost as often they fail at this.

When, in early 1968, *Time* magazine published a letter
from the authors referring to the misery of Guatemala's
masses, AGA demanded equal time and offered this rebuttal:

No human being has to be a priest to be on the side of the poor,
and Guatemala, under no circumstance, is the most impoverished
nation in the world, nor are we indifferent to wanting to improve
the conditions of our poor. The program "Against Poverty" of
President Johnson shows that many fellow citizens of Thomas Melville live in greater necessity and poverty than many Guatemalans.
We have here more than 417,344 owners of plantations and lands,

and if each one of these represents a family of five members, it signifies that more than half of our people own their own lands.[2]

Thus AGA, representative of the landowners' mentality, consoles itself that Guatemala is not the poorest country in the world, and that some United States citizens are worse off than some Guatemalan citizens, both facts that cannot be denied. But the cynicism of this defense can be seen in the claim that more than half of all Guatemalans are property owners, while there is no mention made of the extension of these holdings, nor whether they are sufficient for supporting a family. No recognition is made that only 7.3 percent of these holdings are legally inscribed, facilitating spontaneous expulsions and thefts. Therefore, when the newspapers report a lack of corn in Huehuetenango, on the western altiplano, with its corresponding hunger,[3] as they did in August of 1967, no relation is made to Guatemala's land tenure pattern. So too in Chiquimula, on the eastern altiplano, it was observed the same month that the "peasants want to give away their children in order to save them from hunger"[4] and the problem can be attributed to the "Will of God." Every year, as more corn has to be imported, and then rice, the basic cause of the problem is still ignored. For the first time in its history, Guatemala imported black beans in 1967,[5] thus winding up with a shortage of all three of the peasants' basic staples.

When someone describes the extent of the problem, he is promptly labeled a Communist and an agitator and becomes open game for rightwing terrorists or for the government itself. Ydígoras refused to allow the publication of a study that attributed 50,000 infant deaths a year to malnutrition, as a "Communist document."[6] When Doctor Moisés Behar, head of INCAP (Institute for Nutrition of Central America and Panama, financed by the OAS), made a declaration on the nutritional state of Guatemalans, he did so in Washington and not in Guatemala City: "The pre-Colombian Maya ate better than the people today."[7]

The question that presents itself then is, how can a problem be resolved that is not recognized as a problem by the very ones causing it? The answer, of course, is obvious: the solution to a given problem is effected by those who struggle under its weight. One must not wait for those who have intentionally created the problem in the first instance, to suddenly repent and solve it.

In a true democracy, the agrarian problem could be solved by electing a president and a congress who recognize the injustice of the existing situation and have the power to do something about it. But Guatemala bears only the facade of democracy, and therefore it is not difficult for 2.1 percent of the population, the wealthy landowners, to control and manipulate their fellow citizens who own insufficient lands and suffer from the consequent poverty. Even when a person such as Julio César Méndez Montenegro, who is progress-oriented, is successful in reaching the presidency, his ability to effect change is sharply limited. Méndez Montenegro was forced to operate under the restrictions imposed by a constitution drawn up by the Military government that preceded him, even though this constitution was declared illegitimate by the Fourth Juridical Congress of Guatemala, since it was "not a product of the popular will."[8]

Even before taking office, Méndez Montenegro's presidential power was curtailed by having to accept the guidelines laid down by the military as the *sine qua non* conditions for averting a coup. Miguel Angel Asturias, Méndez Montenegro's ambassador to France and winner of the Nobel Prize for Literature for 1967, says that:

a military manuever was to come out of the situation created by the Northamerican fondness . . . for the civilian candidate (Méndez Montenegro) . . . in what was a virtual ultimatum that was presented to Méndez Montenegro consisting of five points: 1) a promise not to change any of the military commands; 2) leave everything related to the military in the exclusive jurisdiction of the Minister of Defense; 3) maintain the prohibition against allowing exiled military men to return to the country; 4) promise not to investigate the activities of the military government; 5) failure to fulfill any of these points would automatically provoke a military coup.[9]

Once in office, Méndez Montenegro immediately began to demonstrate his puppet status by visiting all the main military bases in the country where he publicly acknowledged his respect for the Army and his willingness to uphold the Armed Forces' "duty and right to safeguard the Constitution."

It is no secret in Guatemala that the Army and the police (under military control) hold the political power of that country. The uneasy, but mutually beneficial, alliance that exists between the Armed Forces and the oligarchy enables the 2.1 percent to rule over, or overrule, the rest of the population. The officer corps is made up mostly of aspiring members of the middle sectors who would like to take their place among the ruling class before or after retirement from the military establishment. It is in their best interest to cooperate with the people who can facilitate that process.

The uneasiness of the power alliance comes from the civilians' inability to judge the extent of influence a given officer wields within the armed forces. The alliances and counter-alliances make the military far from the monolithic structure that some outsiders seem to think it is. Thus it was indispensable for Méndez Montenegro to visit each commander throughout the country and proclaim his respect for each one of them personally and not confine himself to talking to his Minister of Defense. The President's condition of dependency on the military was obvious to the public who observed him making his visits around the country, a .45 calibre pistol strapped to his hip, while the Minister of Defense, Col. Arriaga Bosque, was just two steps behind, watching every one Méndez Montenegro spoke to. The macabre joke was made, not without subsequent evidence of truth, that the .45 pistol was carried by Méndez Montenegro more to protect himself from Arriaga Bosque and his friends, than from any wild-eyed assassin.

But the alliances within the armed forces, based on what

is commonly called *personalismo* (personal relationships rather than ideological ones), can be used by a clever politician to his advantage. Méndez Montenegro, while certainly not a clever politician, was able to take advantage of a political blunder and, counting on the competing loyalties within the military establishment, to rid himself of its apparently strongest bloc and his biggest threat.

This blunder was the kidnapping of Archbishop Mario Casariego in March, 1968, which was seen by the Guatemalan people as obvious collusion between the right-wing terrorists and the army. The army and police had immediately accused the left-wing guerrillas but this was popularly viewed as a smoke screen. It was not hard to guess who was responsible, it was only a question of their motivation.

Mario Monteforte Toledo[10] says that there were three reasons for the kidnapping of the Archbishop: Casariego did not align himself with the Liberation Party and the privileges of the wealthy, as did his predecessor, Archbishop Rossell; Casariego had not lent himself to the antiCommunist campaign, nor to condemning guerrillas as if they were the only ones responsible for the deplorable national conditions; and most importantly, the kidnapping would produce an outpouring of public revulsion and thus the citizens, expressing their lack of confidence in Méndez Montenegro, could have publicly demanded a military coup that would then have been easily executed.[11]

The plan backfired for several reasons. Church authorities remained calm and asked the country to do likewise. Archbishop Casariego is not a popular man in Guatemala, and even among the clergy, the kidnapping was greeted with more bemusement than outrage.

The right-wing terrorist-military collusion was confirmed after a few days when it was discovered that the archbishop had been held prisoner in the home of the former secretary of information of the Castillo Armas government, Dr. Carlos Cifuentes Díaz. Furthermore, any doubts that may have lingered were dissipated when the Minister of Defense refused to

heed Méndez Montenegro's request to cut short his visit to the
United States and return home. Arriaga Bosque was visiting
the Pentagon and other U.S. military installations[12] where
Guatemalans were training, making public statements denying his relationship to right-wing extremist groups.[13] He prolonged his visit five days beyond Casariego's kidnapping and
in effect told the President that he would return only when the
army requested it, and not as Minister of Defense, but as head
of a new military government.

Méndez Montenegro moved fast. Congress censured the
Vice President, Marroquín Rojas, a staunch backer of Arriaga
Bosque and a vociferous defender of right-wing terrorism, for
his editorials justifying the kidnapping. Then Méndez Montenegro sought and obtained promises of support from various
quarters, reportedly the Air Force, the Mariscal Zavala Brigade in the capital and Colonel Chinchilla Aguilar, the Minister of Education. He checked out his plans with the U.S.
Embassy, and finally confronted the three men who were most
often linked to the right-wing extremists: Colonel Rafael
Arriaga Bosque, as Minister of Defense was responsible for
the indiscriminate arrests and executions perpetrated by the
army; Colonel Carlos Arana Osorio made efficient use of
terrorist bands against purported guerrilla sympathizers in the
Zacapa area; Colonel Manuel Sosa Avila was accountable for
the hundreds of arrested citizens who could not be located in
any police detention center.

From the day he was sworn into office, the President had
found these three men to be his most powerful opponents on
the right and the watchdogs of his administration. When the
Liberation Party issued a repeated call to the country to join
the "national crusade in order to demonstrate to the Castroite
subversives that the government, the people and the army,
have joined to form a single combat force,"[14] the true meaning
was only vaguely hidden:

In view of the government's indolence in confronting with decision
the challenge of the armed rebels, and in view of the lenience of

the courts in judging them, diverse sections of the citizenry, reacting justifiably to the growing leftist offensive, have spontaneously organized themselves, have adopted a posture of self-defense, and have begun to respond to the enemy with the same arms and the same tactics.[15]

It had been openly commented on by both the radio and the press that the army and police forces were involved in the right-wing terrorist activities sponsored by various antiCommunist groups. The relationship could hardly be hidden; why else the law of amnesty passed as the final act of Peralta's Congress "for all members of the army, all policemen and their superiors, for those acts committed in the repression of subversive activities?"[16] Arriaga Bosque himself came close to admitting the relationship in December, 1966, when he stated that he was "grateful to the public for their help in fighting Communism" but added that he could not make deals with these secret organizations since this was "prohibited by the Constitution."[17] The kidnapping of Archbishop Casariego, however, was just one act, although the most blatant, in a whole series of subversive and murderous right-wing activities that could not have been accomplished without the cooperation of military and police authorities.

The President supported by Chinchilla Aguilar and the U.S. Embassy, told the trio he was removing them from their posts, but he offered them compensations: they could pick any of several diplomatic posts. Arriaga Bosque decided to accept the post of Guatemalan Consul in Miami and Arana Osorio became Ambassador to Nicaragua. Both places are centers for Latin American intrigue and plots, the temporary homes for political exiles from many nations. Arriaga Bosque made a last effort to save himself appealing to the armed forces to "remain united in their fight against Communism."[18] The ploy did not work and no one rallied to his side. Méndez Montenegro, in an attempt to salvage some of the tarnished image of the military, explained the changes as "democratic removals" that occur regularly within the armed forces.[19] No one was deceived.

Colonel Chinchilla Aguilar was then elevated to the position of the country's number one strong-man, replacing Arriaga Bosque as Minister of Defense. Not long afterwards, the newspapers were commenting on the fact that Chinchilla Aguilar was Méndez Montenegro's choice as the P.R.'s presidential candidate for the 1970 election. It was also said that he was favored by the U.S. Embassy. It looked as if Méndez Montenegro had built himself an alliance within the military that would give him greater powers over his government's policies.

The seeming ascendancy of the president over the military was short-lived, however. By November, Col. Carlos Arana Osorio, speaking from Nicaragua, was announcing that he was the Liberation Party's candidate for the presidency in the 1970 elections.[20] He had been in Nicaragua only eight months, but this was sufficient time to make some necessary alliances. Coincidentally, the same day as Arana's announcement, Méndez Montenegro visited the CONDECA headquarters (Central American Defense Command) and was quoted as saying: "Central Americanism is not just a platitude, but a reality."[21]

CONDECA had ostensibly been established to facilitate cooperative military training exercises and to coordinate an appropriate military response in case of a foreign invasion. Its efforts were more concerned with internal security, however, and it was acknowledged that the participating governments would aid one another in case the pacification of the citizens of one or other nation was more than the respective government could handle. Said Guatemala's Minister of Defense, Col. Chinchilla Aguilar,[22] when he was named President of CONDECA in July, 1968:

CONDECA embraces not only actions that are purely military for the defense of democratic institutions of our countries, the maintenance of our territorial integrity, independence and liberty, but it also involves the maintenance of an environment of peace and security that will permit the respective governments and inhabitants to begin (sic) the development of economic, social and cultural programs.[23]

CONDECA, then, is really an international police force meant to be used to keep the citizens of Central America in line. Not that such a force would actually be deployed physically, except in case of extraordinary need, but rather because the psychological advantage gained by such a threat is very real and should not be underestimated. Individuals or groups who are political fugitives from the internal security forces of their own country realize that if they are captured in a neighboring country, their fate is no more apt to be determined by legal considerations than if they were back home. Thus it is that the international alliances established among the individual military commanders of Central America (also based on *personalismo*) are certainly secondary to the domestic alliances, yet do play an important role in determining the political standing of a particular officer in his native country.

It is only in the light of these military alliances, especially with the armed forces of the Somoza family, that Arana's ambassadorship to Nicaragua and his subsequent political comeback can be understood. Méndez Montenegro's statement, on the day Arana's candidacy was announced, contained a bitter core of truth for the president: "Central Americanism is not just a platitude, but a reality."

Arriaga Bosque went to Miami. Aviateca, the Guatemalan national airline, has two flights a week to Miami. It is a good place to be if one has to be out of the country and wants to maintain close contacts. Hundreds of thousands of Cuban exiles float around Miami, dreaming of going back to their fatherland some day, ready and willing to cooperate with anyone who might facilitate the undertaking. Many of them were trained for the Bay of Pigs invasion in Guatemala and are friends and acquaintances of Arriaga Bosque. Many others have invested in Guatemala what they were able to get out of Cuba. General Wessin y Wessin was there too, an old anti-Communist fighter from the Dominican Republic, exiled from his country on much the same basis as Arriaga, preparing to go back as the presidential candidate of his country's right-wing forces. Roberto Alejos, accused of implication in the kidnapping of Archbishop Casariego and owner of the Helvetia plantation (training ground for the Cuban invasion troops), hand picked successor of Ydígoras for the presidency, also spends much time in Miami as principal stockholder of one of the city's main banks. Arriaga Bosque's desire to be Guatemalan consul in Miami was not an idle one.

Such a view of the military-political alliances of Central America and the Caribbean also lends perspective to the visit of the top brass of CONDECA to Miami in March, 1969.[24] Present were General Doroteo Reyes Santa Cruz, who replaced Chinchilla Aguilar as Minister of Defense in Guatemala; Colonel Florencio Iraheta of Salvador; Colonel Samuel Cárcamo from Nicaragua; and Colonel José de la Cruz Hernández of Honduras. Ostensibly, the reunion was for the purpose of pinning a medal on Col. Enrique Peralta Azurdia, former military dictator in Guatemala, for "his extraordinary and relevant contribution to the common defense and military solidarity of Central America."[25] It would have been more proper that Col. Peralta Azurdia receive his medal in Guatemala or in some other Central American city, except perhaps that some of the participants in the meetings in Miami were not Central Americans, and their presence in Central America would have made foreign involvement even more obvious than having CONDECA travel to the United States.

Be that as it may, two months after the meeting, Colonel Arana Osorio was beginning his political campaign in Guatemala with the self-confidence of a man already elected. Roberto Alejos had withdrawn his candidacy for PID in favor of Arana Osorio in order to form an "alliance of all the anti-Communist and patriotic sectors of the nation." The mistake of

1966 was not to be repeated. Arana lashed out at the Revolutionary Party and blamed them for dragging their feet on suppression of the guerrillas.[26] Daily, his pronouncements on sundry subjects were repeated in full detail in the press. One day he was condemning the new immorality of motion pictures and the next he was announcing that the MLN and the PID would co-sponsor the bill in Congress for the exoneration of export duties on coffee.

The real measure of Arana's new power was soon demonstrated. His old nemesis, Colonel Chinchilla Aguilar, had already been sent into political exile as Ambassador to Spain, when Arana came back to Guatemala. On June 11, 1969, the Liberation candidate visited the President, accompanied by many of his high-level backers. After an hour alone with Méndez Montenegro (his retinue waited in the foyer), the Colonel told reporters: "We exchanged impressions in order to find a formula that would permit the coming elections to take place in a climate of peace and tranquility."[27]

The next day it became clear what the climate consisted of. The Liberation Party sent a declaration to the newspapers:

The MLN views with sorrow the increase of negative forces which, aided by the little efficacy or total lack of it, on the part of the authorities charged with maintaining order and security, frightens the citizenry preparing for the 1970 elections. If these groups continue in this destructive and discouraging work, the citizenry itself will have to take into its own hands the means of self protection and then Guatemala will enter the worst of anarchies.[28]

The Liberation Party's accusations of lack of efficacy in supressing the guerrillas and left-wing terrorists were aimed at the Minister of the Interior, Mansilla Pinto. It was he that Arana was referring to in his first attack on the government and it was he that the Colonel had demanded be replaced in his meeting with the President on June 11. There were immediate rumors throughout the capital that Mansilla Pinto was out and that none other than Colonel Manuel Sosa Avila was back in power, not as head of the national police, but now as Minister of the Interior.

Mansilla Pinto had been a target of the right-wing extremists since his appointment. The Mano Blanca, one of the many right-wing terrorist organizations, but one whose connections to the police department were particularly strong, published a flier stating:

Is not President Méndez Montenegro responsible for what happens when his Minister of the Interior is shown to have obvious sympathies for Communism and is completely incapable of fulfilling his obligations? Licenciado Mansilla Pinto is undermining the stability of the government with his incompetence and it is absurd to think that the Revolutionary Party is not aware of the dissatisfaction and lack of tranquility that is noticeable among the people.[29]

The publication went on to state what it believed to be the proper attitude of the Minister of Interior or any other government official:

The question that the MANO poses is this: On which side is the Revolutionary Party? A third position will not help to solve the problem. Either one aids the Communists or one is against them. This bloody situation, this war unto death, will only terminate when one of the two bands in this struggle triumphs completely over the other.[30]

When, only three days after Arana's visit, the private secretary of the President announced the appointment of Colonel Sosa Avila as the new Minister of Interior, he qualified the change of Ministers as a "routine appointment in a democratic system,[31] reminiscent of the very words used a year before when Col. Sosa Avila and his two companions had first been fired.

The new Minister took office promising to do all in his power to establish law and order. He denied any connections with right-wing terrorist groups, but not everyone believed him. The University Students Association protested the appointment.[32] And in Miami and Washington, Cuban exiles were openly jubilant about what they referred to as "our first coup."

This, then, is the democracy of Guatemala: The sovereignty, the liberty and the freedom of Guatemala are the sovereignty, the liberty and the freedom of the Guatemalan army and oligarchy. Whoever is on top in the armed forces is also on top in the country. Is it correct to talk about the military being the guardian of the country's constitutionality when it has thrown out two constitutions in the last 16 years and rewritten them to suit its purposes and those of the oligarchy?

It is no wonder that Méndez Montenegro felt that it was quite a feat for him to finish his term. This he was able to accomplish because he did what he was told. He did nothing serious enough to anger a sufficient number of the army officer corps or the ruling class.

Any interested observer, sympathetic to the plight of the Guatemalan peasants, cannot avoid wondering what will be the resolution of this centuries-old conflict of values and needs. The oligarchy has virtually all the economic power, all the political power and all the physical power (represented by the armed forces and the police) that is needed to control the peasants' lives. They also have a high degree of intellectual, cultural and spiritual control over the *campesinos,* which is maintained by denying them an adequate educational system, by constantly insisting that the Maya recognize his "natural inferiority," and by cynically using the teachings of the Catholic Church to justify poverty, misery and injustice.

There are indications, however, that the vice-like grip is finally being loosened, as the educational processes begun by the social developments under the Arévelo and Arbenz governments penetrate deeper and deeper into the national consciousness, aided by the proliferation of transistor radios that tune in with equal facility "Radio Habana, Cuba" or the "Voice of America." The politicization created by the insurgency and counter-insurgency struggle, the awakening social-conscience in some members of the Church, and the alarm caused in some segments of the population as they see this fratricidal conflict and attempt to explain its causes, are also playing a significant role. The peasants are learning that they have certain inalienable rights that have in fact been alienated and that are not going to be obtained and retained without some kind of struggle.

In the 1970 election campaign this fact was acknowledged by all three presidential candidates: Mario Fuentes Pieruccini of the PR, Jorge Lucas Caballeros of the DCG, and Carlos Arana Osorio of the MLN–PID.

Mario Fuentes Pieruccini began slowly by tramping through the countryside promising every citizen a pair of shoes, a new health campaign to eliminate common peasant sicknesses and the suppression of the *mecapal* (the leather or fiber band that goes across the forehead and is used to support one-hundred pound cargo weights on peasant backs). He also promised:

My government will give land to the peasants: to every peasant who is interested in cultivating and producing more. But we will not take lands away from private owners, because this would amount to "stripping one saint's statue to dress another."[33]

When he went to Zacapa and was met by thousands of peasants who had been firsthand witnesses of Arana Osorio's counter-insurgency tactics, he told his listeners:

The Revolutionary Party has been decimated here in the eastern part of the country. We have learned with pain and sorrow how they tried to erase from the map all of us who have been struggling peacefully since 1944 for a dynamic revolution, but they made a mistake here, in Izabal, Chiquimula and Jutiapa.[34]

In Quiché, Fuentes Pieruccini told his assembled audience that he would establish a new cabinet post: Attorney General for Mayan Affairs.[35] In this office there would be twenty-two accredited assistants, each one of whom would speak one of the twenty-two distinct indigenous tongues, and who would be in direct communication with the new president. But as the campaign progressed, Fuentes Pieruccini emphasized the theme of agrarian reform:

We will take steps to end the abuses that thousands of you suffer each year when you go to work on the plantations, living there for several months in terrible conditions, only to return home with a few cents and malaria . . . With the highways we are building, we are going to open up huge extensions of lands that we will give out to the peasants and other farmers who want them.[36]

A few weeks later, the official party candidate was quoted as saying: "What is Guatemala's biggest problem? It is that there are many men asking for lands, and much land asking for men."[37] But conscious of the furor being created by the Christian Democratic candidate who was advocating agrarian reform in much more militant terms and of Arana Osorio who was just as militantly opposed to it, Fuentes Pieruccini clarified exactly what he meant by agrarian reform: "My government will give land to everyone who wants land, even if it means that we have to buy land so that every peasant can be a landowner."[38]

Fuentes Pieruccini was in a bind. The mystique of the electoral campaign of his predecessor, Julio César Méndez Montenegro, had been the 1944 revolution and agrarian reform. After four years in the presidency, when Méndez Montenegro listed the accomplishments of his regime, he had not been able to mention land reform.[39] He could not because a PR controlled congress passed a law in August, 1969, assuring *latifundismo* in the Petén lands which were to be distributed by the incoming government. It was not easy for Fuentes Pieruccini to campaign on this same platform, and his attempts to do so left him open to severe criticism by his opponents. Jorge Lucas Caballeros, running under the banner of the Christian Democrats, said:

All of us candidates should be very clear on this point and tell the people exactly what we mean by 'agrarian reform'. More than five centuries ago, the first word to be heard when this continent was discovered was: LAND, LAND, and our peasants are still waiting for land. Many try to fool the peasants by giving out small plots at a pace that won't guarantee our peasants land until the year 2100, when other men will be cultivating the moon and Mars. No! We will make the political decision to effect a complete and rapid agrarian reform, with the object of increasing the productivity of the peasant by means of a redistribution of the land, water rights, technical assistance and credits . . .[40]

As Lucas Caballeros repeated the message again and again, making land reform his first priority, he created much apprehension among his opponents. He had taken over Fuentes Pieruccini's issue and the latter had no solid platform to stand on.

Arana Osorio, running on a "law and order" platform with the backing of the military and oligarchy, began to charge the Christian Democrats with "Communism" and to denounce Lucas Caballeros for his willingness to plunge the country into bloodshed. A group of Arana's adherents published their leader's viewpoints on the land issue and tried to twist the meaning of the DCG's approach:

While Señor Lucas offers radical and violent change in order to fool the people, Colonel Arana promises stability and reform. Stability means that the peasant who has land, some irrigation, pasture, or a small home, will be guaranteed that he will continue to own it, and that he can count on getting easy credit from Arana's government.[41]

With the issues of Communism and violence introduced into the campaign, accusations of similar nature increased in number and stridency with every passing day. Lucas Caballeros maintained that:

Under the present government, the attitudes of the PR and the MLN have been identical. Thus it is that a new system of government was implanted: to govern with the aid of bands of outlaws which are established, patronized and protected by the official powers-that-be. These bands were the creation of the PR as much as of the MLN. It does not matter if they are called the *Mano Blanca* or the *Centurions,* because all of them, whether organized by the PR or the MLN, were created under the eye of the government and with its help: irresponsibly distributing arms among them, giving them carte blanche to kidnap, threaten, torture and assassinate all those who do not agree with the government, amassing a toll of victims which in other Latin American countries would be considered unspeakable. More than 6,000 Guatemalans assassinated in two years is really genocide, and both Parties are equally responsible, especially their leaders.[42]

Arana Osorio defended himself by maintaining that everything he had done in the northeast had been at the orders of Méndez Montenegro:

as an Army officer, I received an order from the President of the Republic, in his capacity as Commander-in-chief of the Army, to fulfill and make others fulfill the Constitution in the northeastern area of the country, which, as everyone knows, was dominated by a subversive group.[43]

Arana acknowledged that the subversion was not all due to "Communist agitation," as he had previously maintained:

Subversive movements which attempt to alter democratic institutions are not dissolved only by bullets. Subversive movements such as we were facing *are also a problem of hunger* (emphasis Arana's) —a problem of injustice that has accumulated over a long period of time—it is the problem of desperation in the face of a life of misery and suffering, since our countrymen live in a world apart, which is sometimes primitive; civilization and progress have not yet come to them, nor has the constructive action of the government.[44]

But Arana was not going to limit himself to a defensive position. On the day preceding the above statement, the MLN had denounced the Christian Democrats as a front party for the FAR:

We affirm that the coalition PGT-URD[45] and its armed branch, the FAR, are the same ones who dominate, direct and decide all and each one of the actions of the "Front-Party", the Christian Democratic Party and its candidates—from their political indoctrination, their preparation of histrionics, to their frightening plans for violence and the alteration of our institutions.[46]

Arana himself made his final major public appearance in the capital city of Zacapa, and spoke to 15,000 people who knew him well:

Four years ago I was a military attaché in Washington, and I used to read in the news about Guatemala being bathed in blood. It was on June 16 that God wanted me to come to Zacapa to receive my military command. The situation then was very difficult, but I found strong hearts, and even more important, I found 'pants' (slang for manliness) and we fought subversion together . . . Now you have three alternatives to choose from, *continuismo* (a continuation of PR policies), *comunismo* (he referred to the Christian Democrats), or liberty by means of a national solution (he meant the MLN-PID, his own party).[47]

Arana ran a more effective campaign than his two opponents. He managed to line up a running mate of impeccable oligarchic credentials, Eduardo Cáceres Lenhoff, and he managed to stay above many of the accusations of political chicanery. Both Lucas Caballeros and Fuentes Pieruccini hurt themselves and each other with recriminating statements. The PR said it would bring Lucas Caballeros to trial immediately after the elections for a coffee sale scandal involving millions of dollars during the Ydígoras government when the DCG's candidate had been Minister of Finance. Lucas Caballeros vehemently denied the accusations, but was never able to explain adequately how he survived Peralta Azurdia's coup as one of the few holdovers from the Ydígoras cabinet. Lucas Caballeros tried to turn the coffee issue against Fuentes Pieruccini by demanding publicly that:

The government of the PR must clarify the coffee affair before a competent tribunal. They have been in office four years and they have not clarified it. If they have not done it, it is because those responsible are precisely those who now support the official party.[48]

The daily accusations of an impending electoral fraud to be perpetrated by the PR and the President were countered by inviting three OAS observers to watch the election proceedings.

Assaults, kidnappings and assassinations occurred with increasing frequency and aided the law and order candidate. The MLN candidate for mayor of Guatemala City, David Guerra Guzmán, who was also a member of Congress, was assassinated in downtown Guatemala City.[49] A leading newspaper editor, Izidoro Zarco, who was actively backing the MLN and accusing the DCG of Communism, was also assassinated.[50] A shootout in the capital between members of the PR and the MLN left a total of three dead (one of them a PR candidate for Congress), and two wounded, and an accusation of murder against an MLN congressman and that party's secretary general.[51]

Three days before the elections, a young man, Vicente Girón Calvillo, was kidnapped on a downtown Guatemala street.[52] Witnesses claimed that plainclothes police were responsible but the police denied any knowledge of the incident.[53] The next day, Fuentes Mohr, the government's Minister of Foreign Relations, was kidnapped by the FAR who said they would exchange him for Girón Calvillo.[54] The government made repeated public broadcasts requesting information on the whereabouts of Girón Calvillo, claiming they had no knowledge of his kidnapping. But government officials feared the guerrillas might kill the foreign minister, so Girón Calvillo was "found" in an isolated prison in Baja Verapaz and was sent off to political asylum in Mexico. A U.S. newspaper reported that:

The kidnapping of Fuentes Mohr laid bare the fact that Guatemala's counter-intelligence forces had, in effect, kidnapped and secreted Girón Calvillo in a remote prison without public announcement and without bringing him before a magistrate.[55]

But Guatemalans are accustomed to this type of event, and when one of the intermediaries in the exchange of Fuentes Mohr for Girón Calvillo was himself, together with his sister, kidnapped by the secret police the very next day, the FAR responded by abducting the United States labor attaché and thereby brought about another successful exchange.[56]

It was in this climate that the electorate went to the polls on March 1, 1970, and gave Colonel Carlos Arana Osorio 42.9 percent of the votes cast, a total of 234,625.[57]

It is not an easy task to interpret this vote in the light of the present political climate and the voting procedures in Guatemala. According to the 1964 census there were 2,054,304 citizens eighteen years and older.[58] Eighteen is the minimum voting age. For the March 1, 1970 elections, "about 1,150,000 citizens" were registered to vote according to the official electoral registrar.[59] Of these, only 46 percent voted. Calculating on projected 1970 population totals, 9.6 percent of the adult population voted for Arana Osorio, 8 percent for Fuentes Pieruccini (194,798 votes), and 4.8 percent for Lucas Caballeros (116,-865 votes).

The claim of U.S. political scientists, that an interpretation of Guatemala's voting pattern is feasible, is put in doubt when one realizes that many of the "colonos" are told how to vote if they want to keep their jobs on the plantations, that the ballot for illiterates is not secret, that votes are bought and sold with impunity, and that the peasants who vote do not split their ticket but vote on the basis of local candidates for mayor. The conclusion of the three OAS observers can certainly be challenged: "The elections in Guatemala give us hope for the future of democracy in Latin America and are a lesson for many countries."[60]

Immediately after the elections, although the secondary election by Congress to legally make him president was still pending, Arana Osorio promised that he would not take revenge on his political opponents. This, of course, was encouraging news for Lucas Caballeros, Fuentes Pieruccini and their respective adherents. It was hardly so for Guatemala's disinherited masses. Arana's promise of "stability" was threat enough which spelled only further degradation for them.

NOTES

1 *El Imparcial,* February 24, 1967.
2 *Prensa Libre,* February 29, 1968.
3 *El Imparcial,* August 8, 1967.
4 *Ibid.,* August 28, 1967.
5 *Ibid.,* November 11, 1967.
6 *Ibid.,* January 6, 1964.
7 *Ibid.,* June 27, 1968.
8 *Ibid.,* September 21, 1966.
9 Miguel Angel Asturias, *Latino América y Otros Ensayos,* Madrid: Guadiana de Publicaciones, 1968, p. 49.
10 Monteforte Toledo was the president of Congress in the government of Juan José Arévalo.
11 CIDOC, *Document 68/61,* Cuernavaca, Mexico, 1968.
12 *El Imparcial* March 13, 1968.
13 *Washington Star,* March 15, 1968.
14 *El Gráfico,* May 16, 1967.
15 *Ibid.*
16 *El Imparcial,* April 28, 1966.
17 *Ibid.,* December 12, 1966.
18 *Ibid.,* March 29, 1968.
19 *Ibid.,* April 9, 1968.
20 *Ibid.,* November 29, 1968.
21 *Ibid.*
22 Previous Minister of Education.
23 *El Imparcial,* July 1, 1968.
24 *Ibid.,* March 13, 1969.
25 *Ibid.*
26 *Ibid.,* May 12, 1969.
27 *Ibid.,* June 12, 1969.
28 *Ibid.,* June 13, 1969.
29 CIDOC, *Dossier #21,* Cuernavaca, Mexico, 1968, p. 4/283.

30 *Ibid.*
31 *Prensa Libre,* June 16, 1969.
32 *Ibid.,* June 17, 1969.
33 *Ibid.,* November 15, 1968.
34 *Ibid.,* December 1, 1969.
35 *Ibid.,* January 12, 1970.
36 *Ibid.,* January 19, 1970.
37 *Ibid.,* February 2, 1970.
38 *Ibid.,* February 23, 1970.
39 *Ibid.,* February 26, 1970.
40 *Ibid.,* February 11, 1970.
41 *Ibid.,* February 2, 1970.
42 *Ibid.,* February 18, 1970.
43 *Ibid.,* February 20, 1970.
44 *Ibid.*
45 Partido Guatemalteco del Trabajo and Unidad Democratica Revolucionaria—supposedly a Communist coalition, which in fact does not exist.
46 *Prensa Libre*, February 19, 1970.
47 *Ibid.,* February 23, 1970. (Parentheses are the authors'.)
48 *Ibid.,* January 28, 1970.
49 *Ibid.,* December 18, 1969.
50 *Ibid.,* January 29, 1970.
51 *Ibid.,* February 26, 27 and 28, 1970
52 *Ibid.,* February 27, 1970.
53 *Ibid.,* February 28, 1970.
54 *Ibid.*
55 *The Washington Star*, March 2, 1970.
56 *Prensa Libre*, March 7, 1970.
57 *Ibid.,* March 3, 1970.
58 División General de Estadística, Ministerio de Economía, *Algunas Características de la Población de Guatemala, 1964.* Guatemala: September, 1968, p. 9.
59 *Prensa Libre*, February 27, 1970.
60 *Ibid.,* March 4, 1970.

It is this influential nucleus of aggressive, ambitious professional military leaders who are the root of American evolving militarism . . . Civilians can scarcely understand or even believe that many ambitious military professionals truly yearn for wars and the opportunity for glory and distinction afforded only in combat . . . Most military people know very little about Communism . . . Defeating "aggression" is a gigantic combat-area competition rather than a crusade to save the world from Communism.

General David M. Schoup
Former Commandant, U.S. Marine Corps

17

opportunity for glory

JOHN F. KENNEDY, in announcing the establishment of the Alliance for Progress, stated: "Those who make peaceful revolution impossible, make violent revolution inevitable." It is obvious that the large landowners, who have resisted integral development in the structures of Guatemala for over four centuries, are not going to change unless someone obliges them to do so. It is also obvious that the long-suffering peasants, who have borne the burden of the day's heat these many years, can no longer afford to accept the quiescence of ages past, as demographic pressures race in tandem with their awakening sense of awareness. Yet it is the policy of the Guatemalan governing elite to attempt to control these pressures and to detour this consciousness. Just as in the days of

Castillo Armas, he who favors meaningful land reform is branded a Communist sympathizer and is ostracized; and he who would dare to actually work for land reform is said to bear the mark of Satan himself on his soul and often does bear the marks of self-proclaimed avenging adversaries of the devil on his flesh. The landowners, in a word, make peaceful revolution impossible.

The military support of the oligarchic structure supplied by the Guatemalan airforce, army and police, is, by itself, insufficient to oppose and control the rising cries for justice that shatter the calm rural atmosphere. This was clearly demonstrated under Peralta Azurdia when the guerrilla bands were able to operate almost with impunity in the Zacapa and Izabal areas. They conducted literacy classes for children and adults, held public meetings to discuss the ills of Guatemalan society and the method of obtaining the political power necessary to cure them. They would also challenge the local soccer teams to games that were often attended by hundreds of people. Most importantly, they settled land disputes in favor of the peasants. These accomplishments often meant staying in one locale, two or three days at a time—a very effective demonstration of confidence in the peasants and disrespect for the national government and its security forces.

The army is perhaps Central America's best, as is also its air force, the former made up of from eight to twelve thousand troops and the latter composed of 500 men. Accurate figures on the police force are hard to come by because of the twilight zone within which many of them operate. Press reports acknowledge the creation of 1,500 new police positions in 1967 and another 2,000 in 1968. From these figures it is possible to estimate that the police department has at least as much personnel as the army. These totals do not seem excessive in a nation of five million people, but it must be remembered that their primary and almost exclusive duty is internal security and not national sovereignty. Yet, their numbers have not been sufficient in the past and they will become less so with every passing year. A remedy, however, has been provided for this deficiency, paradoxically by the very government that suggests basic changes be made in the power structure of the nation: the United States of America. And the United States president who foresaw the inevitability of violent revolution where peaceful revolution is rendered impossible, himself initiated the program called "counterinsurgency" that not only makes peaceful revolution impossible but assures an ever increasing level of violence in any attempted reform.

The program is ostensibly based on the following premises: all insurgents are Communists or Communist-dupes; all Communists or Communist-dupes are the sworn enemies of the U.S.; all sworn enemies must be defeated because they constitute a threat to U.S. national sovereignty. We must look deeper, however, for the real rationale of United States foreign policy, because this equation is too simplistic for the educated policy-makers of the United States government.

The United States has had for decades a very special interest in Central America, and Guatemala is the heart of Central America. Since the U.S. became a naval power in the last century, one president after another has given protectorate status to the Caribbean, and that much abused concept of international power politics, "sphere of influence," has nowhere been applied with such aggressiveness as by the United States in the Central American-Caribbean area. From 1900 to the present, the United States has engaged in "twenty-eight military actions"[1] and of these, eighteen have been invasions of Central American and Caribbean nations; this total does not include such CIA projects as the Arbenz overthrow or the Bay of Pigs invasion. Central to this interest, of course, is the Panama Canal, begun when President Theodore Roosevelt aided an independence movement which resulted in Panama separating itself from Colombia in 1903.

Since that time, Central America has proved to be a small but profitable market for United States investment:

Central America was one of the first areas of the World to attract extensive U.S. investment. Early investors were involved in mining and railroads. Later, large investments were made in agriculture, especially bananas, and after W.W.I investments were added in utilities, aviation, trade, insurance, banking and manufacturing. The Department of Commerce estimates that the total accumulated value of direct U.S. private investment in Central America at the end of 1963 was $375 million, with a market value slightly over $1 billion.[2]

The formation of the Central American Common Market in 1960 has enhanced the prospects for United States capital in the area. The Peter Grace company has bought up food-processing plants in Guatemala and owns large agricultural enterprises there; three U.S. cosmetics firms have located there and two new oil refineries involving an investment of over $13 million were recently built by two major United States companies. Foremost Company is the largest producer and retailer of milk, butter, cheese and ice-cream; International Nickel is in the process of investing $70 million in mining in the Izabal area; and Monsanto Chemical is mining sulphur in Alta Verapaz. All U.S. pharmaceutical firms that have gone into Central America in the last five years have located in Guatemala, and even as the United Fruit Company liquidates its land holdings in the Pacific Coast, it is opening up new areas for production in the central part of the country.

All these investors, now over 100 U.S. Companies, demand one thing: stability—

Political stability, not democracy, is the important criterion. The U.S. investor is not concerned with abstract political theory. Any government approximating or to the right of our own politically, is acceptable. The impressive record of 35 years of political and economic stability in Nicaragua under Somoza family rule proves a definite asset to its industrial promoters. In the last year, Guatemala has experenced a slowdown in the number of investments it is attracting relative to the other market partners and much of this decline is attributable to widely publicized government instability and guerrilla activity.[3]

Thus it is imperative that the United States defeat the "Communist aggression" posed by the Guatemalan masses, because if Guatemala goes, Honduras goes, El Salvador goes, and so forth.

General William Westmoreland, in his speech to the VIII Conference of American Armies in Rio de Janeiro on September 25, 1968, said:

I was pleased to accept this invitation because as military men, I believe that we, perhaps more than any other profession in the public service, recognize the immediate threat to the countries and people we serve that is posed by the sort of thing which is taking place today in Southeast Asia. We know that South Vietnam is a Communist laboratory. We know that if aggression under the guise of "national liberation" succeeds there, it is ready to be marketed.[4]

The General then proceeded to tell his listeners that "aggression under the guise of national liberation" will not only fail in Vietnam but will also fail in Latin America because the lessons of Vietnam will be marketed in Latin America, not by the guerrillas, but by the United States and the Latin American Armies.[5] The speech, of course, was consistent with what was and is the United States policy in Guatemala. In November, 1967, when United States Ambassador, John Gordon Mein, presented the Guatemalan Armed Forces with new armored vehicles, grenade launchers, training and radio equipment and several HU-1B jet powered helicopters, he publicly stated:

These articles, especially the helicopters, are not easy to obtain at this time since they are being utilized by our forces in defense of the cause of liberty in other parts of the world. But liberty must be defended wherever it is threatened and that liberty is now being threatened in Guatemala.[6]

Thus it should not have come as such a shocking surprise when Guatemalan rebels interpreted Ambassador Mein as they interpret their own officials when the latter talk of liberty, justice and democracy. They ask: whose liberty? whose justice? and whose democracy? and hear the answer booming in their daily lives. When Ambassador Mein was assassinated in August of 1968 by left-wing guerrillas, the United States characterized the killing as a "foul, cowardly act."[7]

The result of such a policy, including the thousands of deaths over the past four years, is to drastically distort the internal dynamics of Guatemalan society. These dynamics operate on a mass psychological level but their effects are very much social and physical. Thus it is that the landed oligarchy, assured of unlimited U.S. support to suppress "Communist guerrillas," makes no accommodations to the just claims of the insurgents, other than a socially insignificant military-civic action program aimed only at giving immediate short-range satisfaction to felt needs and thus temporarily removing insurgency incentives. It also means that the desperate social conditions that ordinarily would push a society toward insurgency and which would serve as a bellwether, are dampened and bottled up by the threat of overwhelming foreign intervention, producing a pressure-cooker effect instead. Arbenz's resignation might exemplify this dynamic. The third result has perhaps the most dangerous implications for both Guatemala and the United States: the insurgent who realizes that he not only faces his own oppressive government but also that of the United States, is obliged to make alliances that he might otherwise prefer to avoid. Castro's Cuba is an oft-cited example of a country backing into Moscow's lap because of the United States government's indiscriminate labeling of all insurgents, socialists and Marxists, as the professed enemies of the people of the United States who must be fought to the death.

The United States Embassy in Guatemala periodically denies the charges of taking sides in internal conflicts. It obviously is not telling the truth. In 1969, the Embassy maintained that only thirty-four members of the Special Forces were working in Guatemala. What this means is that on the day the announcement was made, there were at least thirty-four Special Forces Troops in Guatemala that the Embassy was willing to acknowledge publicly. The claim demands no more belief than Henry Cabot Lodge's statement in 1954: "the situation does not involve aggression but is a revolt of Guatemalans against Guatemalans,"[8] or the repeated denials of complicity in the training of Cuban rebels at Retalhuleu.

Guatemalans have other indications also: a Green Beret from Ohio, by the name of Hornberger, just returned from Vietnam in early 1966, made a mysterious trip to Washington in August of that same year and then left for Guatemala the following month telling his family that he was off to hunt Communists. Without any seemingly prior knowledge of the country, he evidently knew just where to go and what to look for. His body and that of a companion were finally recovered from guerrilla territory in January, 1967.[9] His apparent mission was the assassination of guerrilla leader Luis Turcios.

Major Bernie Westfall perished in September, 1967, in the crash of a Guatemalan airforce jet that he was piloting. The official notices stated that the U.S. airman was "testing" the airplane.[10] That statement may have been true, but it is also true that it was a common and public topic of conversation at Guatemala's Aurora Air Base that the Major often "tested" Guatemalan aircraft in strafing and bombing runs against guerrilla encampments in the Northeastern territory.

When Colonel John Webber and Lt. Commander Ernest Munro were assassinated in January, 1968, and two U.S. military advisors were wounded in the same attack, Colonel Manuel Sosa Avila, head of the national police, claimed that "the plot was hatched at last year's meeting of OLAS,* hosted by Castro in Havana."[11] Another "informed source" was quoted as saying that FAR had slain the Americans "to get into the limelight again and put pressure on Castro to extend more help."[12] This is the usual tack taken by the Guatemalan government and one that is guaranteed to get a reflex response from the U.S. Ambassador. Ignored was FAR's own reason for the killings: "The U.S. military mission is helping the Guate-

* Organization of Latin American Solidarity.

malan government in pursuing the guerrillas."[13] Colonel
Webber had gone to Guatemala as military attaché to the
Embassy as soon as Méndez Montenegro had taken over and
he immediately expanded the counterinsurgency forces, obtaining from the United States more jeeps, arms, helicopters, communications equipment and advisors. He made no secret of the
fact that it was his idea and at his instigation that the technique
of counterterror had been implemented by the Guatemalan
army in the Zacapa and Izabal areas. When the advisability of
arming civilian collaborators and paying them to kill Communists and "potential guerrillas" was questioned, Webber
had justified the tactic saying: "That's the way this country is.
The Communists are using everything they have, including
terror. And it must be met."[14]

In November of 1967, there was quite a squabble going on
between United States helicopter pilots and the Guatemalan
airforce. The Americans were being used by Guatemala's
Geodetic Survey under contract to AID to map all the jungle
areas of Petén and surrounding regions, and the Guatemalan
pilots felt that they should be given the job. All the U.S. pilots
were veterans of Vietnam and one of them confided to this
author: "If anything ever happens in this country, we'll know
the terrain better than the Guatemalans." The training, money
and arms used by rebels are always attributed to Castro, yet
the two outstanding leaders of the guerrilla movement, Yon
Sosa and Luis Turcios, were trained at Ft. Gulick and Ft.
Bragg, respectively. The guerrillas themselves claim that the
money obtained from local kidnappings is adequate enough for
rebel purposes and that it would be a dangerous tactic, un-
necessarily executed, to look to Moscow and Havana as additional sources of finances. The arms captured from rebel bands
are consistently of United States manufacture, indicating that
they are either captured from or given by the government
forces to the rebels. Both rebel bands have broken with and
denounced the Communist Party (PGT) and Moscow has declared its disfavor of them.

From May 27–31, 1968, the Southern Command Forces

of the United States stationed in Panama conducted joint military operations with the Nicaraguan and Guatemalan armies in the Department of Izabal, Yon Sosa's base of operations. The "training exercises," as they were so euphemistically called, were fittingly and officially designated as "Operation Hawk."[15] No one in the area failed to get the message.

The United States Embassy claims that every visit of General Robert Porter, Jr., or his successor, General George Mather, from United States Southern Command, is "routine."[16] They also state that all the Guatemalan officials trained in Ft. Gulick,[17] all the special police hired with Alliance for Progress funds (3,500 in 1967 and 1968), and the "model police programs" developed by AID consultor Peter Costello and implemented with AID money,[18] are no more than what is done by "similar United States missions in various Latin American countries."[19] According to Pentagon figures, "Guatemala received $2.2 million in military aid for the year 1967 and from $1 million to $3 million annually in the years since 1962 . . . Total civilian aid for 1967 was put at $3 million in grants . . . Of the grants, $625,000 was for training and equipping the police."[20] Yet the helicopters alone given by Ambassador Mein in 1967 were valued at more than $1.5 million. It may mean that the Department of Defense and the CIA do not inform the State Department of everything they do, nor what it costs them, since their finances and operations are not open to Congressional scrutiny. These facts and figures do not explain everything that occurs in Guatemala with a United States label on it. It may mean that the special missions of men like Hornberger, Westfall and Webber are not considered within the concept of ordinary military assistance. But then, how are we to explain the counterinsurgency base in Mariscos, Izabal?[21] or the unmarked C-47 filled with U.S. paratroopers which was forced down at Aurora?[22] or the presence of the Green Berets confirmed by the police chief,[23] or the participants in "Operation Hawk"?[24] or the special group of "Huey instructors who visited Guatemala recently"[25] and "trained" Guatemalan pilots? How does the U.S. government calculate the value of the three

HU-1B's "given" in 1967 by Ambassador Mein or the C-47's and the helicopters "donated" by Mein's successor, Ambassador Nathaniel Davis, in June and December, 1969? Is any account made of the five million dollars worth of arms left behind on Roberto Alejos's plantation after the CIA-trained Cuban rebels left?[26]

All these materials may not seem like an overpowering military force, but a very important concept is involved. The Guatemalan citizen who understands what is going on, be he of leftist or rightist political orientation, believes that even if the figures admitted by the State Department actually represented the truth, it would only be because such quantities and qualities are sufficient at this time for its purposes. Given the United States policy toward Guatemala (and the rest of Latin America) most inhabitants of that country recognize that all the assistance that their government needs to maintain stability (read *status quo*) both in men and arms, will be forthcoming from the United States.

And there is no reason for them to think otherwise, now that Richard M. Nixon is in the White House. His political career has been built on the championing of right-wing causes, and it is erroneous to think that his fears of "Communism" in Latin America will be any more sophisticated than his knowledge or appreciation of the dynamics of Vietnamese society (c.f. his speech on the history of the Vietnam War, November 3, 1969, on national television). The first foreign visitor welcomed to the White House after his inauguration was Galo Plaza, Secretary General of the OAS, former president of Ecuador, one of that country's largest landowners and ardent defender of the United Fruit operations in Latin America.[27]

After months of silence as regards his new Latin America policy, exemplified by the ill-advised and tumultuous Rockefeller "fact-finding mission," President Nixon broke his silence on October 31, 1969. The tone of his remarks indicated that his "new" policy was not so different from the old:

I would be less than honest if I did not express my concern over examples of liberty compromised, of justice denied, or rights infringed. Nevertheless, we recognize that enormous, sometimes explosive, forces for change are operating in Latin America. These create instabilities and bring changes in governments. On the diplomatic level, we must deal realistically with governments in the inter-American system as they are. We have, of course, a preference for democratic procedures, and we hope that each government will help its people to move forward toward a better, a fuller and a freer life.[28]

What President Nixon is in effect saying is that the United States government is not adverse to dealing with dictatorships even though it would "prefer" democratic procedures. To be sure that such a frank and public blessing of Latin American dictatorships not be misunderstood as an unqualified blessing of all dictatorships, the President immediately indicated that he excluded Cuba from his remarks; that Castro's government was one government in the inter-American system that would not be "dealt with realistically as it is":

In this connection, however, I would stress one other point. We cannot have a peaceful community of nations if one nation sponsors armed subversion in another's territory.[29]

It is doubtful that President Nixon was referring to the United States intervention in Guatemala in 1954, or in Cuba in 1961 (both prepared while he was Vice-president) or in the Dominican Republic in 1965. None of these can be called "subversion" since the interference was so open and massive. He was rather referring to the few Cubans involved in guerrilla activities in Venezuela and Bolivia. So it is that the United States government continues to accept the "examples of liberty compromised, of justice denied, of rights infringed," just so long as it is done in the name of a minority that exploits the majority. If the dictatorship is on the left, a dictatorship in the name of the impoverished majority, the United States will not tolerate it, because such a government would oppose the exploitative enterprises of United States business interests.

The President's speech came a few days prior to the official release of the Rockefeller Report, and was obviously based on many of Rockefeller's conclusions. Those parts of Nixon's speech already cited seem to portend some implementation of the recommendations for military aid to Latin American nations:

(a) Creation of a multi-national Western Hemisphere Security Council.
(b) Increase in U.S. military training grants.
(c) Provision of jeeps, helicopters, communications equipment and small arms for internal security support.
(d) Removal of congressional curbs to permit more sales of U.S. military equipment which otherwise will be purchased from other sources East or West.[30]

Rockefeller used the same rationale as that used for depriving the Vietnamese of their right of self-determination: "Forces of anarchy, terror and subversion are loose in the Americas. The subversive capabilities of these Communist forces are increasing."[31] When the governor of New York was asked by a reporter whether he was not offering a prescription for new Vietnams in Latin America, Rockefeller said that he found the analogy "utterly irrelevant."[32] The report, entitled "Quality of Life in the Americas," does in fact demonstrate that the reporter's analogy is very relevant as it gives more insight into Nixon's statement to the effect that the United States will not tolerate "export of revolution which is intervention."[33] Since it is impossible for a revolutionary movement to develop in the twentieth century without many involved persons having read Marx and been influenced by him, all revolutions are, by definition, "exports" and "interventions." And then there is the fact that practically all peasant societies, among them certainly the Maya, have had communal land-owning patterns and communistic value systems for thousands of years before the world ever heard of Karl Marx. Yet, this is equated to the International Communist conspiracy and therefore becomes the rationale for propping up the Latin military, even though they be antidemocratic. For as Rockefeller believes, "few Latin countries have the sufficiently advanced economic and social systems required to support a consistently democratic system."[34] So if the United States has to support antidemocratic governments, like that of Thieu and Ky in Vietnam, better it be in favor of the small minority that will look out for U.S. interests such as United Fruit, Grace and Texaco, rather than those governments of the left that will use their national resources for the benefit of all their own people. As a further palliative, trade concessions will also be granted by the U.S. which are intended to increase the gross national products of Latin nations, but not their distribution.

And what of the Maya and his poverty-stricken *Ladino* cousin, who now eat worse than their preColumbian ancestors? What are they to think of their government and that of the United States? They must believe that insurgency is a useless gesture unless they are ready to "create two, three, or more Vietnams." And who is to say that they never will?

NOTES

1 *The World Almanac,* 1970. p. 165.
2 *Studies in Law and Economic Development,* Vol. 1, No. 2, September 1966. "The U.S. Private Investor and the Central American Common Market" by Sheldon L. Schreiberg, p. 140.
3 *Ibid.,* p. 147.
4 Text available from the Pentagon's Office of Information.
5 *Ibid.*
6 *El Imparcial,* November 10, 1967.
7 *The Washington Post,* Editorial, August 30, 1968.
8 U.S. Department of State, *Op. Cit.,* p. 14.

9 *El Imparcial*, January 2, 1967.
10 *Ibid.*, September 26, 1967.
11 Theodore A. Ediger, UPI Dispatch, January 19, 1968.
12 *Ibid.*
13 *Ibid.*
14 *Time*, January 26, 1968, p. 23.
15 *El Imparcial*, June 1, 1968.
16 *Ibid.*, February 22 and November 10, 1967; June 1 and November 6, 1968; *Prensa Libre*, February 25, 1969.
17 *Prensa Libre*, April 10, 1969.
18 *La Hora*, December 13, 1967; *Prensa Libre*, March 3, 1969.
19 UPI dispatch, Theodore Ediger, January 19, 1968.
20 *The Washington Post*, February 4, 1968.
21 *El Imparcial*, May 17, 1962.
22 *Ibid.*, January 14, 1963.
23 *Ibid.*, December 13, 1966.
24 *Ibid.*, June 1, 1968.
25 *Prensa Libre*, June 26, 1969.
26 *El Imparcial*, April 3, 1963.
27 See his book: Plaza Lasso, Galo and Stacey May, *The United Fruit Company in Latin America*. Washington: National Planning Association, 1958.
28 *The Washington Post*, November 1, 1969.
29 *Ibid.*
30 *Ibid.*, November 9, 1969.
31 *Ibid.*
32 *Ibid.*
33 *Ibid.*, November 1, 1969.
34 *Ibid.*, November 13, 1969.

authors' postscript

THE AUTHORS refrain from speculating as to what is going to happen in Guatemala during and after President Arana Osorio's term of office. The facts speak for themselves: The internal conflicts of the existing social order in that country demonstrate that its institutions are on a collision course with history. The present U.S. foreign policy only exacerbates the death and destruction that will result therefrom. It is now a question of deciding where their loyalties lie for those who, even though not the protagonists, have been concerned with the conflict. The authors recognize our own obligation to assist the peasants, not only because of the many close friends we have among them whom we hope never to see included in one of the Pentagon's "body counts," but also because for too long we fronted for the oppressors.

We do not expect the casual reader to share our concern or our commitment. Nevertheless, whether the U.S. government sends an all-volunteer force or simply war material to Guatemala (or Colombia or the Dominican Republic or Brazil) in ever-increasing amounts to keep an archaic politico-economic system functioning spasmodically, this aid represents every U.S. taxpayer. Such a fact admits of no neutral observers.

Many would have us believe that Vietnam has taught us a lesson and that a similar blunder will not soon be repeated elsewhere. We see no basis for such optimism, neither in the history of international power politics and even less in the concept, so popularly accepted, that the real mistake in Vietnam was involving U.S. forces at such tremendous cost in an unwinnable war. The reduced expenses and continuing successes of U.S. efforts* in Latin America preclude any substantial public outcry against our policies there. It may be many years before the Guatemalan peasants and those of other Latin American countries can mount a resistance even remotely comparable in intensity and effectiveness to that of the Vietnamese. U.S. policy in Latin America is established, functioning, and, so far (except in the case of Cuba), successful.

If "no more Vietnams" has any other meaning than the misleading Guam (Nixon) Doctrine or the Vietnamization Program, then we must begin to realize that even the most minute aid to Guatemala's oligarchy in order to help it continue its dehumanized and dehumanizing control over the impoverished masses makes a mockery of our own proclaimed moral heritage as expressed in the Declaration of Independence and in our Constitution. The results of the 1954 CIA-sponsored overthrow in Guatemala are not just history, they are the daily inheritance of Guatemala's destitute.

* Chile, Peru and Bolivia notwithstanding.

appendix 1

MAN—LAND RELATIONSHIP

IN ORDER to get an exact statistical picture of the man–land relationship in Guatemala, we will use the figures of the CIDA report published in 1965.[1] This report is based on the data of the 1950 census and uses projected figures for 1965, since the results of the 1964 census were still not available at that time. The authors believe that the CIDA report paints a more accurate picture of the actual situation than that represented by the published results of the 1964 census. The purpose of the 1950 census, made while Arévalo was president, was to get a detailed and exact description of the physical and social state of the nation to better understand the implications of the goals of the then ongoing revolution. The purpose of the 1964 census, made under a military dictatorship, was to prove that tremendous strides had been made in "modernizing" the country during the preceding fourteen years. It was hoped that this "modernization" would be reflected by reducing the percentage of indigenous peoples from 56 percent to 43 percent; by changing the criteria for determining rural and urban population which resulted in a 9 percent increase in "urbanization"; and the standard for literates in the 1950 census was the ability to read and write, while in the 1964 census it was the capacity to sign one's name.

GEOGRAPHICAL DIVISIONS

Guatemala's total land area is 108,889 square kilometers of which approximately one-half is mountainous, the *Cordillera de los Andes* (Mountain Range of the Andes) which forms the highlands that extend from the Mexican border on the west, through the central regions, to the Salvadorean and Honduran borders on the south and east. This splits the country into a number of distinct geographical entities with a variety of climatic conditions, elevations and land fertility that makes Guatemala eminently agricultural, with the capacity to produce almost any crop at some time or another during the yearly cycle. For the purpose of this study, we would limit these divisions to the six named by CIDA in their excellent work, and enumerate them here: (See Maps #1 and #2)

(a) West-Central Highlands. From 1,500 to 3,000 meters above sea level; very broken terrain with mostly moderate temperatures that dip below freezing during December and January in the higher elevations; a markedly dry period from November to May, while the rest of the year constitutes the rainy season (winter depends on rain, not temperature); the people there are largely of Maya stock and *minifundismo* (tiny farms) predominates; there is much deforestation and erosion; the main crops: corn, wheat and black beans.

(b) Eastern Highlands. Mostly below 2,000 meters elevation; the terrain is also very broken, but much drier than the western highlands; there is less fragmentation of land holdings, but the lands are even less productive; its main crops are fruits, tomatoes and grass for cattle grazing; mostly poor *Ladino* population; needs irrigation.

(c) The Pacific Slopes. From 200 to 2,000 meters elevation; very humid; here lie the best soils in the country and it is the most important area in the national economy; its main products are coffee (in the higher lands), fruits and pasture. Large landholdings predominate.

(d) The Pacific Plains. A band of fertile lands 20 to 40 kilometers wide extending practically at sea level from the coast to the foothills of the cordillera, in an unbroken stretch along the Pacific Ocean; the climate is tropical with much rain, except along the immediate coast. Almost exclusively, large holdings with crops of cotton, sugar, bananas, fruits, rubber and cattle pasture.

MAP 1
POLITICAL DIVISION OF THE COUNTRY

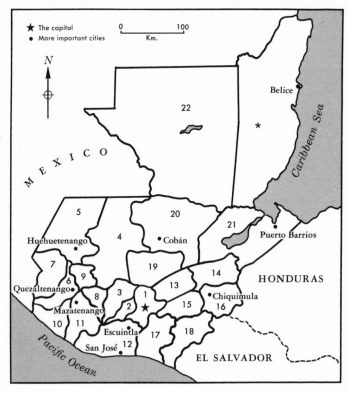

★ The capital
● More important cities

0   100
Km.

N

Belice

*

Caribbean Sea

MEXICO

22

5

20

21

Puerto Barrios

Huehuetenango

4

●Cobán

7

19

14

HONDURAS

6 9

Quezaltenango●

8   3   13

1

●Chiquimula

Mazatenango

2 ★

15

16

10   11

Escuintla

17   18

San José   12

Pacific Ocean

EL SALVADOR

DEPARTMENTS

Central:
1. Guatemala
2. Sacatepéquez
West:
3. Chimaltenango
4. El Quiché
5. Huehuetenango
6. Quezaltenango
7. San Marcos
8. Sololá
9. Totonicapán

South:
10. Retalhuleu
11. Suchitepéquez
12. Escuintla
East:
13. El Progreso
14. Zacapa
15. Jalapa
16. Chiquimula
17. Santa Rosa
18. Jutiapa

North Central:
19. Baja Verapaz
20. Alta Verapaz
North:
21. Izabal
22. El Petén

* Territory claimed by Guatemala

MAP 2
NATURAL REGIONS OF GUATEMALA

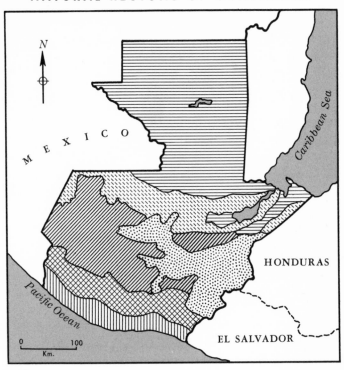

- ▨ (West-central Highlands)
- ▨ (Eastern Highlands)
- ▨ (Southern or Pacific Slopes)
- ▨ (Northern Slopes)
- ▥ (Southern or Pacific Plains)
- ▤ (Northern Lowlands)

(e) The Northern Slopes. Much like the Pacific slopes, but wider and less fertile; perhaps less broken also but there are few roads and poor communications; good coffee country, especially in Alta Verapaz, above 600 meters; the *Zona Reina* of northern Huehuetenango and Quiché holds much promise once roads open up the area.

(f) Lowlands of the North. Consists mostly of the Department of Petén, as well as parts of Alta Verapaz and Izabal; comprises one-third of the country's total area, and holds less than three percent of the population; its terrain is largely unbroken, under 200 meters high and with a tropical climate. The tropical rains have made this a jungle forest on washed lands of low fertility; few roads; crops are chicle, pepper and fine lumbers.

POPULATION: LOCATION

In 1964 there were 4,284,473 people in Guatemala,[2] with 43.3 percent listed as indigenous. The authors believe the actual percentage to be much higher than this. Since census figures are drawn up on a Departmental basis (political divisions) and not according to the geographical divisions we have offered, the location of the population is given accordingly but can be easily related to the terrains described previously, by using Maps #1 and #2 in conjunction.

Two and a half percent of the population lives in the Departments of Petén and Izabal (mostly the northern lowlands); 11.3 percent lives in the Departments of Retalhuleu, Suchitepéquez and Escuintla (fertile southern plains) and the vast majority, 86.2 percent, lives in the other Departments, comprising mainly the two highland areas.

POPULATION: COMPOSITION

The population is largely rural, 75.1 percent; a percentage that is decreasing very slowly, and even by 1980, it is calculated that 68% will still be rural—a figure that means that, with an expanding population, there will be a far greater number of small farmers than exist today. It is interesting to note that of the urban population, about 40 percent lives in the capital city, while the second largest city, Quezaltenango, does not even reach 10 percent of the population of the capital itself. This concentration of sophisticated urbanites and trained professionals in Guatemala City has adverse effects on the development of the rural areas. The population explosion in Guatemala City is due largely to the migration of landless peasants looking for work.

The percentage of illiteracy is 72 percent; 41 percent of the urban population is without education, while twice that figure, or 82 percent of the rural population, is illiterate.

CHART 1
URBAN AND RURAL ILLITERACY

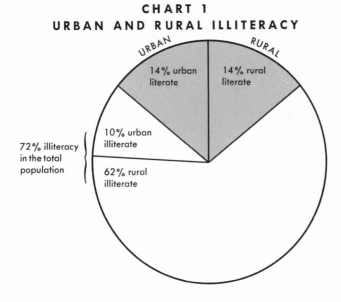

POPULATION: MAN–LAND RELATIONSHIP

There is an absolute scarcity of land in the *altiplano* (See Map #3), where the lands are poorest, necessitating an intensive use that results in more and more deforestation and

MAP 3
RELATION BETWEEN FARMLAND AREA AND THE RURAL POPULATION ACCORDING TO THE 1964 CENSUS

PERCENTAGE OF TOTAL
RURAL POPULATION

48% [▦] Less than 2 manzanas per rural inhabitant
34% [▦] From 2 to 3.9 manzanas per rural inhabitant
18% [ ] 4 manzanas and more per rural inhabitant

more and more erosion. This can be seen from the figures on the population density for the five most populated Departments. Guatemala is highest with 366 inhabitants per square kilometer (due mainly to the Capital itself); Sacatepéquez has 170 per square kilometer; Quezaltenango, 136 per square kilometer; Totonicapán, 134 per square kilometer; and Sololá, 102 per square kilometer. All are located in the *altiplano*.[3]

The implications of all these figures and percentages are obvious, a few of which we underline here. Guatemala is an underdeveloped nation whose primary resources are its people and its land. The people are largely uneducated, existing on the worst lands in the country—mountain lands. The majority of these people are Maya, a race and culture that is viewed as inferior, and whose destiny, according to the ruling class, is to serve forever.

LAND OWNERSHIP: TYPE OF HOLDINGS

A further implication of these figures, and one that is related to the whole process of development, is ownership. We must break these figures down even further, and determine who owns what and where, and how he is using it. For this purpose, we will also use the classifications of the CIDA work, which are the five following categories of land holdings: microfarms, subfamily farms, family farms, medium multifamily farms and large multifamily farms.[4]

The first two of these are commonly called *minifundios* while the latter two are referred to as *latifundios*. The microfarms have less than one manzana (1.7 acres); and the large multifamily farms are larger than 1,280 manzanas (2,176 acres).[5] The *minifundios* then are farms that are too small to sustain an average family, and the head of the house must seek outside work to make ends meet. We use this CIDA definition because subsistence means more than warding off starvation; it includes the means to pay for simple medical needs, a roof over one's head and a shirt on one's back. The average family of five in the highlands needs approximately one quintal

Table 1.—Land Area According to Size of Holdings and Use[6]
(in Hectares)

Size of farm	Total area	Utilized	Not used	Unusable
Micro	28,575	27,125	—	1,450
Subfamily	504,556	400,503	74,010	30,043
Family	500,830	250,498	205,647	44,685
Medium Multifamily	1,167,532	574,996	502,701	89,835
Large Multifamily	1,519,339	433,239	922,175	163,925
TOTALS	3,720,832	1,686,361	1,704,533	329,938

(100 lbs.) of corn a week, or 52 quintales a year, since its diet is almost exclusively made up of this cereal. The average highland yield is a quintal to a cuerda (approximately 625 sq. meters) which means that 52 cuerdas or 5.5 acres are needed just to supply a family's corn needs and nothing more. The CIDA classification of microfarms and subfamily farms having less than 10 manzanas (17 acres) seems amply justified.

It can be seen from Table 2 that the *minifundistas* take

Table 2.—Use of Land: Percentages[7]

Size of farm	Total area	Utilized	Not used	Unusable
Micro	100%	94.9%	—	5.1%
Subfamily	100%	79.4%	14.7%	5.9%
Family	100%	50.0%	41.1%	8.9%
Medium Multifamily	100%	49.2%	43.1%	7.7%
Large Multifamily	100%	28.5%	60.7%	10.8%
TOTALS	100%	45.3%	45.8%	8.9%

advantage of between 80 percent to 95 percent of their available lands, that is, practically all of them. The big land owners, on the other hand, only utilize a small part of theirs. We can also observe (Table 3) that the *minifundios* (micro and subfamily farms) represent 88.4 percent of the total farms and together possess 14.3 percent of the land area. The *latifundios* (medium and large multifamily farms) represent 2.1 percent of the total number of farms and together possess 72.2 percent of the lands. The picture that these figures represent is not even as stark as reality itself, if we take into con-

Table 3.—Number of Farms, Area and Percentages According to Size of Holdings[8]

Size of farm	Number	Percentage	Area	Percentage	Average-size
Micro	74,270	21.3%	28,575	0.8%	0.4 Hec.
Subfamily	233,800	67.1%	504,556	13.5%	2.2 Hec.
Family	33,040	9.5%	500,830	13.5%	15.2 Hec.
Medium Multifamily	7,060	2.0%	1,167,532	31.4%	165.4 Hec.
Large Multifamily	520	0.1%	1,519,339	40.8%	2,921.9 Hec.
TOTALS	348,690	100.0%	3,720,832	100.0%	

(These totals were based largely on figures from the 1950 census since the 1964 census was not available when the report was written. If anything, the situation is worse today than that indicated by the 1950 census or the 1965 CIDA report.)

sideration that all cultivated land is classified as "utilized" where much of it, in the highlands, should be classified as "unusable," because the peasants there are forced to use lands that the large landowners would never touch. There are many stories of peasants who have fallen out of their cornfields and been killed, and though this may seem like an exaggeration, a trip down the Pan-American highway through the Department of Huehuetenango will convince one of the danger of working the fields high up the mountain sides. Often the incline exceeds 60°, better for skiing (although there is no snow) than for planting. If figures were available on the utilization of usable land only, many of the peasants would get percentages of 100 plus. In many areas, small patch farming is common up to the very peaks of steep rocky mountains (see Chart 2).

Such an inequitable distribution of the land in regard to the population has many historical causes, as we have shown. One additional cause is the healthy climatic conditions of the mountains that give the sickness-prone and weak physical condition of the peasant added protection against disease. But this, his need for such protection, is an effect of his poverty, not its cause, and it is not sufficient explanation for his remaining in the highlands, while unused lands abound on the south coastal plains, and the northern jungle areas, as well as on the Pacific and northern slopes. He stays there largely because the ruling class wants him there. It is hard to conjecture how much

CHART 2
FARM-LAND DISTRIBUTION

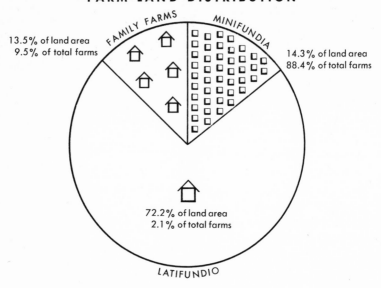

longer he can afford to remain there, for all other considerations aside, the population is growing at the alarming rate of
over 3 percent per year, about 100,000 net increase annually.
Projecting these rates, Guatemalan population will increase
sixteen times in the next 100 years.

Charles Wagley, an anthropologist who has studied Guatemala, said that the present agriculture problem is "having too
many sons," which means that there is not enough land for each
under the present land system and within the finite boundaries
of each municipality. "The solution," he says, "lies in either
contraception, infanticide, land reform or a return to the old
communal land system."[9]

POPULATION DENSITY

It is necessary to consider that in the western mountain region,
the density of the rural population in 1964 was forty-three

persons per square kilometer, a figure that will reach seventy persons per square kilometer by 1980, thus creating tremendous pressures. Since even today there is not enough land for minimal subsistence, it is of the utmost necessity that migration be made possible. This is something the people will have to do for themselves and they must be prepared to overcome opposition to it.

NOTES

1 Comité Interamericano de Desarrollo Agrícola, *Tenencia de la tierra y desarrollo socio-económico del sector agrícola: Guatemala.* Washington, D.C.: Pan American Union, 1965.
2 The statistics given here are from: Guatemala: Dirección General de Estadística, *Censo de Población de 1964,* published in 1966.
3 Guatemala: *Censo de Población de 1964,* p. 14.
4 CIDA, *Op. Cit.,* p. 19.
5 *Ibid.*
6 *Ibid.*
7 *Ibid.,* p. 20.
8 *Ibid.,* p. 58.
9 Wagley, Charles, "The Economics of a Guatemalan Village," *American Anthropologist,* 1941, p. 81.

ABBREVIATIONS

AEU — Association of University Students
AGA — General Association of Agriculturalists (large land-owners)
AID — Agency for International Development
CIDA — Interamerican Committee of Agricultural Development (sponsored by the UN, the OAS and others)
CGTG — General Confederation of Labor Unions
CNCG — National Confederation of Guatemalan Peasants
DAN — National Agrarian Department
DGAA — Department of Agrarian Affairs
FAO — Food and Agriculture Organization
FAR — Armed Forces of Rebellion (guerrilla forces)
FYDEP — Institute for the Promotion and Development of the Petén
INCAP — Nutritional Institute for Central America and Panama
INFOP — National Institute for the Development of Production
INRA — National Institute of Agrarian Reform
INTA — National Institute for Agrarian Transformation
IRCA — International Railroads of Central America
MLN — National Liberation Movement (Party and government of Castillo Armas)
MR–13 — 13 of November Movement (guerrilla forces)
OAS — Organization of American States
PGT — Guatemalan Labor Party (communist party)
PR — Revolutionary Party
PID — Institutional Democratic Party
Q. — Quetzal (national currency equivalent to the dollar)

SPANISH TERMS

Acuerdo	—Agreement; used for governmental declarations that do not have the matter or force of law.
Arrendamiento forzoso	—Forced rental
Campesino	—Peasant
Colonos	—Tenant farmers who pay for the use of land with labor
Ejido	—Communal landholding
Especie	—Goods or produce
Fiesta	—Feastday or holiday usually celebrated like a fair
Finca	—Plantation
Finquero	—Plantation owner
Jornalero	—Day laborer, usually a migrant worker
Ladino	—A non-Indian, of Western culture
Latifundio	—Extensive landholding
Latifundista	—Owner of a large landholding
Minifundio	—Less than a subsistence landholding
Minifundista	—Owner of a minifundio
Patrono	—Landlord
Sindicato	—Labor union
Zona agrícola	—Agrarian zone for colonization

MEASUREMENTS

1 Caballería	=	64.4 manzanas
		109.8 acres
1 Manzana	=	16 cuerdas
		.7 hectares
		1.7 acres
1 Hectare	=	0.022 Caballerías
		1.43 manzanas
		2.47 acres
1 Acre	=	9.4 cuerdas

index